'Ferguson's Gang" to be Disbanded

"FERGUSON'S GANG," mysterious body of philanthropists, is soon to be disbanded. During the past five years it raised thousands of pounds for the National Trust for Places of Historic Interest or Natural Beauty.

The members sign themselves by such names as "'Erb the Smasher," "Red Biddy," "Black Mary," "Bill Stickers," "Nark," and "Silent O'Moyle."

The chief is "Ferguson," who broadcast a year ago, but even then his identity was not revealed. There are believed to be 10 or 12 members.

When "Silent O'Moyle" handed over £500 in Bank of England notes for the purchase of Newtown Old Town Hall, Isle of Wight, in 1935, he appeared at the offices of the trust in Buckingham Palace-road with a handkerchief over the lower part of his face.

"RED BIDDY'S" VISIT

Only last week the "gang" added its gift of Mayon Cliffs and 24 acres of land, between the village of Sennen and Land's End, a further 15½ acres.

Mr. D. M. Matheson, secretary of the trust, told a *Daily Mail* reporter yesterday : "When 'Red Biddy,' the first member of the gang to visit us came

FERGUSON GANG'S £100 BOMB

A NEW and pleasanter kind of bomb exploit gave Mr. D. M. Matheson, secretary of the National Trust, a surprise yesterday.

When the annual meeting of the trust at Gray's Inn Hall was about to begin a sinister-looking imitation "pineapple " was pushed into his hand by a messenger boy. A label attached to it read :

From Ferguson's Gang:
*Open this fruit and you will find
A kernel greatly to your mind.*"

The kernel was a £100 note. No one at the National Trust has the faintest idea who Ferguson's gang are," Mr. Matheson told the News Chronicle. "The latest gift makes about £2,100 in direct money given to us in this way by the Gang."

MORE BEAUTY-SPOTS

Projected or completed are the National Trust, announced by the Zetland, are 160 acres including part of Wenlock Edge (Sussex). 21¼ acres ... for the protection of ... land, Cornwall, and a ... of woodlands and open ... adjoining Toys Hill, Brasted ...

FERGUSON'S GANG BUSY AGAIN

Mystery Band With Terrible Names Completes Endowment of Beauty Spot

Ferguson's Gang has been at it again.

... National Trust. ... Shalford Mill, on the ... near Guildford, and ... National Trust. Mo... into a condition of ... endow it with a su...

Then early this ... calling herself Red ... of the Trust and ... silver coins. It wa... instalment on the ... Now the second ... been paid.

This time the representative ... Gang sent up his card as though he were a commercial traveller. On it were the cryptic words "'Erb the Smasher, representative, Ferguson's Gang."

But, in spite of his name, he handed over £200 in Bankof England notes, together with an illuminated and sealed document signed by all the members of the gang announcing the discharge of their debt.

"We have not the faintest idea who they are," said Mr. S. H. Hamer, secretary of the National Trust, to the *Daily Sketch* last night. "In addition to Red Biddy and 'Erb the Smasher there are Uncle Gregory, Sister Agatha, the Sanguinary Bishop, Old Paul of Paddington and Bill Sticker. Altogether they have raised £600.

"No, I would not like to say that they have finished—as a matter of fact I think they have something else in mind. What it is I cannot say. No doubt Red Biddy and 'Erb the Smasher know."

£100 NOTE ROUND A CIGAR

ANONYMOUS GIFTS TO TRUST FUND

THE PRESERVATION OF BEAUTY SPOTS

LONDON, Friday.—A body of anonymous well-wishers of the work of the National Trust for the preservation of beauty spots, who call themselves "Ferguson's Gang," have given to the trust money for the purchase of a further 15½ acres of cliff lands near Land's End. As on former occasions no information is given as to the source of the money out of which the land has been purchased.

Other contributions have been made by the "gang" in original ways. On one occasion masked men handed over bags of currency to the officers of the trust. On another occasion, last month, a messenger arrived at the annual dinner of the trust with a cigar, round which a note for £100 was wrapped for the president ...

Woman in Mask ... O'BRIEN ... NARK"

... woman went to the ... in Buckingham ... yesterday.

On the ... presented was written, " Kate O'Brien, the Nark."

She was shown to the room of Mr. Matheson the secretary, and handed him a bank note for £500, in part payment of purchase and endowment of the Newport old town hall, I.o.W. which " Ferguson's Gang " is presenting to the Trust.

Kate O'Brien left without removing her mask or disclosing her identity.

Some time ago, the gang bought and endowed Shalford Mill, near Guildford, for the Trust.

In respect of that gift, the money was brought to the office by masked members of the gang, "Red Biddy" and "'Erb the Smasher"

Now little more than a hamlet, Newtown once had two members of Parliament. The most famous were John Churchill, afterwards the great Duke of Marlborough, and George Canning, the famous Foreign Minister.

Ferguson Gang
"Jealousy" Prompts £100 Gift

AFTER a rather longer hibernation than usual, the "Ferguson Gang" has made its beneficient appearance again, having left a £100 note with the National Trust for the Avebury Appeal.

It is suggested that the gang has been reawakened by jealousy of a rival gang, "The Black Atropine Sisterhood," which recently presented a sum of money to the Trust for the preservation of Dovedale.

Ferguson's latest gift is towards preserving the prehistoric stone circle at Avebury and the scenery about it. Bigger than Stonehenge, the Avebury stone circle is estimated to be 3,000 or 4,000 years old.

GANG'S PARCHMENT

With the £100 note was an

" handed £200 in notes ... cretary, together with a ... ated document, signed by a ... members of the gang—inclu... ed Biddy "—announcing th... ge of their debt.

Smasher " left, as he arrive... gnised.

FERGUSON'S GANG

POLLY BAGNALL AND SALLY BECK

This book is dedicated to my grandfather,
John Eric Miers Macgregor, a gentle, generous and loving man,
known to me as Poppa.
Polly

Also dedicated to my family the Becks, the Fehls
and the Gilmans, who will appreciate many of the
characters and events in this book.
Sally

And the Gang:
Bill Stickers   Margaret 'Peggy' Pollard neé Gladstone (1904–1996)
Sister Agatha   Brynhild 'Brynnie' Jervis-Read neé Granger (1908–2004)
Red Biddy, White Biddy   Rachel Pinney (1909–1995)
The Lord Beershop of the Gladstone Islands and Mercator's Projection
Ruth Sherwood (1907–1990)
Kate O'Brien the Nark   Mabel Joy Gaze neé Maw (1907–1983)
Shot Biddy   Eileen Souter née Bertram Moffat (1910–2002)

First published in the United
Kingdom in 2015 by
National Trust Books
1 Gower Street
London WC1E 6HD

An imprint of Pavilion Books
Company Ltd
© National Trust Books, 2015
Text © Polly Bagnall & Sally Beck, 2015

ISBN: 9781909881716

A CIP catalogue record for this book is
available from the British Library.

10 9 8 7 6 5 4 3 2 1

Design by Lee-May Lim
Reproduction by ColourDepth, UK
Printed and bound by Bookwell, Finland

Printed on PREPS (Publishers'
Responsible Environmental
Paper Sourcing) compliant paper.

This book can be ordered direct from
the publisher at the website
www.pavilionbooks.com, or try your
local bookshop. Also available at
National Trust shops, including
www.nationaltrustbooks.co.uk.

FOREWORD

Ars longa, vita brevis
(Art is long, life is short)

In 2011, a small group of American visitors contacted the National
Trust and asked if they could see the room at Shalford Mill, near
Guildford, Surrey that had been used by the mysterious group of
women, Ferguson's Gang. The room had been the Gang's headquarters from 1932, when my family began to live at the Mill, until the
1960s, when they no longer needed it and handed it over to us. My
father, Brian Bagnall, a cartoonist for the satirical magazine *Private
Eye*, turned it into his studio and it was full of his old computer and
drawing equipment. I cleared it up as best I could. Rummaging about
in the cupboards I found a ceremonial staff belonging to the Bludy
Beershop, a Gang member, which had been used to stir distemper, and
the Gang's secret money box into which they had saved their booty.

Although my family often talked about the Gang, and I had met
some of them, I realised that when my mother and her sisters passed
away much of this history would be lost forever. My mother had known
them and even been there when they had their Ritual Hauntings and
meetings at the Mill.

The true story of Ferguson's Gang is incredible and yet, until now,
almost unknown, as they adopted pseudonyms, and with the exception of the Gang's leader, Bill Stickers, chose to remain anonymous.
To record their story, in 2012 I curated an exhibition at Shalford
Mill called 'Taming the Tentacles'. With help from my niece Megan
Clark-Bagnall, we curated a site-specific art exhibition at which
many of the artefacts belonging to the Gang were shown publicly for
the first time.

My research for the exhibition set me on a path of discovery. My
mother knew the real names of the Gang's inner circle and told me that
her own parents were active members. Her father, my grandfather, the
architect John Eric Miers Macgregor, was nicknamed the Artichoke

and became a close associate member, deeply involved in the Gang's activities, sharing their vision and ethos.

Ferguson's Gang was formed in 1927. Their aim to protect rural England was inspired by the work of the architect Clough Williams-Ellis whose book, *England and the Octopus*, was an impassioned plea against the onslaught of unchecked urban development spreading across the country in the 1920s.

What made the Gang unique was the way it set about fighting 'the Octopus'. Using pseudonyms and dressed in disguise they delivered funds to the National Trust, garnering enormous publicity for their cause. All their missions bar one were reported in the national press.

The women brought together spectacle and performance with-activism in a way not seen before and became forerunners of modern-day female activist groups such as Guerrilla Girls and Pussy Riot. They raised money and acquired property, land and notoriety, all of which went to advance awareness of rural conservation.

Ferguson's Gang opened their doors to any number of subscribing members, forming a diverse group. Radical activists worked side by side with landed gentry, communists with conservatives, suited men from the National Trust with barefooted bisexuals. The strength and creative potential of the Gang was in uniting with others who must have held sometimes diametrically opposing opinions. But who were they? And why don't we know more about them?

Although I had written a booklet to accompany the exhibition, it was meeting journalist and writer Sally Beck that became the catalyst for this book.

I understood the essence of the Gang. I had grown up in the Mill and played in the same underground passageways and corn bins that the Gang had known. The Mill itself absorbed the Gang's anarchic spirit. Over the years it has reverberated with the thunderous feet of friends and family as they charged up and down its wooden ladders. It was always an open-house full of oddballs, and growing up there we delighted in the absurd and unconventional. Country walks were spent peering through cottage windows as my father, aunt and grandfather, all architects, discussed the merits of a flagstone floor, the south-facing light, or the aspect of a certain building. No village, church or cathedral was passed without us having to inspect the traces of a fresco in the nave, or making a sketch of a Romanesque arch. My grandfather, the

Artichoke, showed me the beauty of simple old buildings and also the thrill of inventing something new, usually with an old cotton reel and some elastic bands. He has been my inspiration.

Sally, on the other hand, was able to question the things I had taken for granted in pursuit of the facts. Together we pieced together information from obscure archives and their cryptic minute book 'The Boo'. Written in 'mockney', deciphering it was a puzzle often proffering more questions than answers. Was Shot Biddy really the same person as White Biddy, or Red Biddy before her? This book answers many such queries. A large part of my initial research had been meeting with friends and relatives of members of the Gang, who showed the warmth, openness and, above all, the great sense of fun that was typical of the Gang. With access to their personal letters and family archives Sally and I were able to build a full understanding of the Gang. The result is a vivid picture of the extraordinary women whose activities began almost a century ago.

Long after the Gang's official activities ceased their spirit remained alive and the women members lived full and long lives.

In the 1970s, as a 70-year-old lady, their leader Bill Stickers decided to embroider a tapestry of all the scenes of the Narnia story. She started and continued single-handed until she had embroidered 1,330 feet of cloth. Unwittingly, she broke a world record. This was typical of a member of the Gang; starting with an idea and not doubting her ability to achieve it. Bill may be a role model for us all, inspiring us to have the confidence to do something positive no matter how uncertain the outcome.

The issues that faced Ferguson's Gang are still current today and we may ask ourselves: 'How do we improve the quality of life for an overwhelmingly urban population? What do we really mean by the countryside? What is Englishness? How does this all fit in with a diverse world?' The problems now, as nearly a hundred years ago, may appear overwhelmingly complicated and inscrutable, but the answer is to remain UNDAUNTED.

Polly Bagnall, 2015

PROLOGUE

On 17 July 1939, the National Trust held their Annual General Meeting at Gray's Inn Hall in London. Despite pre-war jitters, the atmosphere seemed calm and civilised. Ladies, gentlemen, lords and landed gentry sipped tea from bone-china cups and ate ginger biscuits as they discussed the demolition of friends' stately homes, or whether or not to build Anderson shelters in their gardens.

Representing the National Trust, among others, were the Chairman Lawrence Dundas, the Second Marquess of Zetland, a Conservative politician who was serving as Secretary of State for India, and James Lees-Milne, Secretary of the Trust's Country House Committee, and a writer and expert on country houses. Lees-Milne was instrumental in the first large-scale transfer of private country houses into ownership of the Trust, using his charm and knowledge to persuade cash-strapped aristocrats to give their homes to the nation rather than have them demolished, as was the fashion of the day. In charge of the meeting was Donald Macleod Matheson, an Oxford-educated Scottish aristocrat who had served in the artillery during the First World War and had been appointed the Trust's Secretary.

The distinguished company was nervous beneath its superficial calm. Just a few weeks before the meeting, massive explosions had hit three targets in London as part of a campaign of terror waged by the Irish Republican Army. So far that year, it had scored 59 direct hits on the capital and 70 in the provinces. Destructive homemade bombs were the weapon of choice, unobtrusive devices mostly left in mundane-looking suitcases that went unnoticed until it was too late. Bridges, post offices, postboxes, a tobacconist's in Piccadilly Circus and a newspaper office had all been bombed. Unsurprisingly, Londoners wondered anxiously who and where would be next.

When the gathering of employees, members and patrons had taken their seats, and as Donald Macleod Matheson readied himself to read the agenda, there was a sudden commotion at the great doors of the Hall. Three mysterious figures in plain black masks had entered and were approaching the table where the National Trust representatives were sitting. With them was a messenger boy carrying a large metal pineapple.

The onlookers were terrified by the sight of what appeared to be desperate terrorists and some kind of dangerous device, and the panel sat rigid in shock as the boy pushed the fake pineapple into the hands of James Lees-Milne. Then the intruders left as quickly as they had come. In a kind of pass-the-parcel game, Lees-Milne immediately shoved the object to Matheson, who quickly passed it on to Lord Zetland. Everybody froze for a heart-stopping moment as he read the label attached to the strange-looking object:

Open this fruit and you will find a kernel greatly to your mind.

At once Lord Zetland realised that this was not a bomb sent by the IRA, and was able to reassure everyone that they had in fact witnessed another donation from the eccentric Ferguson's Gang, who only ever appeared masked and disguised. There was an audible sigh of relief from the gathering and a ripple of excitement as the pineapple was opened to reveal the 'kernel', a £100 note.

All was well but the incident was alarming enough to be reported in the papers the next day. The *Daily Telegraph* had the headline: 'Beneficent Bomb'. This was followed by: 'The annual meeting of the National Trust was enlivened yesterday by the attentions of "Ferguson's Gang," an anonymous group of good-cause helpers.

'During the proceedings a curious red-and-white metal container was handed up to Lord Zetland, the chairman. He jokingly suggested that the I.R.A. might have begun to take an interest in the National Trust.' The *News Chronicle* added: 'No one at the Trust has the faintest idea who Ferguson's Gang are.' Then Matheson was quoted as saying: 'This latest gift makes about £2,100 in direct money given us this way by the Gang.' The average annual income at that time was around £200 a year so the sum of £2,100 was equivalent to a year's wages for just over 10 people.

Back at their headquarters, five of the Gang met to discuss the day's events. Present were the leader and founder, Bill Stickers, along with Sister Agatha, Shot Biddy, the Bludy Beershop and Kate O'Brien the Nark. The Gang was elated. They had pulled off another coup and made the headlines again, just as they had hoped.

The incident at Gray's Inn Hall was recorded in their minute book in barely punctuated 'mockney', their version of Cockney. In their lingo, they referred to money or notes, as 'goats', and growing pots of money as 'kids'. Typewriters were 'tripewriters' and rooms were 'cells'. In the minute book, a record known as 'The Boo', their entry for that day was particularly gleeful:

TRIPLE DELIVERY BY BLACK MARY BILL STICKERS & SISTER AGATHA, July 17 1939

...Bill kept opping up and down and shouting Look, e's got the goat, and jobbling peoples elbows, so that it was a wonder we wasnt spotted ... [Bill] ... thrust the goat at Lees-Milne but it butted him over and rushed up to Matheson and buried its mustle in Lord Zetland's hand whereon Lord Z shot up both I.brouse into his hair and the Press all noticed. Lord Z. held up the fruit what the goat come in, and read out that it was not an IRA bomb but us. We ad put a vurss on it with a old Cornish tripewriter what cant be traced.

The £100 contained in the pineapple was a deposit for the purchase of their third acquisition for the Trust. The Gang had delivered another blow in the struggle to which they were dedicated: saving rural England by endowing important but small properties that were in danger of being ignored and destroyed. Yet again, their stunt brought their cause to the attention of the nation.

The Press attention they received was purely accidental; they never set out to court it, public relations was in its infancy then, but they never objected to it either. They were clever enough to realise that it brought national awareness to their cause, which in turn helped the National Trust gain members and raise money. Accordingly, they made sure they always executed headline-grabbing capers.

Only once pre-war did a stunt go unreported, and during the war they were quiet, but post-war, they were back in the headlines. The Press did try to discover their identities (not even the Trust knew all the members' real names) and although the odd journalist knew who Bill Stickers and Red Biddy were, they played the game and never outed them in the newspapers. In the end, only Bill Stickers formally revealed herself, and then only in 1996, after her death at the age of 92, in a letter sent to *The Times* on her instructions. The others never officially came out from behind their masks and carried their secret to their graves.

In its day, the Gang might have appeared childish to outsiders but there was nothing childish about its intentions. On the contrary, its members were deadly serious about their aims. Even so, they never wanted to do anything in a mundane way because they loved the fun, and 'going quietly' wasn't their style.

Their missions had to be eccentric and playful. Dressing up was paramount and they bought their masks from Harrods. They dined well with food from Fortnum & Mason delivered to their meetings, and made sure that they enjoyed themselves hugely, whatever they were up to. That love of fun and desire to play should not obscure the importance of what they did, and the brilliant, highly educated and unconventional people they were.

The women in Ferguson's Gang were all strong and non-conformist, as robust as the threads of their lisle stockings. From the upper, and upper-middle classes, with distinguished forebears in their family trees, they were educated, enquiring and brave. They were also inclusive and non-judgemental and, although they shared interests, they were a diverse group: some members were lesbian, others bisexual or hetero-sexual. They may have been outspoken, upsetting the status quo, but together they made use of their individual differences and strengths to become a formidable force.

Today, the generosity of Ferguson's Gang is worth tens of millions of pounds. They left another invaluable legacy too: they helped put the National Trust, a small and underfunded body in its early years, with a fraction of the four million members it has today, well and truly on the map. This is their story.

CHAPTER ONE
Bill Stickers – Peggy Gladstone

Every gang needs a mastermind, someone unorthodox with the intellectual capability to organise a mob. Ferguson's Gang had as its leader Peggy Pollard née Gladstone. She was a woman with a formidable intellect who taught herself Sanskrit at the age of 16, won a scholarship to Cambridge at 17, and became the first female student there to gain a Double First in Oriental languages.

Unconventional, with a surreal sense of humour, Peggy delighted in the absurd. Make-believe was part of her psyche, a tool she had acquired during childhood. Although she and her younger brother Bobby lived in an impressive house, were waited on by a staff of 22 servants, and enjoyed a lavish lifestyle, they were also isolated and lonely. Elaborate, make-believe games alleviated the boredom and provided Peggy, at least, with a gateway to otherwise inaccessible worlds.

Born on 1 March 1904, and christened Margaret Steuart Gladstone, she was the great great-niece of the Liberal Prime Minister William Ewart Gladstone. Affectionately known as Peggy, she was the first child born to her parents, John and Margaret Steuart Gladstone.

Their home had the prestigious address of 2 Whitehall Court, London, SW1, a stone's throw from Buckingham Palace and the Houses of Parliament. To the south of their house was a foggy scene Monet painted in the same year Peggy was born. *London, the Houses of Parliament. The Sun Shining through the Fog* was characterised by its blue and amber hues silhouetting the Palace of Westminster, Big Ben and Westminster Bridge.

Next door to their home was a turreted, Gothic-style building that housed the gentlemen-only National Liberal Club, established by Gladstone in 1882.

William Ewart Gladstone was a formidable character who served as Prime Minister on four separate occasions between 1868 and 1894, as well as serving as Chancellor of the Exchequer four times between 1853 and 1882. As Prime Minister, his policies were designed to improve individual liberty and to loosen political and economic restraints. His spectacular political career spanned 60 years and he became Britain's oldest Prime Minister, resigning aged 84. Naturally, his influence was felt throughout the Gladstone family.

Peggy's father John Steuart Gladstone was the son of William Gladstone's niece Mary. John was a partner in the family firm of Gillanders Arbuthnot & Co Ltd, a trading company based in Calcutta. He had spent time in Burma, where he became immersed in Eastern culture. That same culture later had a considerable influence on his intelligent and curious daughter.

Peggy's mother was the daughter of Gerald FitzGibbon, an outstanding scholar and eminent lawyer who became the Lord Justice of the Irish Court of Appeal and Queen's Counsel, one of the most distinguished judges in Irish legal history. Margaret was known as Anne, and grew up in Dublin in a fine house that was the hub of a glittering social life that included British and Irish lawyers and politicians.

In 1907, when Peggy was nearly three, her brother Robert was born, but everyone called him Bobby. In 1911, when Peggy was seven and Bobby four, the family left the hustle and bustle of London for a quieter setting near the village of Cranleigh in Surrey. Their new home, Nanhurst, was a luxurious, three-storey, Edwardian house built in red brick with garret windows. In the fireplace of the huge drawing room with its carved oak walls was a fireback that, it was said, had been pinched from Hampton Court. The property covered almost one hundred acres. Its sloping, south-facing lawns reflected John's fascination with the East and were peppered with statues and carvings of Egyptian, Greek, Chinese and Japanese gods, as well as a huge stone statue of Buddha. It was an idyllic setting, but, Peggy hated it and her frustration was revealed in notes she made about her life and privileged childhood.

She called her father 'the Da', and her mother 'Mammy'. A highly intelligent woman, Mammy had been brought up at the heart of Irish political life, but with little outlet for her intellect, she suffered badly with boredom. Bitter at her own lack of opportunity, Mammy made it clear to her daughter that Peggy should not become idle and spoilt. She wanted more for her than simply to marry well, and live in a fine house.

While Europe descended into turmoil with the outbreak of the First World War, at Nanhurst, the Gladstone family barely noticed. Peggy wrote:

The war did not bother us much. The under gardener joined up and that was our lot. I lived what would now be considered the Life of Riley.

The remaining servants included a head housemaid, two under-housemaids, head parlourmaid, second parlourmaid, cook, kitchenmaid, scullery maid, nurse, nurserymaid, head gardener, two under-gardeners and a chauffeur. There was no butler as the Da refused to keep one, ditto his elder brother Arthur, because they vehemently resented the tax on manservants. Peggy had her own maid though, called Jessie, who looked after her clothes, 'and that kind of thing, but I scarcely remember her at all,' she said.

The trappings of wealth made their childhood no less isolated. Peggy and Bobby had no local friends to play with and only the occasional cousin came to stay, so to pass the time they spent their afternoons inventing make-believe games in a private wood opposite their home, bought for their amusement by the Da. As a self-contained unit the two children grew incredibly close and unusually for siblings, rarely argued.

They stuck with a small repertoire of favourite games, the first being hide and seek, and the second, inventing imaginary families. Bobby often took the role of a lost baby who needed a home, and Peggy was the kindly matriarch who offered him one.

Peggy appointed herself Bobby's protector as he was a child with many phobias. The housemaids' pantry window scared him, as did the creaking armchair, and he was utterly terrified of the Drainpipe Man who lurked in the bathroom. He refused to sit at the tap end of the bath, fearful of what might gurgle up the plughole.

On rainy days, they spent glorious times in the attic in a twin-bedded room they named Paris. It became their 'Den of Iniquity' and a place where they hid State Express cigarettes under the mattress. When they fancied a smoke, they locked themselves in, lay down and puffed until they choked.

They were isolated but not imprisoned and twice a week headed for Guildford swimming baths, which they loved. It was a safe existence and one of the most dramatic things that happened to Bobby was when the chauffeur's son taught him the 'f' word.

Their day began at about 8.15am when a housemaid silently entered Peggy's room with a brass can of hot water, drew the curtains and vanished. Bobby never washed in the morning. Having had a hot bath the night before, he didn't see the point, but he always poured the water into the basin to set a good example to the servants. 'I didn't even bother to do that,' wrote Peggy.

At 9am, they gathered in the dining room for breakfast, where the sideboard groaned under enough food to last poorer families a month. There was a whole ham, a glazed tongue poised on its base, and an assortment of porridge, scrambled eggs, bacon and sausages.

> The Da always had a boiled egg which, if very soft, he would hold in one hand and suck out of the shell, a feat which Bobby and I loved to watch. The toast had to be quite perfect, or else the Da would make snide remarks about 'ironclad armour-plated toast' and demand more.

After breakfast, Mammy devoted most of the morning to teaching Peggy French and German, or plain sewing. Peggy reflected that her reading was curiously chosen and included Dostoevsky's *Crime and Punishment*, which made an indelible impression on her, particularly the scene where a horse is beaten to death.

She unkindly described herself as fat, with sallow, spotty skin, but a portrait of her shows a pretty child with pale skin, blooming cheeks and large, soulful eyes. Her face was framed by thick, chestnut-coloured hair which she found hard to tame, often coiling plaits round her ears like snails' shells, which would spring loose at the first opportunity.

They dressed for dinner. Bobby and the Da wore dinner-jackets and stiff shirts, while Peggy and Mammy dressed in heavy silk, two-piece, Burmese loongyees.

Most of the child-rearing was done by Nanny Pepper, who seemed to be kind and strict in equal measures. Peggy and Bobby had misbehaved one evening and were sent to bed, where they lay, expecting the worst. Nanny Pepper kept an assortment of sticks behind her washstand and lashed out with them when she saw fit.

On this occasion, Peggy and Bobby had been lying in bed for some time, wondering what manner of wrath would descend, when the door opened and the vast form of Nanny Pepper loomed into view. She said: 'Here's a punishment for you, naughty boy. Here's a punishment for you, naughty girl...' and handed each of them a saucer of strawberry ice-cream. From that day on, all punishments were referred to as ices.

Peggy worshipped her father and considered him a demi-god. The Da loved her, but he held traditional views on raising girls; a well-bred daughter was kept at home and out of mischief. Mammy, on the other hand, was far more demanding and their relationship was strained. In later years Peggy would suffer a migraine and be physically sick before a visit from her mother. These violent, debilitating headaches ceased the day her mother died.

Some of the strain came from Mammy's dissatisfaction with her own life. Peggy described her as 'beautiful, highly intellectual, intelligent, bored, discontented, ambitious, frustrated and resentful'.

Mammy loathed the landed gentry and was furious that she was barred from all activities except bridge, tea parties and gardening, while the men in her family enjoyed glittering legal careers.

She had married a man 15 years her senior in an attempt to escape the confines of her life but, Peggy observed wryly, marriage had not answered her prayers. Her parents appeared to have little to say to each other, although they never argued – at least not in front of the children and servants.

Mammy had dreamt of going to college and making a career for herself, but the only respectable career for a woman in the early 20th century was as a governess or nurse, neither of which was suitable. After Peggy was born, she made a resolution that she stuck to: that her daughter should not lead an idle and useless life. She planted the idea in Peggy's head early on that she should go to Cambridge University, a grand ambition which the Da would never consent to, but Mammy was determined.

Peggy's formal education began at Eversley School, a boarding school near Dover. Like many girls' schools, it provided a social rather than an academic education, unhelpful if a place at Cambridge was your aim.

Eversley's headmistress was Miss Kate White, a woman who always wore a black hat with ostrich feathers that Peggy supposed she even went to bed in. At bedtime, the girls came to Miss White in a queue and kissed her respectfully on her proffered cheek.

Peggy was a natural intellectual, became head girl and outgrew Eversley rapidly. Although the school extended the curriculum and created a fifth form solely to accommodate her, it was not enough: 'I had no chance whatever of passing the [Cambridge entrance] exam from there, nobody ever had.'

Mammy let Peggy know that the Da did not care a 'blow' about her future. She said that Cambridge would enable her to distinguish herself and, with any luck, make a match with a celebrated professor. The other option, according to Mammy, was to become an unmarried and unoccupied spinster, like the Da's sisters Margaret and Mary, maiden aunts who lived together in London. The prospect of being left on the shelf frightened and galvanised Peggy, but there was still opposition from the Da.

The Da objected, but Mammy took Peggy out of Eversley and hired masters to teach her maths and Latin. She learned English literature by correspondence and found no problem speaking French.

> I got through that sort of thing like lightning and still had lots of time to waste. I had no friends. I used to go off by myself and invent gods and supernatural companions and religions of my own. Whereas the Da and Mammy were both atheists – or rather the Da was a polytheist – I had a built-in desire for a god of some sort and if one was not forthcoming I would make one, that's all.

She was happy studying at home and began to teach herself Sanskrit from one of the Da's many leather-bound books. The Da couldn't help but be impressed, despite his dislike of education for women. He was pleased and encouraging as Peggy laboriously worked out the Sanskrit alphabet.

Peggy could see that her mother's dissatisfaction with her own frivolous life bubbled away under the surface, but could not talk to her about it. It caused Peggy a lot of anxiety so she retreated: 'This is why I had to create a world of my own to live in,' she said. Make-believe permeated her personality to such a degree that it became a permanent part of her adult life. Later, Ferguson's Gang was simply an extension of that.

In 1920, when Peggy was 16, two devastating things happened. The first was that Bobby, now aged 13, was sent to board at Eton. The move had a dramatic effect on their relationship. While 16-year-old Peggy mourned that their fantasy world had come to an end, Bobby retreated further into himself. His worried housemaster, Mr Slater, sent a letter home. Slater described Bobby as: '...a very lonely boy who failed to participate in the life of the school or in any social life'.

The second event was the Da's death at the early age of 52. Peggy was devastated, as was Bobby who became even more of a loner. Peggy said: 'He became a positive oyster who no longer confided in anyone. From that time no living person, I think, had any effectual contact with him.'

John's death did mean that the locked battle over her future disappeared and she had no reason not apply to Cambridge. She was now free to pursue an academic career.

As the time for the entrance exam for Cambridge drew near, Peggy fell in love with Vishnu, praying to her father's statue of the Hindu God and avidly read anything she could about him. She continued to work hard until her much-anticipated interview with Miss Blanche Athena Clough, principal of Newnham College at Cambridge, known to her students as B. A..

Founded in 1871, Newnham was the second women-only college in Cambridge, Girton being the first. Pressure on the few available places was heavy and the bar set high. Cambridge would only admit women who were academically exceptional and reached scholarship standard.

Initially, Peggy planned to study French and English, but at the interview her mother made the course-of-history-turning remark that her daughter was really interested in Sanskrit.

Miss Clough was overjoyed, springing from her chair with the words: 'Is she indeed? Then she must do Sanskrit!'

Peggy sat the entrance exam, was accepted to study Sanskrit and was introduced to her Oriental languages tutor, Professor Rapson, who promised to teach her as much as he could by correspondence before the beginning of term.

It was 1921, and Peggy was 17 when she went up to Cambridge.

Three years had passed since the end of the Great War and England was in the grip of a depression. The only women applying to Cambridge were those with money who did not necessarily need the secure financial future a marriage would provide. Those women who gained a place were brilliant in their subjects and competitive with their male counterparts. As Peggy said: 'All we could do was beat the men and this we lived to do; we took life desperately seriously.'

Their brilliance was not the only reason Cambridge opened its doors to them. Women students were a new avenue of funding.

They might have studied the same as the men, but they were not afforded the same privileges. For example, women were banned from having a vote in college affairs and were only awarded titular degrees.

Male undergraduates were defensive in the presence of these formidable female students. As Peggy started her student life at Cambridge, she found herself confronted by male undergraduates angrily demonstrating against the admission of women. The men staged violent demonstrations, battering the bronze gates to Newnham with a hefty handcart. One overzealous undergraduate was beaten back by a Principal known as Bogey Alice, who flung open the gates, stood in the middle and addressed the marauders.

Peggy noted:

> After two minutes of the vitriolic eloquence of Bogey Alice, they were hurting each other to get away... But I lived in constant apprehension, having a room on the ground floor, and one evening I came in after dark, and suddenly the light of an electric torch flashed up at me from the garden bed. I dropped everything I was carrying, dashed out of the room in panic, and raced madly up about eight flights of stairs till I reached the topmost room of the tower, which was inhabited by one K Winterton. I banged on the door and screamed for help. When she let me in I exclaimed that we were invaded, that we should all be raped, murdered, etc... which did not seem to bother K Winterton unduly. She produced the standard Newnham hospitality which was cocoa and biscuits (it has to be said that as much cocoa was drunk every night in Newnham as would fill the inverted dome of St Paul's) and said: 'If he gets up here I will offer him some cocoa.'

Still shaking, the next day, Peggy had her first tutorial with Professor Rapson whom she described as 'a beaming fat little Father Christmas'.

She organised her working day to give herself the maximum amount of leisure time, waking at 6.30am, and working 'like fury' until 10am in the college library. For the rest of the day she had nothing to do, except for tutorials. 'I led a lonely life as every possible friend was working flat out all day with "engaged" up on the door. I used to go down town and eat ices.'

This lack of activity led Peggy to dreaming up an imaginative practical joke: a brief but successful art fraud. An accomplished artist, Peggy drew a number of pictures that she described as 'mildly pornographic sketches'. The most spectacular was entitled *La Fille aux Punaises*, 'Girl with Bedbugs'. Peggy told everyone they were by a malnourished young artist called Gustave Majal (Majal was the name of a friend's French governess), a friend of her aunt's, who had found him starved to death in the lift of their apartment block. Peggy said that the concierge gave her his drawings, which were scattered on the floor and she sent some to Peggy.

The hoax brought her to the attention of three rich, notable lesbians, Sheila Stoney-Archer, Prascovia Shoubersky and the Countess Vanuuci-Pompei, who reputedly kept a bottle of Vermouth hidden under her bed.

They invited her to tea in their room, thick with cigarette smoke. Stoney-Archer was spread out on a sofa like Madame Récamier, puffing clouds of smoke out of a yard-long ebony cigarette-holder, according to Peggy. They served ginger and banana sandwiches, and Earl Grey tea with slices of lemon, whilst Peggy produced the sheaf of risqué drawings.

> The career of Gustave Majal lasted some three weeks, during which the Newnham Intelligentsia were beautifully deluded and they all came to call on me asking to see the drawings of Gustave Majal, whose untimely death was lamented as a real tragedy for art. This encouraged my aunt to discover another cache of drawings up the chimney, but finally, the truth leaked out as too many were in on the secret and I was running out of inspiration.

Despite this prank, Peggy still led a sheltered life, even at Cambridge. Her 'dear old' Professor Rapson, coming suddenly upon a Sanskrit text that smacked of sex, would say, 'We'll skip the next paragraph, Miss Gladstone,' and Peggy quickly lost her place trying to read it. She said that sex was positively as blank a secret to her as nuclear physics but claimed to be not that curious, after Mammy had jumped on her for an innocent question she considered awkward.

Life was monastic according to Peggy, 'not least because we were issued with a small iron workhouse type bedstead, which had a sagging wire support for a thin mattress which then gave way when you lay down.' Even so, she admitted to liaisons with fellow women students.

I had two very brief affairs, scarcely to be dignified by the term, with one Sally Keigwin, a fat girl with a blonde bob and a South African background, reading History in which she got a Double First; and Polly Falcon, a tall slender beauty with red hair. Compared with Sally, who had a bust like a sack of potatoes, and the dead flat Polly, I was the contemporary ideal and thought no small beer of my figure.

By the end of her first year, the power of her interior life emerged true to form with her invention of the Bloggs family. Peggy's chief aide in the game was Isabelle Granger, a second-year student who kept a private punt on the Upper River. Isabelle took on the identity of Dulcie Dumbledore. The Bloggs dressed up, paraded a battered pram with a baby made of towels and made derogatory remarks about students and lecturers, to whom they gave nicknames. The porter, rather luckily, never discovered he had attracted the name Lord Shortage of Intillecht.

Newnham itself was drawn into the game, The Old Hall became Caterham-on-the-Cheap, which years later Peggy described as a sort of sinister Ambridge, and the dining hall became known as a pub called the Clutch and Gearbox.

It was childish and innocent, but there was no shortage of students willing to participate.

In her first year Peggy joined everything and in her second, resigned from them all, apart from the Clare Hall Music Society (CHMS), which was run by King's College choirmaster and organist Boris Ord. Her contralto voice, good ear and ability to sight-read were considered useful and she began work with them on Bach's B Minor Mass, later performed in Ely Cathedral.

But more interesting to her was being given a part in a little masque produced by Dennis Arundell, who later became an actor and opera scholar. Dennis was openly gay and his boyfriend was the beautiful Cecil Beaton, later a celebrated photographer and designer.

Peggy began to soften towards male undergraduates and remarked on the good looks of one Ian Rolleston of King's College. 'It was the first time I began to take notice of males in any other respect than a potential menace. However, it was a case of adoring from afar, they were Brahmins and we were Untouchables.' In the case of Rolleston, perhaps it was as well for Peggy he showed no interest as, after graduating, he joined the Colonial police and was murdered in a riot in Zanzibar.

It was fashionable to blur gender boundaries at that time, with women making their appearance mannish by wearing trousers, cropping their hair and adopting cigarette holders. A modish man wearing Oxford bags and Fair Isle jumpers was considered effete. In Bohemian circles it was de rigueur to dabble with homosexuality, both male and female, as long as it was kept private.

Peggy aimed at the masculine look and bobbed her hair into an Eton crop that some said gave her the look of the handsome film star Ivor Novello. She wore a hunting kilt, heavy brogue shoes or a gent's golf hose and was sometimes mistaken for a man.

One night, walking home late from Jesus College, escorted by Geoffrey Gorer, who later became a well-known anthropologist and author, and Arthur Elton, later Sir Arthur Elton, a baronet who made his name pioneering British documentary film-making (during the Second World War, he was Supervisor of Films at the Ministry of Information), three silhouettes appeared, one wearing the hat and gown of the Senior Proctor.

'Are you a member of the University, Sir?' the Senior Proctor asked Peggy. (Men were supposed to wear a cap and gown but Peggy was required to wear neither.)

Overcome with fright, she could not reply, but Gorer stepped in, declaring indignantly: 'This is a LADY!'

The Senior Proctor swept off his headgear, bowed and fled, her escorts burst out laughing and the incident was reported in the local paper the next day.

Not as eccentric, when Bobby visited Peggy at Cambridge he was embarrassed by Peggy's Jesus College male friends, Gorer, Elton and

Humphrey Trevelyan (later an author and British diplomat in Beijing, Egypt and Iraq). Peggy admitted: 'They were such notorious alleged perverts that their rooms were frequently wrecked by hearties out to vindicate the good name of the College. I liked them all very much and even in a way shared their dangers, for once Arthur Elton invited me to his College Ball on condition I came in a crinoline with a white curled wig.'

A true sport, she arrived bewigged, in a silver lamé crinoline. She later learned she was in danger of being publicly stripped naked by a gang of rowing men from Jesus who thought she was a boyfriend of Arthur's.*

At the time, Frank Pollard was editing Cambridge's alternative student magazine the *Gownsman*, later to be retitled the *Gownsman and Undergraduette*, with his friend Frank G. G. Carr. Both were keen sailors (Frank Carr later became director of the National Maritime Museum at Greenwich) and both were studying law at Trinity College. Pollard and Carr met Peggy over lunch and suggested she could help with the magazine. Peggy, the *Undergraduette*, began to write what she described as a series of libellous stories about Newnham College. Pollard thought these hilarious and told her candidly that he liked her as she was so unlike a woman.

While Pollard edited the magazine he also wrote for it, using his nom de plume 'Uncle Gregory'. He illustrated the magazine with macabre woodcuts of hanged men, gallows and inebriated writers. Peggy wrote lighthearted tracts and a column as Auntie Lavender in the 'mockney' that would later characterise the Gang's minute book, 'The Boo'. Auntie Lavender advises a 'Veuve Joyeuse' who writes: 'I cannot afford the fashionable "boiled leg" hose (pink stockings) and unless I feel fashionable I cannot work. What am I to do?' Auntie Lavender replies: 'Try Nature's way, dearie. Immerse nether limbs in hot water, bring to the boil. Let simmer ..., remove quickly and rush to lecture. The effect will be striking.'

Peggy spent much of her time with Pollard, but it was Arthur Elton who unexpectedly proposed. Surprised, Peggy accepted his opal engagement ring. Although she preferred Pollard, it seemed Elton was a better prospect and her family would approve.

It was probably on account of my masculine airs, Arthur was sufficiently attracted to make me an offer of marriage,

21

though if I had been more percipient I might have seen it was by no means wholehearted... Alas, scarcely had Arthur Elton offered me his hand in marriage than Pollard himself came forward with a declaration. It never rains but it pours... Reluctantly I opted for Arthur Elton who was the son of a baronet and would have a stately home, Clevedon Court, [a 14th-century manor house near Bristol that was later donated to the National Trust in lieu of death duties] one day.

It amused Peggy that Elton was attracted by her masculinity, but the novelty wore off. She remained friends with Pollard and wrote to him expressing her concerns: '... it seems it may be a long time before I get married. I may have to take matters into my own hands... I don't like assuming responsibilities, nor do I like the male characteristics expected in me and approved in me so much by Arthur. I know he'd rather have been a woman and for me to have been a man, he's often said so, but the physical facts remain.'

Rather ungallantly, Elton soon had second thoughts about marriage, but lacked the courage to call off the engagement. 'It was Pollard I finally married as Arthur Elton ... with desperate resourcefulness went to see Pollard and asked whether in the circumstances he would take over, as it were...'

Peggy accepted Pollard as her fiancé and graduated from Cambridge in 1924.

Her private life might have been less than ideal, but academically she was formidable and achieved first-class honours in both parts of the Oriental languages tripos, the first woman at Cambridge ever to do so. Most of the women that year were brilliant in their subjects and there was an impressive crop of Double Firsts.

Her studies continued. Peggy was awarded the Caroline Turle scholarship to undertake further research on *'The Indian Experiences of Vishnu from the Rigveda down to the Puranas'*, spending her last two years under the tutelage of Dr Barrett at the London School of Oriental Languages.

She kept her promise to write a book on Vishnu and was later awarded a PhD for it. Only two copies were published; one was held in Room Lamba at the British Museum and the other she used as a footstool.

'I do not believe any other woman ever got a Double First in Oriental Languages, or that anybody else has written a Life of the God Vishnu,' she said.

* Elton remained a bachelor until 20 years later when in 1948 he married the Canadian historian Margaret Ann Bjornson. They had three children.

CHAPTER TWO
Ferguson's Gang is born

After she left Cambridge, Peggy decided against living with her mother, who had moved to the Isle of Wight, choosing to move to London instead.

In the early 1920s, the capital was emerging from its post-war depression and was anything but sleepy, as busy then as it is now. Four thousand open-topped red buses ferried around some of its seven million population. Black cabs dodged the odd horse and cart and were hailed by smart flappers fashionably dressed in pastels. The roads were chock-a-block with traffic and hundreds of people walked shoulder to shoulder in the streets.

Strong-minded and independent, but also a country girl, Peggy was surprised to find she loved the city. She wrote to Pollard: 'London is the most wonderful place in the world. I've no reason to like it; I don't frequent theatres, night clubs or social functions: I know it's vulgar compared with Stockholm, which is comparably beautiful, but the more misadventures that befall me in London the better I like it.'

Financially secure, Peggy was lucky enough to be able to enjoy herself with an annual private income of £400 (the average labourer earned around £105 annually): '£400 a year was nuts and figs when you had nothing to spend it on but your private pleasures,' she said.

She found historic London fascinating: it was not the main tourist attractions such as Big Ben and the Tower of London, but the marginalised and little documented obscure parts that resonated with her. Peggy was particularly interested in anything connected with women's history and its place in the fabric of the city, and together with a new circle of friends, set out to uncover London's hidden water wells, priories, prisons, holy shrines, ducking-pond fields and underground rivers. These friends shared her eccentricities and growing interest in historical and rural Britain.

Peggy's fascination with hidden waterways emerged because her flat in Pimlico was built above what was the southern end of the Tachbrook.

It had long ceased to function as a river and was now an underground sewer, prone to flooding in bad weather.

Inspired by this watery network, she sketched a map of London's underground rivers, which the Ferguson's Gang's artist would later illustrate. The map included places such as the site of Bedlam, a south London hospital for leprous maidens; Bunhill Fields, an old burial ground in north London; the spring of Agnes le Clair; and the south-east London Church of St Saviour and St Mary Overie, which is now Southwark Cathedral.

The first of her new acquaintances was 'Brynnie', Brynhild Catherine Granger, the younger sister of her Cambridge chum Isabelle Granger who had been Dulcie Dumbledore in the Bloggs family.

Their relationship did not gel immediately so Brynnie pursued Peggy, rather like a beau courting a young lady. She won her over one afternoon during a trip to the zoo when they both dressed up as nuns.

Peggy gleefully recorded their outing:

> At first I thought she was rather an idiot but undeterred by my coolness she kept asking me out until in the end I began to like her and we pretended to be nuns. I was Mother Angelice and she was Sister Agatha and we decided to go in disguise one Thursday to the zoo and have ices at Selfridges afterwards. We agreed to meet in a little tea-shop. I took a lot of pains with my dress and carefully made a sort of coif with a veil of black casement cloth; I stuck my head through the elastic waist of an old accordion-pleated skirt which came down nearly to my hips, and added a good long full skirt of black casement cloth and looked quite passably nun-like. Anyway, I got safely to the tea-shop and waited for Sister Agatha to arrive. When she did I nearly disowned her and fled. I never saw anything so daft in my life.
>
> Ag had put on, over a bright blue cloth coat and pink stockings, a pair of college gowns back to back and for a quimp had round her neck a filthy damask table napkin stained with obvious cabbage or cauliflower marks; her beaming face peered out of the leg of a pair of white bloomers, which were no means fresh from the laundry... When we got to the zoo

we were a bit disappointed as the deer and antelopes, which we liked best, fled from us in terror.

We felt a bit nervous about ices at Selfridges and went straight to Fortnum and Mason to buy stuffed quails.

Brynnie was from an upper middle-class fruit-farming family in Essex but despite their different backgrounds their personalities were complementary. While Peggy could be intimidating, dictatorial and overly direct at times, Brynnie was gentle, easy-going and eager to please. They became firm allies and friends, and with their enthusiasm for adventure, formed the foundation stone of Ferguson's Gang.

While Brynnie was studying at King's College for Women she met the bright, fun-loving Joy Maw, who had recently moved to London from Shropshire. They studied the same course and shared a room at Queen Mary's Hostel, the college halls of residence in Campden Hill, Kensington.

Accustomed to boarding school life the girls bonded and became friends with Rachel Pinney, an old school friend of Bryn's. When they were first introduced, Rachel was studying at Bristol University but would later continue her education at King's.

Suitably eccentric, Rachel had already formed a clique at Bristol called 'The Family', much like Peggy's Bloggs family. She was from the same kind of distinguished upper-class background as Peggy and, like her, bore the scars of a traumatic childhood. The four were from diverse backgrounds, with varying degrees of wealth, but class proved no barrier to their friendship.

Their personalities and troubled backgrounds made them ripe to share in Peggy's imaginative games. They had come to the city to study and establish themselves independently, but had no desire to be alone.

They did not know yet that they would become a gang. Ferguson's Gang was Peggy's creation. She and her brother were enjoying themselves at a Hunt Ball on the Isle of Wight with a fellow Etonian friend of Bobby's, known only as 'pore old Arris'. They were chatting, when Arris ran in screaming like a banshee. 'We were all sloshed,' said Peggy. 'Then pore old Arris came rushing in and hid behind the curtains. "Ferguson's after me. Ferguson's going to get me," he said. We laughed ourselves into fits and at last he fell on the floor and hid under the table. Into my mind came the idea of Ferguson's Gang and we started it there and then.' Whether Ferguson was real or imagined she did not say, but if he was real, he was only ever represented by proxy.

CHAPTER THREE
Stonehenge

It was a clear, sunny day in 1927 when Peggy told Rachel, Bryn and Joy about Ferguson's Gang, during a picnic at Tothill Fields, the site of a former prison for women and young boys. They were sitting by the Thames, remarking on how the landscape of the city and the country was changing. Around them, new buildings were going up as fast as old ones were being demolished and they wondered how long the little green space of Tothill Fields would survive.

Two other future members were there that day. One was Poolcat, who made the picnic, and the other was See Me Run, the Heathen Chinee who was important early on in the life of the Gang but was mysteriously excommunicated as a 'traitor and a nark' before the Gang's first acquisition.

References in The Boo suggest that Poolcat was George Macaulay Trevelyan, an important influence on the Gang and their thinking, and a vital link to the National Trust.

Born in 1876, Trevelyan was a member of the Cambridge Apostles, a secret society of the university's most influential undergraduates. Other Apostles included the composer Ralph Vaughan Williams and the novelist E. M. Forster, both enthusiastic supporters of rural conservation.

On that day, Trevelyan was a year into his 23-year stint working for the National Trust, or the National Trust for Places of Historic Interest and Natural Beauty as it was wordily known then, and later, in 1931, he helped found the Youth Hostel Association in Great Britain.

Trevelyan's thinking was very much in line with the Gang's attitude to the countryside and he felt, like them, it should be there for all to enjoy. His rousing pleas to protect it were inspiring and in an essay called 'Must England's Beauty Perish?' he wrote:

> In an age when beauty, especially beauty of nature and landscape, is being destroyed with unexampled rapidity by

modern inventions and economic residential developments, the desire to save beloved places from ruin is much more widely and intensely felt than ever before.

The women were also aware of the threat of the growing metropolis, and although the Gang had no constitution or specific aim, involving themselves with conservation provided a common cause.

London was exciting and offered them much in the way of clubs, cafés and a wild Bohemian subculture, but it was also noisy, busy and polluted, with a thick layer of soot blackening its buildings. Escape was a growing trend for those living in cities, and in the 1920s and 30s, an awareness of the need to protect green spaces began to emerge. Suburban towns and cities throughout the United Kingdom were growing at an unprecedented rate. The roads and railways linking them to metropolitan zones were increasing and within a short time people realised that the remaining green spaces might soon be filled in with houses.

The National Trust had been founded by Octavia Hill in 1895, initially to preserve parks and fields in the city. Hill had her roots in social reform. She was a strong and impressive woman and a natural role model for Ferguson's Gang. By the end of the 19th century, Hill had started a campaign to improve the urban environment. She then persuaded the influential art critic and social reformer John Ruskin to buy slum dwellings in Marylebone, London, and transform them into good social housing. Once the transformation was complete, Ruskin planted trees in the adjoining wasteland and turned it into a playground.

Open spaces were sacrosanct to Hill and among the many high-profile places she helped save were tracts of Hampstead Heath and Parliament Hill Fields in London.

The accelerated rate of house building following the First World War was in danger of obliterating common lands and had a catastrophic impact on rural life. A burgeoning urban population became divorced from the countryside.

In the first half of the 20th century there were few nationwide laws to protect green spaces and it was left to charitable trusts to take up the baton. They also highlighted buildings that were of historic interest and saved them when their owners either did not have the resources nor the will to do it themselves.

The women had read about the National Trust's work and discussed it at their picnic. They were particularly struck by the Trust's campaign to protect Stonehenge from development and very excited that the Trust were trying to save 4,000 acres of farmland around Stonehenge, trying to prevent that ancient monument suffering piecemeal encroachment.

The National Appeal to save Stonehenge was launched that same year, by Prime Minister Stanley Baldwin. Until then, the vulnerability of the 5,000-year-old Mesolithic monument, one of the world's most important prehistoric structures, was unknown to most Britons. The truth was that the stones had been badly neglected and were in danger of complete collapse.

The story of their sad demise had begun 30 years earlier when the site was owned by Sir Edmund Antrobus, 4th baronet and colonel in the Coldstream Guards, who had absolutely no interest in their welfare. He was required by the 1882 Ancient Monuments Act to conserve Stonehenge, but had not done so, despite the valiant efforts of Augustus Pitt Rivers, Inspector of Ancient Monuments, to persuade him. Pitt Rivers found himself impotent when trying to impose any action, as Antrobus refused either to repair or sell the site.

Consequently, Stonehenge was utterly unprotected, and when tourists visited and wanted a souvenir, they simply went to a kiosk, hired a hammer and chisel, and chipped off slivers of the stones. Even if Antrobus had agreed to sell the monument, there was a fear that public custodianship might mean the site becoming a theme park, as portrayed in a *Punch* cartoon of the time, where the stones were used as banqueting tables and to house fairground attractions.

In 1900, the feared collapse of one of the great sarsen stones actually occurred, and finally Antrobus was forced to allow access to the site. An advisory committee worked with him to re-establish the stone.

The stones were by no means saved and there was further concern for them. Canadian troops based in Larkhill, a garrison town 1 mile north of the site, practised their manoeuvres beside the stones, and the landmine tests they carried out were responsible for cracking one of them. That was bad enough but the Royal Air Force constructed an aerodrome within sight of the circle and the stones became a playground for First World War fighter-pilots who practised aerobatics above them. Photographs show their displays of derring-do as they flew as close as possible to Stonehenge on their way to the airfield at Stonehenge Down.

Fate stepped in when Antrobus died in 1915. The estate was then sold at auction and bought by Cecil Chubb, a wealthy resident from Shrewton, a village 4 miles west of the stones. He paid £6,600 for them on a whim as a present for his wife and became the last private owner of the stones. She was less than impressed, so in 1918, Chubb donated them to the British Government for posterity, ensuring their preservation for the nation forever, and received a knighthood from the King in gratitude.

Even with intervention, the 40-tonne stones were leaning at perilous angles, with unsightly wooden props erected to prevent them toppling over. Salisbury Plain, where the stones stand, was still private property. Within sight of the circle was an aerodrome, a pig farm, and two cottages for Stonehenge custodians, all of which had been built too close to the site. When an enterprising restaurateur erected the Stonehenge Café, their true vulnerability became clear.

A Stonehenge Protection Committee was formed with cooperation from all the political parties. High-profile advocates included the Conservative Prime Minister Stanley Baldwin; Ramsay MacDonald, the former Labour Prime Minister; the Viscount Grey of Fallodon, who was Vice-President of the National Trust; and Jacob Pleydell-Bouverie, 6th Earl of Radnor and the Lord-Lieutenant of Wiltshire.

They were joined by the National Trust, which stepped in to help and they issued a joint campaign leaflet in 1927 that read:

The land of the Plain around the stones however, is still private property. So long as it remains in private hands, there is an obvious danger that the setting of Stonehenge may be ruined and the stones dwarfed by the erection of unsightly buildings on the Plain... The conditions of modern transport make it extremely likely that this structure, if no preventive measures be adopted, will be the first of many, and that the monoliths will in time be surrounded by all the accessories of a popular holiday resort. The Stonehenge ring, as every British child has learnt to picture it from his earliest years, will no longer exist. The solitude of Stonehenge should be restored, and precautions taken to ensure that our posterity will see it against the sky in the lonely majesty before which our ancestors have stood in awe throughout all our recorded history.

The Committee secured options to buy the 1,444 acres of land surrounding Stonehenge with a budget of £35,000 to complete the purchase. By 1928, all the buildings had been removed and the stones stood proudly in a grassland setting.

Success meant that Stonehenge never had to face a block of high-rise flats, a low-rise bungalow, hotel or shopping complex. It stood, as intended, a majestic monument surrounded by countryside, visible from far and wide, thanks to a well-orchestrated conservation campaign.

The women were inspired that such a small organisation as the National Trust had managed to save a monument of worldwide importance and felt compelled to make their own contribution to conservation.

They discussed Stonehenge at Tothill Fields that day and the image of Stonehenge was so important to Ferguson's Gang it would become part of their emblem. It also became a favourite pilgrimage, a place they visited as often as they could.

Gang funds were essential if they were to achieve anything of note. Since the picnic, collecting Victorian coins had become a game and one they decided to continue in order to raise money. At meetings, all members were asked to surrender any coinage printed with Queen Victoria's image to use for future Gang activities. But the bulk of the money came mostly from Peggy and her mother. 'What everyone else contributed wouldn't have bought a pound of toffee,' Peggy wrote.

Unsure what to save first, their 'swag' languished in Bill Stickers' underwear drawer, hidden beneath her silk petticoats.

Peggy chose pseudonyms for the Gang and they pledged to remain anonymous for their lifetimes. Peggy became Bill Stickers, a name taken most likely from the sign 'Bill Stickers will be prosecuted', put up to prevent people from pasting advertising posters onto walls. Brynnie was Sister Agatha, as she had dressed in a nun's habit on that quasi-religious trip to the zoo with Peggy. Rachel, with her Communist leanings, was initially known as Red Biddy, and Joy became Kate O'Brien the Nark. She shared the name with Kate O'Brien, the Irish lesbian novelist, as well as Peggy's friend Kate O'Brien who lived in Cornwall and had allegedly been a gun-runner for the IRA.

Hiding their identities suggested they were rebellious and prepared to operate illegally, but they were never anything other than benevolent. There was never any doubt that they were a gang of friends with a common cause, not a gang of criminals.

As a gang they never fell foul of the law, or perhaps never needed to, but individually, however, they did commit small and larger misdemeanours.

There was a suggestion that Peggy stole some ancient objects from the Fitzwilliam Museum in Cambridge, but they said they had not noticed if she had. However, the Gang's archive contains a few mysterious objects whose provenance cannot be confirmed, including a primitive oil lamp and a jade ring. One Gang member did fall foul of the law making what she thought was a benevolent gesture. Much much later, Rachel was sent to prison for kidnap.

Peggy, Rachel, Brynnie and Joy became the first permanent members of the Gang's inner circle. It would be a year before they were joined by a fifth core member, art student Ruth Sherwood.

CHAPTER FOUR
The newlyweds

Peggy may have achieved independence by moving to London and doing as she liked, but in 1928 there was still an expectation that upper-class and middle-class women married. Women generally pursued work or a career only if they needed to earn money. Peggy had an income of £400 a year, which would double to £800 when she married, so she was under no pressure to find work.

She had enjoyed flirtations with women at Cambridge and her independent spirit seemed indisposed to marriage. Nevertheless, she left Cambridge engaged to Frank Pollard, and after four years, they married.

Frank Pollard was born in 1906 and was christened George Francis Gifford Pollard. He read law at Trinity College because he was the son of a prominent solicitor but had no real passion for it.

Pollard failed his law degree, eventually graduating from Cambridge with a 'Special' in English; a gateway permitted to the men but not the women.

This failure was irrelevant to Peggy, who considered him exceptionally bright. 'Pollard carried heavier intellectual guns than anybody I ever knew, and I with my Double First and PhD was an intellectual dwarf by comparison. He was a walking *Encyclopaedia Britannica* and could talk about things like mediaeval iconography or architecture or pretty well anything and make circles round anybody he was talking to, he just didn't happen to be good at exams, and I did.'

His intellect did not impress her family, who lamented his lack of status. 'I invited him to the Isle of Wight, and to Mammy's infinite disgust and in the face of Bobby's discreet but evident disapproval I did marry Pollard, who had neither money or prospects.'

Peggy and the penniless Pollard married in 1928 at St Margaret's Church, Westminster, the church favoured by society and members of the Royal Family, and where Peggy had been christened 24 years before.

It was not a glittering high-society wedding, but several members of the Gladstone family were there. Pollard's friend Bill Bailey was the best man (and the only guest in morning dress). For some reason he timed the ceremony, reporting it had taken ten minutes and 30 seconds. The wedding party was held some time later where Peggy asked guests to sign a tablecloth and then preserved their signatures by embroidering them. These included previous beau Arthur Elton, the famous ballerina Marie Rambert and the members of Ferguson's Gang.

After the ceremony, Mr and Mrs Pollard left Westminster and travelled to the luxurious Tregenna Hotel in St Ives, Cornwall, for their honeymoon. For Peggy, the honeymoon was an anticlimax. Pollard's only interest during their week away was sailing, a passion not shared by his spouse. 'At this prospect I felt a mixture of resignation, depression and determination; however, I needed all these qualities on the wedding night, when Pollard informed me that he did not feel energetic, rolled over and went fast asleep.'

The rejection was crushing. Although Peggy had no desire to have children (she'd made sure no references to them were made in the marriage service and the works of Dr Marie Stopes, an expert on contraception, were part of her trousseau), she was excited by the prospect of consummating her marriage. Pollard was 6 foot 2 inches in height, attractive, and a powerfully built rowing man, so why wouldn't she? But he simply had no interest in sex, or in women, whom he considered generally inferior.

Afraid that the disastrous wedding night was somehow her fault, and worried that Pollard would begin looking for a mistress, Peggy decided that her best course of action was to make him comfortable, buy him a yacht if she could afford it, and learn the art of cooking. 'We might well manage a platonic relationship as we had any amount in common including our cynical attitude to religion and our Cambridge background. As for sex, well, I could take it or leave it. I would settle for what I could get, and there's an endo't.' Peggy returned to London still a virgin.

Mammy could have afforded to buy Peggy a flat in Kensington or Chelsea but home was a 'damp, prehistoric basement in a rather criminal part of London.' Their only view was the feet and ankles of passers-by and the flat was so gloomy that the light was kept on all day. It was built over the underground River Tachbrook (but luckily, was not affected when it flooded), located in Denbigh Street, Pimlico. Its previous tenant was Pollard's best man Bill Bailey, who had lived there with his communist spouse. Mrs Bailey refused to wear a wedding ring. To prove they were married they carried a green marble clock everywhere as it was inscribed by the firm where Bailey worked. 'You don't get marble clocks for living in sin,' they assured suspicious landladies.

The newlywed Pollards shared the building with a woman who led a colourful life, spending her days in her dressing gown admitting gentlemen callers. She earned the disapproval of the Pollards' charwoman, a formidable Roman Catholic Scot.

The char's wages were ten shillings a week, and for that, she arrived early, made breakfast, cleaned the house and argued with Peggy about religion before going home. Between arguments, she taught Peggy basic housework, showing her how to wash and iron and to cook. She was unimpressed with the food Peggy purchased and snorted with derision at the offal she brought home from Strutton Ground Market, swearing that her family would not touch it.

Peggy was no chef and her culinary skills needed practice. She once undercooked a rabbit, rendering Pollard prostrate with food poisoning for two days. Pollard was not a bit upset and found the idea that his wife might be prosecuted for murdering him hilarious. 'He was easily amused,' she said. 'I attribute the undoubted success of our weird marriage to the fact that I could always make him laugh.'

To outsiders it would have seemed a romantic existence, as Peggy wrote plays and poems for Pollard, while he lived the life of a writer. As law was now out of the question, he concentrated on journalism and wrote novels, achieving a modicum of critical acclaim. Published by Grant Richards, his books were Boys' Own dramas based at sea. *All in the Downs* was the story of a convoy to the West Indies and the erotic intrigues of wealthy merchants. *East Indiaman* was the next, chronicling the maritime, commercial and amorous adventures of a young officer in the service of the East India Company. It received blanket reviews, but they were mixed.

The *Daily Mail* loved it and wrote: 'Mr Pollard has an astonishing gift for recapturing the spirit of the 18th-century; he writes with wit and vigour.' The *Observer* was quite unflattering. It said: 'Mr Pollard has evidently studied his period very carefully, and he can carry his story along with picturesque details and accurate descriptions when all else fails him. And as a general rule plot fails him.'

It was Grant Richards who had introduced the couple to Marie Rambert and her husband, the playwright Ashley Dukes. Rambert, a Polish dancer from Warsaw, had studied in Paris, where she was employed by Serge Diaghilev as assistant choreographer in his Ballet Russes. On settling in London, she established a dance school in Notting Hill, West London, which evolved into the Rambert Dance Company. During the 1920s, Rambert dancers performed in nighttime revue shows at various venues around London. When Rambert re-established the troupe in 1930 as the Ballet Club at the Mercury Theatre in Notting Hill, the first classical ballet company to appear in Britain, she invited Peggy and Pollard to be founder members.

A Rambert dancer was an artist, technically brilliant and beautiful, and these creatures seemed to love Pollard, especially the English ballerina Alicia Markova who worked as a 'guest' artist at the company. Pollard loved the dancers as much as they loved him and, after a performance, he would hail a taxi and travel home with an ethereal ballerina sitting on his knee, arms wrapped around his neck. 'I did not mind at all. I adored them myself. They were as beautiful as angels,' said Peggy.

Peggy occasionally cast off her masculine clothes and could dress as beautifully as a debutante if she needed to. She owned at least one couture dress: 'I did buy a model, it was designed by Princess Yousoupoff... It was a black chiffon sheath, with a front panel painted in futuristic flowers, crimson, green and blue, sprinkled with silvery dust. There was a six foot long black scarf with painted ends which you knotted round your neck. In this with my Eton crop, I really looked good for once in my life and people would visibly jump when I entered a ballroom. And under it I wore Nothing At All ... mark ye my words, Nothing At All.'

They led a happy life doing practically nothing and settled into a routine, which included Pollard reading, writing and smoking his pipe, while Peggy cooked, sewed and played the piano. Pollard, like the Da, liked to be played to and was particularly fond of Wagner. Brynnie visited once a week for supper and a trip to the zoo, while another evening was spent at the Ballet Club, with another being designated to the theatre.

It was a twilight existence in many ways, punctuated with weekends away visiting Peggy's mother on the Isle of Wight. After her husband's death, Anne sold Nanhurst and moved to The Briary, a Victorian villa in Freshwater Bay built by the painter G. F. Watts. Peggy much preferred this new home and the artistic enclave of Freshwater. Lord Tennyson had lived in Freshwater, as had the pioneering photographer Julia Margaret Cameron.

They did not always head for The Briary – they sometimes stayed with their old friends the Godwin-Austens in Surrey. They no idea then, but Arthur Godwin-Austen would become an important catalyst for the first major purchase for Ferguson's Gang.

During those weekends they horrified their hosts with the travails of their 'low neighbourhood' where residents regularly made headlines. Notable anecdotes included a man who murdered his grandparents with fire-irons, the police chasing a jewel robber, and a young couple who gassed themselves in the adjacent street.

These stories may have been entertaining but nothing could convince Pollard that city living was for him. He hankered after a boat and Peggy said generously that he could buy one as long as it was not 'ruinously expensive'. They heard of a boat called a Plymouth hooker that had been abandoned in distress off the Isle of Wight and was listing in Yarmouth harbour, and Peggy allowed herself to be convinced to buy her. Discarding the original name of *Sula*, they renamed her *Bellatrix*. She was a wreck, a major restoration project that they worked on together, pumping her dry and patching her hull while Pollard began talking enthusiastically about long-distance cruising.

Peggy came to the conclusion that although all yachtsmen were delightful, they employed a class of downtrodden and overworked serf: a combination of cook, cabin-boy, first mate and able seaman who was expected to do everything, and the serf was usually the wife. She observed that although these women were resigned, obedient, willing and devoted, almost none were particularly enthusiastic. She said they had acquired a serenity that came from feeling sure that life could hold no more nasty surprises.

Still, Peggy gamely manned the galley, and once the *Bellatrix* was seaworthy, embarked on a maiden voyage to Norway. Pollard would go on to captain many ships but this one was a disaster and the boat sank.

The sea was calm on their first night but he became extremely seasick. 'This startled and shocked me,' Peggy said. 'But he told me

Nelson was always sick on every voyage.' She manned the tiller in a thick fog while Pollard went below.

Suddenly startled by a steamer that came from nowhere, she lost control and the *Bellatrix* careered into the side of another yacht. 'It all happened in seconds. I heard the hiss of the bow wave and even the rattle of the crockery as if the crew were getting breakfast. Then out of the fog loomed a steamer that looked as big as the *Titanic*, passing within yards of us.'

The *Bellatrix* went down just outside Lyme Bay and Peggy found the experience so traumatic, she never put to open sea again.

Although she never found her sea legs, it was inevitable, given Pollard's passion, and Peggy's love of the countryside, that they would leave London. By 1931 they had settled in the perfect village in St Mawes on the south Cornish coast, a pretty place with a large harbour. Peggy bought one of four small stone and slate cottages in The Rope Walk, a tiny cul de sac behind Our Lady Star of the Sea and St Anthony Catholic Church. She paid £300, receiving a generous discount because its greenhouse had blown away in a gale.

Writing about their life in St Mawes, she said: 'It seemed ideal to me. Just to waste time delightfully, have nice people to stay and go cruising in the summer… Pollard was the perfect companion if not everybody's idea of the perfect husband. I now had a good idea of what he liked and didn't like to eat, and never once in my life have I asked him to put down that paper as he hasn't heard a word I've been saying.

'I made a comfortable framework for him financially and whole-heartedly admired him; compared with which a few odd infidelities [Peggy's] don't really seem to count. And when he got terribly into debt, as periodically happened, for he was utterly reckless about buying books and clothes, I bailed him out. I can't say I was in love with him, and I don't fancy he was with me. We just got along awfully well.'

Pollard was purportedly involved with the Gang and his pseudo-nym was his old nom de plume Uncle Gregory from his *Gownsman* writing days. It often appeared on the Gang's leaflets and minutes, but in reality, he did very little. Pollard was happier writing adventure novels, sailing and entertaining the locals in the pub with his stories.

CHAPTER FIVE
The bird of paradise and his octopus

To understand the Gang's passion for rural England it is vital to understand what was happening to the countryside, to trace the birth of conservation as we know it and who was involved. In 1928, a year after Ferguson's Gang was formed, maverick architect Bertram Clough Williams-Ellis published *England and the Octopus*, a book attacking building policy, or lack of it. Clough was an eccentric and a nonconformist, exactly the kind of character Peggy was drawn to.

The Gang were excited that someone had identified many of their own concerns for the future of the British countryside and had written a book spelling them out. Peggy attended one of Clough's lectures and the sight of him in a loud bow tie, canary-yellow stockings and breeches, reminded her of a 'bird of paradise'. She developed a deep respect for Clough, and wrote to him subsequently. It was the first of many letters they exchanged over the next 50 years, until Clough's death in 1978.

Clough Williams-Ellis was witty and original, a flamboyant and charismatic Renaissance man. He was 45 when they met and Peggy was 24. She was in awe of him and he had nothing but respect for her. On the flyleaf of her personal copy of *England and the Octopus* he wrote: 'To Peggy Pollard, to whom I would have Dedicated this Angry Little Book had she been known to me when I wrote it.'

England and the Octopus was angry with good reason. In it, Clough lamented the sprawl of post-war urban development and described London as: 'An octopus spreading its tentacles across the countryside.' Building was out of control, he said, not just in London, but nationwide.

The absence of planning controls meant that anyone could build anything anywhere, and frequently did. He complained about ribbon developments: houses springing up by roadsides, creating suburban sprawl and traffic congestion. He disliked pepper-pot developments too, where homes were sprinkled haphazardly across open country with no consideration for their surroundings.

After the First World War, urban development was rife. England tried to revitalise its flailing economy by building its way out of recession. Between 1927 and 1935, four million houses were built, translating to 38,000 acres a year being developed, with the highest concentration in the South East and the Midlands. How best to contain urban sprawl was a hot debate. There were very few centralised systems for planning and building consent. It was a landowner's prerogative to develop his land as he wished, and trust and a respect for tradition were his only restraints. The real question was how to preserve a rural landscape that was so rapidly changing.

Clough could see that liberty to build anywhere led to a hotchpotch form of development that benefited no one. Positioning himself at the centre of the debate about building control, he wrote: 'We need direction and leadership now as never before, because now, in this generation, a new England is being made, its form is being hastily cast in a mould that no one has considered as a whole... If there is no master-founder, no co-related plan, we may well live to be aghast at what we have made – a hash of our civilisation and a desert of our country.'

He had no desire to preserve the countryside in aspic, but he could not bear to see England's lush fields and ancient woodlands disappear under a mishmash of ill-constructed, ill-considered housing, advertising hoardings and wooden telegraph poles.

In *The Face of the Land*, the 1929–30 yearbook for the Design and Industries Association, Clough wrote an impassioned plea:

We English may be a great people... But if we're to be judged by that which we are so feverishly yet carelessly constructing as the background of our lives, we should surely be counted as quite lamentable muddlers, making a sad mess of our country, with very little sense of order, seemliness, dignity, or even efficiency, and none at all of that discipline without which there can be no assured or permanent freedom.

England, as I verily believe, stood forth as the loveliest thing that God and man had ever made between them. There is a cloud of witness to this effect, the painters Canaletto, Scott, Gainsborough, Constable, Morland, Turner, Willson, Crome, Cotman, Cox and the rest and writers and poets without number. They pictured what they loved and what we have largely lost forever.

If God had made the countryside, then man had contributed to its beauty, building the great churches and cathedrals of England but also the stately homes, castles and magnificent houses that had housed its nobility, statesmen and clergy over the centuries.

Clough was not just paying lip-service; his aim was to achieve harmony between old and new, and he showcased his utopia in the Italianate folly he built overlooking the sea on the dramatic hillsides in Gwynedd, North Wales, which he named Portmeirion. He began building it in 1925 and skilfully mixed architectural styles from different periods and from different countries, using ornamental salvage from demolished stately homes, and continued working on it for the next 60 years.

Clough's was not a lone voice. In 1877, William Morris, the most influential designer of the 19th century, had set up the Society for the Protection of Ancient Buildings (SPAB) with notable members of the Pre-Raphaelite Brotherhood. Over the years, the society attracted prominent supporters, both inside and outside the world of conservation, including Thomas Hardy, John Ruskin, Beatrix Potter, Sir Arthur Conan Doyle and John Betjeman, all of whom were members.

The Society's mission was to raise awareness of how old buildings should be conserved, both aesthetically and to maintain their historical integrity and authenticity. Overzealous restorations led to eyesores like thatched cottages having half-thatch half-slate roofs. The Society's advice to architects was not to make a pastiche of the past or try to disguise the new to look old, but to conserve what was old and ensure that new additions didn't overwhelm or camouflage the original. Conservation work should make use of similar, local, handmade materials they said. This created continuity and helped the property blend into the fabric of its surroundings.

The only government provision to protect any kind of property was the Ancient Monuments Protection Act passed in 1882, which allowed landowners with ancient monuments on their land to enter into an agreement with civil authorities to place their property under public guardianship. The authority then had an obligation to maintain and preserve the monument for the nation. The Act excluded inhabited residences and, in the event, only 69 monuments, all prehistoric, were identified in England, Scotland, Wales and Ireland. Until 1896, when the National Trust was founded, there was little public interest in preserving residential buildings.

Big houses were expensive to run and often had few modern amenities. During the years of war and economic hardship, aristocrats and landed gentry were crippled by financial decline and Estate Tax (death duties), which had risen from a maximum of 8 per cent at the turn of the century to a maximum of 50 per cent by 1930.

After the First World War, with the economy in tatters, rural landowners could barely balance their account ledgers, and some tenant farmers, unable to compete with cheaper food imports brought from abroad in refrigerated ships, were unable to find the rent. Redundant homes, if demolished, could not be valued for probate duty and the land was then available to sell for development, so demolition became the preferred option. The destruction of unaffordable, crumbling country seats became a spectator sport with groups of people gathering to watch stately homes being razed to the ground. The effect was devastating. By 1945, 178 houses of architectural importance had been destroyed.

Some stately homes were deconstructed and shipped to America, like the half-timbered Elizabethan manor house Agecroft Hall, from Lancashire, which was sold at auction in 1925 and re-erected in Richmond, Virginia. It had fallen into disrepair after coal pits were opened around the estate and a railway line cut through it.

Change was slow, but against the odds there was pressure to save some very important historic buildings such as Tattershall Castle in Lincolnshire, which was handed to the National Trust in 1925. Originally built by Robert de Tattershall in 1231, it had been owned in the 15th century by Ralph, 3rd Lord Cromwell, Treasurer of England, who expanded it greatly. It was put up for sale after falling into neglect. Its greatest feature was its huge Gothic fireplaces and these were bought by an American millionaire who packaged them up ready to be shipped to the States. The National Trust attempted to buy them back, but the public showed little interest and they failed to raise the funds. It was a debacle dubbed the 'Tattershall Vandalism'. The furore did attract some attention and motivated Conservative statesman and Viceroy of India Lord Curzon of Kedleston to step in at the eleventh hour. He bought the castle and after a nationwide hunt the fireplaces were tracked down to a shipyard in London. Lord Curzon retrieved them and restored the castle under the supervision of Scottish architect William Weir.* It is now one of the three most important surviving brick castles of the mid-15th century. Coincidentally, Weir's apprentice was a young architect called John Macgregor, who later had a major role in Ferguson's Gang.

Deeply affected by what might have happened to Tattershall and other properties, Clough did not shy away from this wanton destruction and contributed to the debate in practical ways, helping to remodel grand estates so that they could serve communities.

In 1922, Stowe in Buckinghamshire, one of the most important houses and estates in the country, worked on by the great designers and architects Vanbrugh, Kent, Gibbs, Pitt, Sloane and Adam, had become too expensive to run and was destined to be demolished. Attitudes towards saving stately homes were still apathetic. *Country Life* magazine dismissed it, saying it had outlived its usefulness, while *The Times* suggested that such buildings assumed grandeur once ruined. The *Spectator* disagreed and reiterated its historical significance and beauty. It was only saved because the educationalist and Church of England clergyman Reverend Percy Warrington read the article and suggested that country houses could easily be converted into public schools. Subsequently, Stowe was bought by a consortium, and Clough was the architect appointed to transform it. He was so passionate about conserving the estate as a whole, that when the owners announced plans to sell off the two-mile Grand Avenue in the grounds, Clough recognised it was as important as the house, and bought it at auction, eventually selling it at a loss to a group of the schools' benefactors, but managing to maintain the integrity of the estate.

Nevertheless, there was little incentive for landowners to conserve property or land when the economy was so unstable and land was so cheap. Freehold bungalow plots in the late 1920s could be bought for 1s 2d a square yard, while a luxury berth on a White Star Lines cruise ship to America cost £38.

Sensitive to the situation, Clough gave financial backing to the Council for the Protection of Rural England (CPRE) with Professor Patrick Abercrombie, a town planner, Arts and Crafts architect Guy Dawber and David Lindsay, Lord Crawford, who turned down a cabinet post and chairmanship of the BBC to concentrate on conservation.

In May 1928 Cough joined the CPRE's Executive Committee and became their de facto spokesman, giving lectures across the country and writing numerous articles for the national and local press. These four men dedicated much of their working lives to protecting the landscape and were later knighted for their efforts.

Not everyone understood the CPRE. Anthony Bertram, in his 1938 book *Design*, published by Penguin, felt the need to defend the organisation, saying: 'There is a grossly unfair tendency to mix up the CPRE with the sort of arid conservatism which tries to mummify the countryside, and that automatically opposes all innovations, all new design, all demolition and reconstruction.'

The Gang derived great pleasure from the countryside. Rachel Pinney describes rambling and sleeping in hayricks with a mutual friend Winifred 'Owlett' Howells, relying on farmers to sell them milk. Rachel and Peggy disliked the restrictions of clothing and preferred, when they could, to wear nothing, particularly outdoors, swimming naked whenever the opportunity arose. They were part of the flourishing open-air movement of which the Youth Hostel Association was a potent symbol, opening its first hostel in 1930.

The Ramblers Association bulldozed their way into the limelight by organising a 'mass trespass' of Kinder Scout, the highest gritstone peak in the Peak District. Like most of the land in Britain, it was privately owned and taking a hike there entailed trespassing. The public felt disgruntled that their environment could be seen but not touched so in 1932, members of the Manchester branch of the British Workers Sports Federation hiked up to the Kinder Edge path where they met a smaller group of ramblers from Sheffield. The Derbyshire Constabulary turned out in force and five men from Manchester, including their leader Benny Rothman, were arrested, but it was a highly successful piece of direct action in making public the call for people's right to access to the countryside.

Other organisations such as the Anti-Noise League, Woodcraft Folk, Scouts and Guides sprang up, all dedicated to the cause of enjoying and preserving the British landscape. The CPRE acted as a support for these smaller campaigning organisations and distributed 600 copies of *England and the Octopus* to schools, but it was probably their Countryside and Footpaths Preservation National Conference in 1928 that most appealed to the Gang. The 'Save the Countryside Exhibition' accompanying it had alarming display boards with photographs illustrating the countryside 'before' and 'after' being despoiled. They printed and gave away patriotic postcards showing 'Saint George for Rural England', suggesting it was a preservationist's duty to stand up against motoring, garages, smoke, advertisements and litter.

A radical socialist suggestion put forward by the Independent Labour Party, of which Clough was a member, was that the State take control away from individual landowners and nationalise ownership of the land. A less radical option for conservationists was that the National Trust take custody of the most treasured parts.

The Trust had the capacity to own property and thus conserve rural England, a facility the CPRE did not have. With the CPRE heading the plethora of campaigning groups and the National Trust taking ownership of vulnerable properties and land, the two organisations formed a strong double-act.

---

* The Scottish architect William Weir opened his independent practice in 1900, chiefly repairing ancient structures. As a young man he spent more time on the road studying buildings than anyone else, riding a penny-farthing because the height of the saddle enabled him to see over walls and hedges.

CHAPTER SIX
First campaign – saving Shalford Mill

When the Gang finally drew up their constitution in 1932, it was no surprise that objective number six required elected members to pronounce publicly: 'I swear to follow Ferguson in preserving England and frustrating the Octopus.'

Before finalising the constitution, they spent time having informal meetings and discussing the challenges facing rural England. They looked for more support and welcomed friends and family as subscribing members as long as they were prepared to surrender Victorian coins to boost the coffers. The donated cash was no longer kept in Peggy's knicker drawer but in a money box which was a miniature wooden dolls' house, impenetrable unless you knew how to activate its secret lock.

The Gang gradually grew stronger and, three years after their legendary picnic, were ready to start acting in earnest. Their first donation, for £5, was delivered to the National Trust on 30 December 1930, the equivalent of three weeks' wages for the average shop assistant. It was for the Trust's general fund and was a gesture of goodwill from the Gang. They proudly pasted the receipt they received from the Trust's headquarters in Buckingham Palace Gardens into 'The Boo'. Handwritten in italics and black ink, it was signed by the Trust's Secretary S. Hamer and made out to: 'Ferguson's Gang (from Red Biddy)'.

The Gang wanted to do something more substantial than send donations. They began to discuss potential projects focussing on smaller rural properties with hidden and eccentric histories. One September day in 1931, Peggy and Brynnie took a trip out of London to visit Arthur Godwin-Austen, the family friend of Peggy's who lived outside Guildford in Surrey. They rode on the little green bus towards Ewhurst and as it trundled its way past Shalford church and the Seahorse pub they spotted a crumbling watermill straddling a trout stream at the end of a narrow lane.

The SPAB had recently announced a public campaign to save endangered mills in *The Times* and the *Daily Mail* so it was no coincidence that an old mill caught their attention. Intrigued, they quizzed their friend about the dilapidated mill over tea to discover that he not only knew of it, it belonged to his family estate, and had been put up for sale, but there were no willing buyers, despite its historical importance. As they began to research its origins, they discovered a tale of riches to rags and grisly incidents that intrigued them.

The Mill had been in the Godwin-Austen family since 1794. Before then there had been a mill on the site since medieval times, with Shalford Mill mentioned in the Domesday book. Before the Godwin-Austens, in 1739, a Quaker miller named John Mildred had refurbished it, adding a fourth floor, which overhung the river. He faced the upper storeys with scalloped tiles, an unusually ornate addition to a utility building.

Shalford Mill had a dark history too and industrial accidents happened there periodically. In 1785, miller Daniel Young was adjusting one of the cogs when his smock became entangled in the tackle, dragging him into the cog wheels. The *Reading Mercury*, the local newspaper at the time, reported that: '...his skull was dashed to pieces and almost all his bones broken before assistance could be given to him.' Any help by this stage was fruitless and Young left a widow and three daughters.

The Mill was in the headlines again 40 years later after miller John Sparkes was arrested for shooting a peasant boy caught stealing barley from his fields. Hit in the head and the leg, miraculously the boy escaped serious injury. Sparkes, however, was taken to court.

This did not affect Shalford Mill's prosperity and, in the boom of the 18th century, the Mill was busy: horse-drawn carts would pull up under the lucam, a gabled extension overhanging the bridge where sacks of wheat were unloaded and heaved up through the trapdoor. Two large wooden waterwheels powered the Mill, one inside the body of the building, and the other outside. The whole operation was run by a miller with help from a boy.

When Sparkes leased the Mill, surrounding land and mill house, there were still good times to be had, but in the late 19th century the rural economy began to decline and the watermills were under threat from the more efficient steam-powered mills. The Corn Laws had protected cereal producers until 1846 but once these were repealed, traditional watermills became too expensive to run. The last miller left Shalford Mill in 1914 and it was turned over to storage, after which the once-glorious flour mill became a dumping ground for discarded furniture and sacks of seed.

When Henry Haversham Godwin-Austen died in 1923, he left the remaining family fortune to his son, Major Robert Arthur. Henry had been a famous explorer, mountaineer and naturalist; K2 was originally named Mount Godwin-Austen after him.

Major Robert Arthur Godwin-Austen, known as Arthur, was considered the proverbial black sheep*, having drunk and gambled his way to expulsion from his Norfolk Regiment. It was a humiliating end to his career and his sullied reputation meant that the estate trustees considered him too unreliable to manage his inheritance. While Arthur became the titular head of the family, the trustees took control of the estate, giving him a monthly allowance and banishing him from Shalford Park, the main house, to the smaller Smithbrook Manor. They then capitalised on the property boom and sold off some of the land, a profitable move for the Godwin-Austin estate. A year before Peggy and Bryn spotted the Mill, the whole 1½ miles of fields and open countryside between Guildford and the village of Shalford had been built upon for residential homes.

The Mill escaped the first round of the big sell-off, but it was a temporary reprieve and the plan was to break it up for valuable timber. Or it could have suffered the same fate as The Malthouse, which stood in a field close by.

The Malthouse was sold to antique dealers who hoped to demolish the building and sell the land as prime real estate. Villagers opposed its demolition, but while talks to secure its preservation took place, the owners, under cover of darkness, removed the main truss supporting the building and the whole structure caved in. Irreparable, the building was gone for ever.

With an ulterior motive Peggy and Brynnie invited Arthur to join the Gang as a subscribing member and, tongue in cheek, gave him the title the Pious Yudhishthira. Yudhishthira is a prince from the Hindu epic *Mahabharata*, and Peggy added the title of Pious because, although the real Yudhishthira did govern with absolute piety, there was nothing pious about Godwin-Austen's unreformed lifestyle.

Inspired to save the Mill, Peggy and Brynnie were excited to see inside. They found a Miss Havisham of buildings. The severely dilapidated mill had not been used for 16 years. The windows were broken, the handmade scalloped clay tiles decorating the top floors were hanging off, many of them damaged, and ivy was beginning to work its way into the fabric of the building.

Peggy and Brynnie saw beyond its tattered exterior and were intrigued by its colourful history. The Gang's fascination with waterways, wells, streams and rivers made the Mill all the more appealing. The Mill sat on the Tillingbourne, a tributary of the Wey, in turn a tributary of the River Thames, which is the confluence of the underground tributaries featured on the Gang's map. Fate seemed to decree that they should save it, so Peggy asked Arthur to sell it to the Gang.

Instead of being dismissive, as most might have been at the time if a woman, particularly one with no experience of restoring or buying property, had proposed to take on the Mill, Godwin-Austen took Peggy seriously. Despite his poor reputation, the Pious Yudhishthira persuaded his trustees that these eccentric women could broker a deal whereby they would raise money to repair the Mill and then endow it to the National Trust for posterity. The Trustees agreed to his proposal, and moreover gave the Mill free of charge to the Gang, selling them a further plot of land, which would become the Mill's garden. The total amount the Gang needed to raise to buy and repair the Mill was agreed at £500, just below the price of the average house.

Undaunted by the scale of the project Ferguson's Gang approached the National Trust and put forward their proposal. After some serious negotiation the Trust agreed to take it on condition that Ferguson's Gang would adopt financial responsibility for its repair. They agreed and immediately deposited £200.

They had made their first important bequest to the nation.

---

* Major Godwin-Austen's nephew, Colonel Robin Godwin-Austen, the present owner of the Godwin-Austen estate had grown up in the belief that this 'black sheep' of the family was some detestable rogue. One afternoon, he cycled down to Smithbrook Manor to visit his unknown uncle. 'I was 16, and went to visit Robert Arthur for tea. A most charming man met me at the door. We had a really fun couple of hours. It was a turning point in my life in not believing all you hear. He couldn't have been a more charming old gentleman.'

CHAPTER SEVEN
Hauntings, raids and 'The Boo'

S halford Mill had survived centuries of war, weather and wear but thanks to vandals and neglect, was in a fragile state. John Macgregor, the architect who had worked with William Weir, was asked by the National Trust to look at the Mill. It was the end of 1931 when he reported that, 'It needs gentle and sensitive repair'. By the beginning of 1932 those repairs were well under way. As John began to dissect the building, wondering how bad the damage was, a collective sigh of relief was released when it was confirmed that the oak mainframe was free of beetle. A top-down conservation programme began with the tiles being stripped from the roof and rehung. The diamond-patterned, leaded windows also needed repair.

As Shalford Mill was slowly restored to its former glory, the vandals returned intent on destruction. When the builders arrived one Monday morning they were greeted with a pitiful sight. The new windows had been smashed and building materials stolen.

John and the Gang realised that once the work was completed, the Mill would be vulnerable all over again, empty and hidden from the main road at the end of a lane. Resourceful as ever, John proposed that to solve the problem, half the Mill should be converted into living space. He and his family would be happy to use it as a weekend home.

The Mill's repairs were completed by early 1932 and cost under £200. A further endowment of £300 covered the price of maintenance and paid for the conversion of the Mill's living quarters. Rather cleverly, John negotiated that his annual rent would be 10 per cent of the cost of the works, which came to £20. The Gang and the Trust were happy with the arrangement and by the latter half of 1932 the Macgregors began using the Mill as a weekend retreat. Elson, the builder, kept an eye on it during the week to make sure the vandals did not return.

The Gang came up with a role for Shalford Mill too. There was a box room in the working part of it that would be suitable as their HQ so they asked the National Trust if they would consider renting it to them. The Trust had no objection and set the rent at £3 per annum.

The Gang met regularly, five or six times a year. Although Shalford train station was close by, they generally arrived chauffeur driven, often followed by a distinctive turquoise and gold Fortnum & Mason's van carrying provisions. The driver would unload their picnic hamper and carry it to the first-floor room. To get to it was a bit of an obstacle course. He entered the large black doors at the front of the Mill groping his way through cobwebs and ducking flour sacks that still hung from the ceiling. A sturdy, well-worn ladder led up to the first floor, a tricky passage with a picnic basket.

They nicknamed their room 'the Cell'. It was in the centre of the mill above the old millwheel. Three horizontal millstones, each housed in a circular wooden frame, were situated just outside. For their meetings, the Gang sat round a huge granite grindstone contemplating their next mission. They could hear the water roaring thunderously, directly under the floorboards. It was tiny, no more than 8 feet by 10 feet, and on the west wall there was a small lead-latticed window overlooking the stream below. Small and sparse, it managed to cater for their needs with room for a butler's sink and stand, a shelf big enough to hold a large teapot and a biscuit barrel, and a small round pine table and four rustic wooden chairs. An oil-fired stove provided a little heat and a place to cook. A bunk bed* crammed up against the wall doubled as a sofa, and whoever missed out on a bed to sleep in, made themselves comfortable on the floor.

There was no access to the house from the Cell, which made the task of spying on the Gang far more exciting for the Macgregor children. Drawn in by their laughter and the occasional waft of exotic cooking smells, they would creep up the stairs, trying not to make the floorboards creak, but inevitably were discovered when they could no longer suppress their giggles. Once caught, the Gang could have talked to them about conservation but simply shooed them away.

The Gang were not confined to their Cell and could use the uninhabited part of the Mill for all their fun and ceremonies. In early summer, around the time of the solstice, they performed a 'Ritual Haunting' when they danced around, howled and chanted Latin verse.

After one haunting, they recorded that they pinched milk from the farm to make coffee. After another, they went skinny dipping:

At 3.5am the first cock went off … we watched a beautiful clear dawn, with the presence of Venus and Capella. We sat by the dawn window and had a think until 4am when Is B and Bill disrobed themselves and went 4 a duck in the Tillingbourne. The water was not at all cold and very soft to feel. Is B and Bill immersed themselves and played about 4 a bit: then they came out and dried themselves. The sun had not yet risen.

On the uppermost floor, at the end of the long gallery that they named the 'Chamber of Horrors', was the 'dawn window', which they crowded round just as the sun began to rise. The hauntings lasted until the early hours and as the watery pink colours of the dawn began to break up the inky sky, they would peer through the window, straining to pick out the shapes and colours of three objects in the garden below. They usually spotted a blue cornflower first, followed by pale wild grasses then a pink rose, and as the gloom lifted, they would allow themselves to go to bed.

When they woke, they would check the view again and what greeted them was tranquil and pastoral. The pretty wooden bridge straddled the stream and when the sun shone through the trees and rested on the surface of the beautifully clear Tillingbourne, filled with wild watercress and trout, it was impossible not to feel a sense of peace.

The five core Gang members, Sister Agatha, the Bludy Beershop, Bill Stickers, Kate O'Brien the Nark and Red Biddy, christened their meeting room on 26 March 1932.

They made sure this meeting and all subsequent meetings were officially minuted in a ruled book nicknamed 'The Boo', purely because Joy had misjudged the amount of space she needed to write 'The Book'. Written in two volumes, it is a comprehensive list of their achievements. Illustrated throughout, it contains a cartoon by Fougasse, the cartoonist and editor of *Punch*, who illustrated National Trust Secretary Sam Hield Hamer's retirement card, photographs, national and local press cuttings, letters, minutes, reports of their 'raids' written in mockney, and, most importantly, receipts for funds deposited with the National Trust and other conservation schemes.

It documents the fun they had, the dinners they enjoyed, their surreal, sophisticated and sometimes childish games and sense of humour, and their commitment to their cause. It modestly underplays their achievements and celebrates their antics, rituals and above all food. There is barely a page in 'The Boo' that does not contain some kind of menu or reference to food.

The Gang made their own coat of arms, seal and constitution. Obviously tongue in cheek, the Bludy Beershop's privy seal, for example, was a boa constrictor's 'footprint'. Their heraldry was a millwheel beneath a holly leaf, topped by a Stonehenge trilith.

The first and second paragraphs of 'The Boo' set the tone:

> Financial statement read by Bill and questions satisfactorily answered. Manifesto to the National Trust read and signed. Story of acquisition of mill related. (And generally believed).

> Mosquito annoying members apparently by order of His Bloodiness who objected to its ill-treatment. On being protested to by the other members and asked to exert proper control over it, he explained that he had sent it for a run.

They discussed the possibility of further acquisitions and the pros and cons of increasing the core membership to eight. Eight would provide them with more money, but it would cost more in train fares to visit proposed acquisitions. Eight was also three too many to fit around the Mill's grindstone where they sat to discuss business. 'The Boo' records:

> Proposition eventually rejected on Red Biddy's brilliant suggestion that the Gang might do its travelling cheaper by car at 25/- a day and remain at its present number.

So train fares were rejected in favour of car hire and more members rejected in favour of a comfortable conference table.

They then pledged allegiance to their favourite monument. Red Biddy passed a resolution that was universally carried: 'That ENGLAND is STONEHENGE, and not Whitehall.'

Ag proposed 'LUNCH' – again universally carried.

Lunch that day was mouthwatering: lobster cutlets, potato salad, raspberry cream and fresh pineapple, all washed down with a bottle of Old Malmsey Madeira.

After dining, they drew up their eight-point constitution and vowed to follow the precepts of Ferguson in destroying and frustrating the Octopus. Active members would be elected by inspection and secret ballot, and upon election, would place one hand on the shaft of the mill and publicly pronounce: 'I swear to follow Ferguson in preserving England and frustrating the Octopus.'

All five were duly sworn in. The minutes were signed by the Bludy Beershop as the Sanguinarius Merc & Glad who ended by casting aspersions on the Gang.

They agreed to admit any number of subscribing members who for 2/6 a year, would be authorised to take a Gang name.

The pseudonyms of the subscribing members were as flamboyant as the Gang's. Family members included Black Mary, who was Peggy's mother, while Joy's father called himself Silent O'Moyle.

Joining Poolcat were Yaller Jake, pore old Arris, Anne of Lothbury (a National Trust benefactor), Granny the Throttler, the Bottle Washer, Volker Jake, Deadly Nell, Black Maria, Old Pol of Paddington, the Public Recorder, Bard Gwas Arthur and Jerry Botham.

At their second meeting, three months later, on 5 June 1932, they made payments towards other conservation schemes. One of these was Watersmeet Valley in Devon, 340 acres of charming river and woodland walks. For fundraising purposes, the land was divided into plots and a £5 donation secured the giver one plot, about a quarter of an acre. The Gang sent a £5 postal order, made up of individual donations ranging from 2s 6d to £3 8s 6d. Red Biddy and Bill also sent 13s 6d to the Golden Valley Appeal, an area in Wales in the Black Mountains that was under threat.

Perhaps the Gang's most important meeting in terms of establishing a Gang tradition, was their third on 16 October 1932. Although it was only their third minuted meeting, they were celebrating their fifth anniversary. They decided a pilgrimage to Stonehenge was the only proper way to honour their achievements.

Rituals and hauntings were to be an integral part of Gang life. Peggy knew about many ritual practices through her study of Eastern cultures and she embraced Ruth's artistic interpretations. The others participated actively and felt uninhibited in each other's company. Ferguson's Gang embraced their pagan ancestry and respected ancient practices. Stonehenge was therefore an important cornerstone in the life of the Gang.

They met at Waterloo Station and caught the 11am train to Salisbury. A taxi then took them the 11 miles to Stonehenge. Peggy wrote in 'The Boo':

> Drove to Stonehenge through lovely unspoilt scenery following course of Avon. Found Stonehenge pretty unspoilt: the nearest buildings not very obtrusive, and clear skyline on nearly all sides. Fortunately no people while ritual in progress. Very impressive moment for us all.

Peggy had her photograph taken next to the 'heel' stone, which was used in ancient times as a marker to record the moment when the sun rises on the summer solstice. As they walked through the stones on that clear autumn afternoon, they affirmed their allegiance to Stonehenge.

They had drawn up a beautifully planned itinerary setting out the order of the day, which was typed by Peggy. The nine-point plan was headed 'Instructions for the guidance of the Beershop'.

Points 1, 2 and 3 covered the Gang's procession and entry into Stonehenge. Is Bludiness was to be at the head, followed by a fictitious Ferguson, then the rest walked behind in pairs; Bill Stickers with Sister Agatha, and Kate O'Brien the Nark with Red Biddy. On reaching the Slaughter Stone, Is Bludiness was to take up a commanding position and would bless the Gang with the words: 'ALE GANG'. The Gang would then reply: 'ALE BEERSHOP'.

After a short ceremony they pledged their allegiance to England, saying:

> WHEN YEW SAY ENGLAND DO YOU MEAN ENGLAND AS REPRESENTED BY WHITEHALL OR ENGLAND AS REPRESENTED BY STONEHENGE? And all the Gang shall reply ceremonially STONEHENGE.

The ritual ended with a minute's silence and the words: 'The Gang shall go home'. They caught the 5.55pm train back to Waterloo and on the journey talked about their upcoming projects and minor conservation successes. Peggy informed everyone that she had fought successfully for a footpath, and Joy had dealt with a litter nuisance at Woolacombe. They emptied their pockets of Victorian coins and the total came to £3 4s 9d, which they added to their fund.

Their mission had begun to attract the attention of the Press. On 23 November 1932, a bulletin appeared in *The Times* announcing that Shalford Mill had been donated to the National Trust. It said: 'This picturesque early eighteenth-century water-mill at Shalford, near Guildford has been handed over to the National Trust by a number of anonymous donors who have also endowed it with a fund for its upkeep.'

---

* The bunk bed was salvaged from the Zeppelin R100. The luxury passenger airship was deemed too costly to maintain after making its first successful transatlantic flight in 1930. In 1932, its interior fixtures and fittings were sold off for scrap.

CHAPTER EIGHT
Who are the 'benevolent gangsters'?

The Gang met for the fourth time that year, on 10 December 1932, and passed several Acts or 'Ags' as they called them. They also adopted different administrative roles.

Peggy became the Gang's Clerk, Brynnie had a more spiritual role as 'Aconite to Is Bludiness', while Joy and Rachel were to be 'Grand Deliverers to the Gang', dutifully depositing any booty with the Trust. Joy was allocated the responsible job of 'Bearer of the Travelling Bag', which contained financial contributions towards the cost of their journeys.

After her success presiding over the ritual at Stonehenge, Ruth was invested as the Gang's spiritual head. Her regalia included an engraved wooden staff and a ceremonial robe, blank on presentation but embroidered over time with mottos and scenes which held significance for the Gang. Bill Stickers bestowed the Beershop with 'ABSOLUTE AUTHORITY'. Ruth would have the final say on personal and political disputes, financial matters and policy. They decreed that:

> It shall be deemed dangerous and reprobable HERESY, SIGN of DISAFFECTION, BACKSLIDING and OCTOPHILLY for any member of the gang to profess … that IS BLUDINESS THE LORD BEERSHOP IS IN THE WRONG.

They discussed an invitation to the Trust's annual dinner and decided that, to retain their anonymity, they would wear masks and black velvet. Lord Beershop then cast aspersions on all present (as he would now at the beginning or end of every meeting) and they passed a resolution to go out for a run.

They were in a healthy financial position and had a further £100 to deliver to the Trust for the Mill. The 'drop' would be made in January and no cheque was involved as they would take cash in half-crown denominations.

The job was prepared and executed with precision. They thought of everything,` from their black bandits' masks (purchased at Harrods) to the getaway vehicle. Their first 'hit' on the Trust was made on 26 January 1933 by Rachel and Joy.

Afterwards, they diligently filed reports for 'The Boo', typing, they said, so that their handwriting could not be traced. Joy's account read:

REPORT OF KATE O'BRIEN THE NARK, G. D.
[Gang Deliverer]

On arrival I found Biddy already there with a lamp having chained her bycle to back of Bank. We went in & presented check. We wer asked to wit 10 mins while they opened a strong room for the swag. The money was given us in a neat sack. Very heavy. We procured a Taxi. Loaded the swag & proceeded towrds Victoria unfollowed. In taxi we removed Biddy's topcoat and fixed mask.

Rachel left Joy sitting in the taxi and climbed the steps to the National Trust building at 7 Buckingham Palace Gardens, not far from Buckingham Palace. After handing the doorman her Ferguson's Gang business card, she was taken to see Sam Hamer, the Trust's Secretary. They exchanged pleasantries, and she handed over the cash. She wrote later:

REPORT OF RED BIDDY, G.D.

Well I sez 'Oi av been instructed by Fergersens Gang to present to you the sum of one hundred pounds & an 'illuminated address.' Well e sez e was very pleased & was it all in pennies & I told im I was strong but not as strong as that, so e laughs. ... we torks of the mill & e sez it is one of the most treasured possessions of the Trust...

He sez e & the staff always are very pleased when they get a letter from the gang. Well then the receipt come & I sez good by... So we shakes ands & part, & I walks quick in case the police see me get into the taxi. All the Trust looks out of the window to try & see me take orf my mask, but I am ready for them & keep it on.

The Trust wrote up the drop in their bulletin published at the end of January.

The newspapers drew on the bulletin, which was distributed to their offices, and the Gang enjoyed pretty much blanket coverage. They appeared in the *Western Morning News, Daily Sketch, Daily Mail,* which sent a reporter to interview the commissionaire, and *The Times.*

The Times report published on 1 February 1933 read:

SOME BENEVOLENT "GANGSTERS"
MASKED LADY WEIGHED DOWN WITH SILVER

Anonymity is a quality not unknown among donors of gifts to the National Trust, but rarely is generosity concealed by a disguise so mysterious as that assumed by the benefactors...

They are known to the Trust as 'Ferguson's Gang'. Experience shows that they are not 'gangsters' of the type that have haunted Chicago or engaged in smash-and-grab raids in the West End and other parts of London, although one of their number, a masked lady, recently astonished officials of the Trust when she made a flying visit to the office in Buckingham Palace Gardens. But she speedily proved that her mission was one of beneficence. Without lifting her mask she gave £100 in silver to the secretary as an instalment of the Shalford Mill endowment and then fled, leaving the officials more mystified than ever concerning the 'gang'.

On 2 February, the drop was also reported in the *Evening News.* The Trust received an unexpected bonus after the reports, as extra donations arrived at their offices.

The Press set about investigating the Gang's identities. The *Evening News* got the number of members and the fact that they were women correct (others were convinced men were the ringleaders). They also hinted that they knew the identity of Bill Stickers, whom they described as the Gang's leader, and those of some of Ferguson Gang's members. They reported:

The 'gang' was formed by a young Society woman who, after a brilliant career at Cambridge University, came to King's College and banded her friends together under the name of the 'Ferguson Gang'. She is the grand-daughter of an Earl whose name is one of the best known in the land. It is nothing like Ferguson!

Her husband is a well-known author, and they live in one of the prettiest spots in Devonshire.

There are now five young Society women in the 'gang'. One is almoner at one of the largest hospitals, and another is 'housekeeper' at a West End hotel... Their wish is to do whatever good in this way they can, and to remain completely anonymous.

It is not clear whether the *Evening News* deliberately mixed up Bill's and Sister Agatha's details, and stated that Bill was the grand-daughter of an Earl rather than the great-great niece of a former prime minister, who lived in Devonshire not Cornwall, but they were definitely on to them. They clearly knew that Bill was Peggy, that Sister Agatha was Brynnie and that Joy was Kate O'Brien, but played along and stopped short of printing names.

An unforeseen consequence of the Gang's fame was that they began to receive fan letters from various sources. One was particularly interesting, so interesting in fact that the Trust reproduced it in their regular bulletin:

The attention drawn to 'Ferguson's Gang' in the Press must be held responsible for the inmate of a mental home writing to ask 'Ferguson's Secret Philanthropic Society' to supply him at once with 10 guineas wherewith to buy books and instruments for the study of 'Chaldean astrol Science.'*

The Gang pasted the cutting in The Boo without recording whether they forwarded the 10 guineas.

The following year, they received a more constructive request. The news editor from British Paramount News wrote via the Trust, asking if they could make a newsreel with the Gang. The letter was signed by the news editor, E. J. H. Wright. He wrote: 'If it can be arranged,

I would like to make a newsreel interview with these good people, who could remain masked for the purpose, in order to preserve their identity.'

The Gang wished to keep their activities private and their personal lives separate, so Peggy did not respond.

By 1933, the Gang had got into their stride, raising money and donating as much as they could to whichever appeal took their fancy. Some of the sums seem small. They *were* small in terms of amounts the Gang donated for their chosen projects, but show a concern for conservation that went above and beyond their own achievements. On 26 March that year they met for the fifth time at the Mill and pledged £1 to the Roman Amphitheatre fund of Chester. 'The Boo' also records donations to Gang funds of £184 towards the Mill. Plans for their next drop to the Trust were under way and this time, no half-crowns were involved. They decided on bigger denominations, declaring that various miniature bottles of liqueurs were to have £50 notes tied to them.

In June, they discussed a proposal from the Pious Yudhishthira, who had offered to sell them the 12-acre millpond field attached to the Mill that was used to regulate its water flow. He suggested a price of £800. Considering the whole Mill and its refurbishment and conversion had only cost £500, Peggy was outraged and annoyed that the Major was trying to cash in and she recorded that his proposal was 'negatived'.

They had raised a grand total of £246 18s 3d. A sum of £200 would be the final payment on Shalford Mill, which left a good deposit for another project. All they needed to do now was to find one.

In the meantime, someone needed to deliver money to the Trust for the final payment on Shalford Mill. It was Bobby's turn to make the drop as his alter ego Erb.

On 3 November 1933, Erb the Smasher arrived in style in his Mercedes Benz at the Trust offices with two £100 bank notes. (The miniature liqueur idea had been abandoned.) Wearing a mask, he handed Hamer the cash, with an illuminated sealed document signed by Ferguson, Red Biddy, the Bludy Beershop, Sister Agatha A. B., Bill Stickers, Erb the Smasher, Kate O'Brien T. N., Uncle Gregory, Black Maria, P.P. pore old Arris and Old Poll of Paddington, announcing that they had discharged their debt on the Mill. He lit a cigarette, nonchalantly waited for a receipt and left in a hurry once he had received it. Later he wrote:

I say I want a receipt afore I gives them ther boodle and they gives it me. I suddenly makes my getaway before they knows wots wot and I'm down Victoria Street doing 80 and thats my story and i ope its alrite.....

The newspapers were delighted. The *Daily Sketch* considered the news so important they ran it on page three:

FERGUSON'S GANG BUSY AGAIN
Mystery Band With Terrible Names Complete Endowment of Beauty Spot
Ferguson's Gang has been at it again. But the strange thing about the gang (nobody knows who they are) is that the only things horrible about them are the names they give themselves. They are full of good works, by stealth.

The Times, *Daily Express*, *Morning Post*, *Daily Sketch* and the *Daily Telegraph* all ran stories.

The *Daily Express* said that: '"The Smasher" left as he arrived, unrecognised.' *The Times* got the payment slightly wrong and reported that 200 £1 Bank of England notes were handed to the Secretary.

Jubilant that the purchase of Shalford Mill was completed, they felt in need of a celebration. The opening of the Gang's official HQ at Shalford was now in order and long overdue – 12 months to be precise.

Peggy, Joy, Brynnie and Rachel met at 'the cell' on 17 December 1933. Lunch was splendid: roast duck, seakale and sprouts, followed by junket and cream, bread and cream cheese and a bottle of sherry Flor de Jerez. Peggy took the role of Ferguson and wrote up the ceremony in 'The Boo':

Ferguson or his plenipotentiary shall advance as far as the door of the room and thus address the Gang:

Ferguson: Ale Gang.

Gang: Ale Ferguson.

Ferguson: Is Ferguson's Gang satisfied that this
  room is a fit and proper place for its ead1/4s?

Gang: It is.

Ferguson: Doth any person within or without this
  room challenge the right of Ferguson's Gang 2 take this
  room 4 its ead1/4s?

(There will in all probability be no reply. This is correct.)

Ferguson: I do there4 claim this room as the ead1/4s of
  Ferguson's Gang, and with the power of the Secular Arm
  I open this room.

The minutes state this meeting was attended by 'White Biddy'. From that point on, Red Biddy is never mentioned again. There is no explanation, but it seems Rachel was both Red and White Biddy.

★ The Chaldeans of Mesopotamia invented the 60s system (i.e. 1 hour = 60 minutes) over 3,000 years ago. They also created the day, month, year, calendar system.

CHAPTER NINE
Sister Agatha – Brynnie Granger

Every ringleader needs a sidekick and Bill Stickers had hers in Sister Agatha. Peggy described 'Ag' quite simply as 'daft' but was delighted that she was prepared to make as much of a spectacle of herself in public as Peggy was.

Brynhild Catherine Granger was born in Maldon, Essex, on 15 February 1908, the younger of two daughters. She did not come from a happy home, as her parents' marriage was strained and unconventional. Her mother Isabella was on intimate terms with a wealthy female friend, Henrietta Sadd.

Isabella Dodd and Henrietta Sadd's relationship began before Isabella married, and nothing changed after her wedding. Brynnie's father, Harold Granger, was an Essex fruit farmer who accepted this triangle whereby he and his wife lived in Henrietta's large house in Maldon. The arrival of children changed nothing so Brynnie and her older sister Isabelle grew up in a ménage à trois.

Both girls were sent away to board at St Felix School in Southwold in Suffolk. It was there they first met Rachel Pinney and Peggy's Cambridge acquaintance Prascovia Shoubersky.

The St Felix ethos was to produce sensible well-rounded women. The headmistress at that time was a Miss Silcox, a charismatic, attractive woman, who was a supporter of women's suffrage and wore colourful flowing dresses. The school encouraged girls to use their initiative and to adopt an individualistic approach. The students they produced were confident, strong-minded and academic, with many girls gaining places at Oxford or Cambridge.

Isabelle won a place at Newnham College, Cambridge, as did Prascovia, and there became part of Peggy's inner circle. Brynnie lacked her sister's intellect and academic success, so Cambridge was out of the question, but she was no fool. She passed her school Matriculation exam, which included English Language and Literature, History, French and Chemistry, and left St Felix at the age of 18.

Brynnie had no trust fund and would need to earn a living because although there was money in the family, her parents and Henrietta believed inheritances should not be relied upon. Her mother made enquiries to King's College for Women, London, regarding Brynnie applying for their BSc in Household and Social Sciences.

A letter from Brynnie's mother written in her chaotic hand to Miss Reynard, the college warden, explains that Brynnie '...was not quite equal to Newnham where my older girl is and tho it has been a disappointment the way seems to point to King's.'

She made arrangements for her and Brynnie to visit the college and instead of taking Brynnie's father, she took Henrietta. Isabella wrote: 'May we come on Thursday morning as my great friend who is like a mother to my daughter will be coming with us, Miss Sadd, and she can only come on Thursday.'

In advance of the interview, Miss Silcox sent Miss Reynard a positive note about Brynnie. It said: 'She is an exceedingly nice girl and full of enthusiasm... I think myself she will do very well indeed... '

Brynnie liked the college as did her mother and Henrietta, so in October 1926, she enrolled for the course. It may sound domestic and narrow, but it was in fact a rigorous three-year degree that included economic history and general economics, business affairs, hygiene, household work and the three sciences: biology, chemistry and physics.

The Halls of Residence, Queen Mary's Hostel, were in Kensington. Students were offered a choice of rooms. The options were: A. Single room with washing cubicle, B. Single room without washing cubicle, or C. Share of a double room. Bryn chose the most expensive, A, a single room with a washing cubicle.

The purpose-built bed-sitting rooms were comfortable and functional, with an open-down desk and a single bed-settee, a large sash window, and a central light with a fringed lampshade, typical of the 1920s. Each room had hot and cold water and a scuttle of coal for the open fire. On sweltering nights in central London, the girls took their mattresses on to the roof and slept outside. For girls used to boarding school, it was more independent, but with all the fun of a dorm.

Brynnie was keen to discover whether the college had a piano she could practise on. A passionate musician, she had learned to play as a child. On 24 March 1926, in a letter to her mother, the College Secretary confirmed that there were two pianos in fact, one in the music room and one in the gallery of the refectory. She said: 'There would be no objection, however, to your daughter bringing one with her if you wish her to do so. You would, of course, arrange for the placing of it in her room and the moving of it, as we could not take any responsibility for it as we have no men here used to that kind of work. Also, your daughter would understand, no doubt, that she could only practise at certain hours.'

The piano correspondence seems insignificant, but Brynnie's passion was not solely for music. She had formed a close relationship with her childhood music teacher who had begun writing to her in earnest just before she left school.

It was as her affair with him was beginning to take on its greatest intensity that Bryn became Sister Agatha, entering with gusto the secret world of Ferguson's Gang.

CHAPTER TEN
Kate O'Brien the Nark – Joy Maw

Kate O'Brien the Nark possessed spectacular organisational skills and became the Gang's fixer. She was born Mabel Joy Maw in Atcham near Shrewsbury in Shropshire on 10 October 1907, and was known by her middle name Joy. Photographs of her show a wholesome looking girl with a direct gaze and a swathe of thick, light brown hair cut into a bob.

Her mother was Agnes Higginson. In 1899, Agnes married Joy's father, Arthur Maw, a handsome, charismatic tile manufacturer from a family of wealthy, socially aware industrialists. Father and daughter were particularly close, principally as her mother was absent for much of her childhood.

Maw & Co., in Worcestershire, was originally a failing tile company bought by Joy's grandfather, Arthur Maw Senior, with his brother George. They transformed it into a profitable business, but when high transport costs threatened to eat into profits, they relocated to Ironbridge Gorge in Shropshire, where good-quality clay, iron ore, coal, water power and skilled workers were readily available. Maw & Co., Encaustic and Majolica Tile Works, specialised in the decorative tiles that were exceedingly popular during the Victorian and Edwardian era for flooring and fireplaces. The business thrived, and in 1871 employed 140 men and boys and 40 women, with Maw & Co. supplying tiles across the British Empire and beyond.

The company enjoyed good employee relations and was considered progressive and enlightened. There was health care support for their workers, with a benefit club that would pay out to subscribers if they became ill.

The factory was at the edge of the Benthall Hall Estate, and in 1853, when the Benthall family moved abroad, the Maws leased their beautiful, stone-built 16th-century country house, near Broseley, Shropshire. The hall itself boasted fine oak panelling, an elaborate carved oak 17th-century staircase and decorated plaster ceilings. The Maw family lived at the hall for three decades until the lease came to an end in 1886. They made their mark. Joy's great-uncle George, a renowned botanist and crocus enthusiast, collected specimens worldwide and was responsible for developing the grounds.

By the time Joy was born, the family had moved to a pretty Georgian terraced house near Shrewsbury. It is an irony, given her conservation work with the National Trust, that Joy never lived at the Hall, as, after five hundred years of ownership, the Benthalls endowed it to the National Trust in 1958.

The Maw family business thrived and, although it was run by the sons, the women inherited the profits. This was forward thinking and fantastic for the women but it meant there were no financial reserves, so each new generation of Maws relied on making the business successful. There was no problem while the business flourished, but there was no contingency plan if things went wrong.

In 1920, Joy began boarding at St Elphin's School in Matlock, Derbyshire. While she was away, the family suffered a series of personal and professional crises precipitated by the worldwide economic depression. The company were supplying the armed forces with functional tiles for their barracks, but the depression that followed the First World War left their finances in dire straits. Joy's brother Jock, who was seven years older than Joy but still only a young man, had taken over the business from his father and grandfather and despite being a true entrepreneur, wasn't able to overcome the bleak economic situation and around 1926 suffered a breakdown brought on by the stress.

The situation at home was not much better, and Joy's parents' marriage was in its death throes. For some years, Joy's mother Agnes had been absent from her life and seemed to be suffering some kind of severe emotional problem. Joy's father Arthur was living separately from the family in temporary accommodation at the Park Hotel in Wellington, Shropshire, which sounds salubrious but was actually a basic inn. At the same time, Joy began to suffer serious health problems, becoming so ill that she was absent from St Elphin's for a chunk of her final year. Her fragile state of health worried her father. They enjoyed a close relationship and he did all he could to help her catch up with lost schooling, hiring a maths tutor to help her pass her Matriculation.

They decided that once she finished school Joy would try for a place at King's studying the same course as Brynnie. Arthur worried that if she failed Maths she might not get a place. Miss Reynard reassured him and said that if the worst happened Joy could retake her exam the following year.

A letter from her headmistress, Miss Flood, to the college suggests that her problems were emotional rather than physical, but despite her poor health, she passed the college medical. The stress of her home life had taken its toll and Miss Flood was extremely concerned. She asked King's to keep a special eye on Joy as 'her brother has completely broken down and for years she has had practically no mother'. Her fondness for Joy is obvious in a complimentary character reference she wrote to Miss Reynard: 'She is enthusiastic and anxious to do well in Household and Social Sciences and she has every encouragement from her father.' In a separate note she stressed that Joy was a most deserving student and wondered whether she could be considered for a scholarship. She was not awarded one, so when it came to accommodation, she chose the cheaper option of sharing a room in Halls rather than having her own.

Joy was 19 when she met Brynnie at King's and, like her friend, enjoyed college life. Despite her health, she became involved with the college sports teams, joining the hockey team in her first year, playing in the 2nd XI. In her second year she joined the lacrosse XII and made the first team. She was a successful student too; her degree included the study of home economics, food analysis, nutrition, book-keeping, taxes and accounts, hygiene and bacteriology.

The course gave a good grounding for a number of jobs, the content reflecting the class structure of the time. Students were taught about tiers of hierarchy: 'the casual labourer, skilled artisan, routine brain workers, the professional classes and the rich and the very rich classes.' That summer, Joy would get to meet them all.

During the long holidays in her second year, she joined a domestic agency called 'Useful Women' run by Miss Lillian Kerr in Dover Street, Piccadilly. The bureau, which served the genteel ladies of Chelsea and Mayfair, described itself as 'An organisation of Gentlewomen, formed with the object of bringing into touch those who want certain kinds of work done with those who are ready and able to do it for them.' Ninety-nine services were offered, including letters written, jewellery cleaned, horticultural shows attended and reports sent to flower lovers, elocution lessons given, packing done, pearls restrung, chiropodists recommended, foreign visitors to London met and helped with shopping, heraldic or genealogical research done, dogs washed, brushed and exercised, knitting of every description, private investigations undertaken, trousseaux chosen, underwear of every description made to order, lace cleaned, repaired and valued, income tax returns prepared, millinery, with embroidered hats a speciality, and zoo parties arranged.

None of the demure ladies who used the service would realise that their ladylike helper had a second life in a secret gang and that within just a few years she would be famous or, perhaps more accurately, infamous.

CHAPTER ELEVEN
Red Biddy – Rachel Pinney

R ed Biddy was the most reckless member of the Gang, the first to deliver money incognito to the Trust and the first to make newspaper headlines. Rachel was prepared to do anything for a good cause, especially if it involved an element of risk.

Born 11 July 1909, Rachel Pinney had, perhaps, the unhappiest life of any Gang member. Depression dogged her throughout her life and drove her to extreme actions. She was troubled, rebellious, kind-hearted and a true eccentric, a headline-grabbing character for the Gang and the only member to gain herself a bona fide criminal record and a spell in prison.

Her aristocratic background should have ensured her a smooth path through life. The second youngest of six children, she was born into a distinguished family. Her Quaker mother Hester was the sister of Henry Head, a highly regarded sensory neurologist and pioneer, who experimented on himself, severing his own nerves in order to map how sensation returned. When Hester met her future husband Reginald Pinney on board a ship to India, he was a mere colonel. By the end of the First World War, he was Major-General Sir Reginald Pinney KCB, immortalised in Siegfried Sassoon's 1917 poem 'The General'. Sassoon had served in the 33rd Division commanded by General Pinney, with his battalion the 2nd Royal Welsh Fusiliers. Sassoon was a war hero, whose near-suicidal missions had earned him the Military Cross and the nickname 'Mad Jack'. He was just the sort of brave and fearless soldier the General admired, but, in fact, Pinney despised him, perhaps because of Sassoon's homosexuality. There was no doubt the feeling was mutual and there is nothing in his blunt poem about Pinney that suggests otherwise.

'Good-morning; good-morning!' the General said
When we met him last week on our way to the line.
Now the soldiers he smiled at are most of 'em dead,

Bill Stickers: Gang mastermind Peggy Gladstone c1926. She became the first woman to gain a double first from Cambridge in Oriental Languages.

Red and White Biddy: Major-General's daughter Rachel Pinney was the only Gang member to fall foul of the law, serving a prison sentence for kidnap.

Sister Agatha: Brynnie Granger was Peggy's right-hand woman. She defied convention by having an affair with her married piano teacher.

Shot Biddy: Fashion designer Eileen Bertram Moffat joined the Gang in 1934 after Rachel Pinney left.

Is B – The Bludy Beershop, self portrait: Ruth Sherwood studied fine art at the Slade and became the Gang's official artist.

Kate O'Brien the Nark in 1926: Joy Maw, whilst studying at King's College for Women in London. She was the most level-headed Gang member.

Uncle Gregory: Frank Pollard proposed to Peggy at Cambridge after her fiancé had second thoughts. Sailing was his first love.

The Artichoke: John Macgregor became the Gang's architect. They shared the same ethos and a mutual respect.

Erb the Smasher: Bobby Gladstone was Peggy's dashing younger brother. He stood in for Ferguson, once broadcasting an appeal on the BBC.

Black Mary: Anne Gladstone, mother to Peggy and Bobby, taken on a Gang picnic in 1937. Anne bankrolled the Gang.

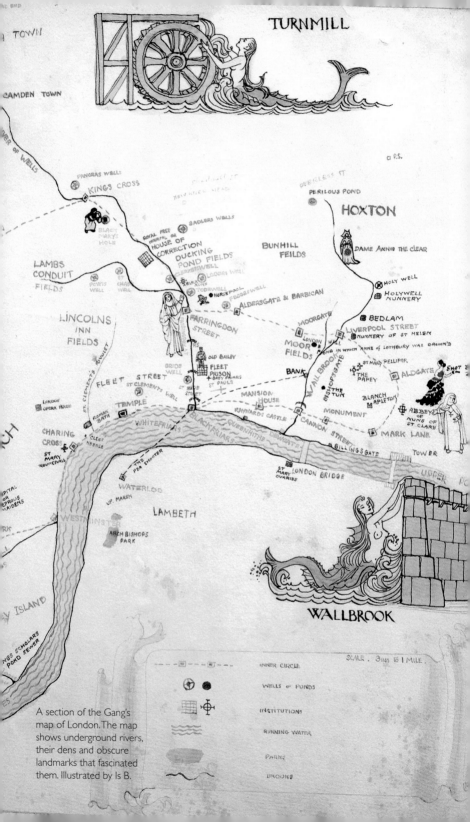

TURNMILL

OR BND

TOWN

CAMDEN TOWN

WER OF WELLS

PANCRAS WELLS

KINGS CROSS

BLACK
MARYS
HOLE

ROYAL FREE
HOSPITAL OR
HOUSE OF
CORRECTION
DUCKING
POND FIELDS
CLERKENWELL

SADLERS WELLS

HOLYWELL HEAD

LOORBS WELL

BLACK
RIVER

TODBWELL

HORSEPOOL

FAGGSWELL

ALDERSGATE & BARBICAN

PERILOUS POND

HOXTON

DAME ANNIS THE CLEAR

HOLY WELL

HOLYWELL
NUNNERY

LAMBS
CONDUIT
FIELDS

POWIS
WELL

ST
CHAD
WELL

BUNHILL
FEILDS

MOORGATE

BEDLAM

LIVERPOOL STREET

NUNNERY OF ST HELEN

LINCOLNS
INN
FIELDS

ST CLEMENTS WELL

FARRINGDON
STREET

OLD BAILEY

FLEET
PRISON

GREY FRIARS

ST PAULS

MOOR
FIELDS

LONDON
WALL

POND IN WHICH ANNE OF LOTHBURY WAS DROWN'D

WALLBROOK

ST MARY PELLIPAR

THE PAPEY

ALDGATE

SHOT

BANK

THE
BISHOPS GATE

THE TUN

BLANCH
APLETON

ABBEY
OF
NUNS OF
ST CLARE

FLEET STREET

LONDON
OPERA HOUSE

BRIDE
WELL

ROMAN
BATH

ST BRIDS
STREET

MANSION
HOUSE

RAYNARDS CASTLE

MONUMENT

MARK LANE

TEMPLE

CHARING
CROSS

CLEOS
NEEDLE

WHITEFRIARS

BLACKFRIARS

QUEENHITHE

CANNON STREET

TOWER

ST MARY
ROUNCEVALL

THE
PEA SHOOTER

BILLINGSGATE

UPPER PO

WATERLOO

UP. MARSH

ST MARY
OVARISE

LONDON BRIDGE

WESTMINSTER

LAMBETH

ARCH BISHOPS
PARK

WALLBROOK

RIS

Y ISLAND

HOSPITAL
OR
LEPROUS
MAIDENS

KINGS SCHOLARS
POND SEWER

A section of the Gang's
map of London. The map
shows underground rivers,
their dens and obscure
landmarks that fascinated
them. Illustrated by Is B.

SCALE . 3 INS TO 1 MILE.

INNER CIRCLE

WELLS or PONDS

INSTITUTIONS

RUNNING WATER

PARKS

BROOKS

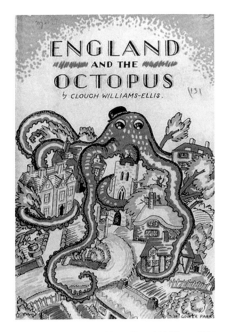

Cover of maverick architect Clough Williams-Ellis'
book *England and the Octopus*, 1928. His 'angry
little book' lamented urban sprawl.

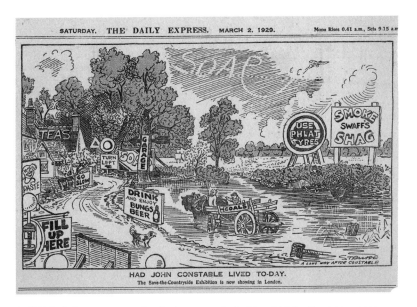

A 1929 *Daily Express* cartoon showing how romantic English artist John Constable might have
painted the countryside cluttered with adverts and signs.

Red Biddy, Sister Agatha and Bill Stickers at the restored Shalford Mill, their first purchase for the Trust (1932).

Right *The Times* was the first national newspaper to report exploits of the 'benevolent gangsters', in 1933.

Shalford Mill, near Guildford in Surrey, before The Artichoke undertook its conservation and repair. C1931.

WE FERGUSONS GANG

With loyal assurance of our de~
votion and future endeavour, Do
thus discharge our debt to the .....
National Trust.

~~~~~~~~~~

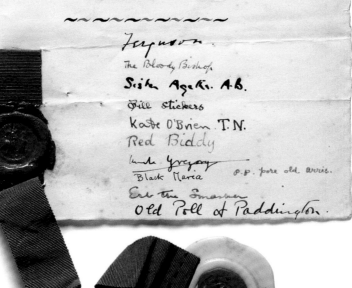

Ferguson.
The Bloody Bishop
Sister Agatha. A.B.
Bill Stickers
Kate O'Brien. T.N.
Red Biddy
Uncle Gregory
Black Maria   p.p. pore old arris.
Erb the Smasher
Old Poll of Paddington.

An illuminated seal, showing the Gang's heraldry, seal and
signatures. Presented by Erb to the National Trust with £200
towards Shalford Mill in 1933.

The tabloids celebrate Red Biddy's £500 'drop' for the Old Town Hall in Newtown. *The People*, 23 December 1934.

Red Biddy (Rachel Pinney) and Luigi Cocuzzi on their wedding day in 1934. Rachel left the Gang shortly afterwards.

Before (1933), and after (1934), pictures of the Old Town Hall in Newtown, Isle of Wight. Ivy nearly destroyed the building, which was close to total collapse.

And we're cursing his staff for incompetent swine.
'He's a cheery old card,' grunted Harry to Jack
As they slogged up to Arras with rifle and pack.

...

But he did for them both by his plan of attack.

Written while recovering from a shoulder injury in Denmark Hill hospital, south London, Sassoon may have thought it unlikely he would meet Pinney again but, around 1925, Henry Head took him to visit Racedown, the Pinneys' family home near Bridport in Dorset. Politely, Sassoon held out his hand to the General and said, 'How do you do, sir? You may remember I was in your division.'

'There were many men in my division,' said Pinney, who turned on his heel and marched back indoors to his study.

Rachel spoke to Sassoon that day and wrote later, in her unpublished memoirs:

> During an interval in the conversation I addressed the visitor as was my wont with: 'Do you play squash?' The answer came, 'I'm sorry, I have more intellectual pursuits.' He was promptly written off by the family and I don't suppose any of us, with the exception of my sister Hester, who herself had more intellectual pursuits, ever read any of his poetry.
>
> We were accustomed to visitors invited by my mother who were VIPs in fields other than sport. We showed our disapproval of them in a number of different ways such as showing them around the farm, making sure that their London shoes were suitably caked with mud.

Racedown, the Pinney family home in Crewkerne, Somerset, had been purchased by sugar merchant John Pinney in 1780 and was, for a while, lent to William Wordsworth and his sister Dorothy. The Pinney family moved briefly to Broadwindsor, Dorset, while Racedown was being extended and there is a memorial plaque to Rachel's mother and father in the parish church there. Once reinstalled in Racedown, a family sport was mocking the Wordsworth pilgrims who came to see where their icon had written 'Salisbury Plain'. The baiting and belittling of visitors by the family was heartily endorsed by General Pinney.

The General was a product of his time, wealthy, upper-class and with a distrust of unmanly men. He was also intensely racist, specifically because his family's sugar plantations in Nevis had been worked by slaves and the Pinneys had fiercely opposed the abolition of slavery.

Lady Pinney deplored racism and loved the arts and the first thing she did after her husband died was entertain black people at their house.

Rachel would have had no idea of any of this and adored her father, who nicknamed her Bachel. Rachel hated her mother and their relationship was strained. 'My mother, as a mother, was son-favouritizing, daughter-rejecting, inaccessible, punitive and frightening,' she said. 'My hatred of her dominated my adolescence. Now she is dead, and I so resemble her, I can understand that she had a relentless driving mission to make things, as they are, conform with her vision of what they ought to be; unfortunately, some of the "things" were "people", who suffered greatly in the process.'

Pinney was a military man through and through and owned a well-stocked gun cabinet, which was always kept unlocked. His children knew how to shoot and how to care for his guns and were at liberty to take one at any time, as long as it was returned cleaned and unloaded.

Rachel was no exception and her first kill was a linnet sitting on a gatepost. Her skill delighted Pinney but her mother simply said, 'Why shoot a linnet?' Rachel felt conflicted – she shared her father's pleasure in sport, yet empathised with her mother's horror at the needless death of a songbird.

This conflict continued throughout her life, as her desire for peace wrestled with her aggressive nature. She was haunted by a story her father related about a battle in the Great War. He said the dead were being thrown into a large circular pit, but when the pit was nearly full, a hand and arm appeared from the centre of the pile of bodies, turning in an attempt to attract attention. Her father ignored it, offering her the explanation that: 'I gave the order to go on with the pit filling. War is war.'

Pinney's motto, according to Rachel, was duty first, sport second and beautiful ladies third. The General indulged in all three to the extent that maids were told never to be alone with him, and were advised that, if they were called to his room, two of them should go. The system was not foolproof and one attractive female member of staff found herself alone and compromised. Yvonne Burns, who the family called Von, had been hired by Lady Pinney as a chauffeur during the war and stayed on. The General had had his eye on her for a while and managed to get her alone one day with the result that she became pregnant. Von gave birth to his daughter Elisabeth in 1923.

The indulgence of his sexual appetite with Von was not enough, however. One day, when Rachel was 11, she was alone with her father and he began to molest her. Rachel wrote:

> I was in the upstairs attic room standing on the west side of the bed when my father started to kiss me. I responded; I loved my father. I put my arms round his neck in a hug, he gently detached my arms and put them down on his penis. As he moved my hands he said, 'No, not there but down there.'
>
> It's hard to say how big an effect that incident had on me, because this whole period was so totally disruptive for me in general. The war was over when I was nine, and the way of life at Racedown changed. The men came home, the Land Army girls left; my father came home, Pilleo, my lifelong friend at that time and our governess, left, and my mother embarked on a campaign of trying to tame me from my wartime freedom on the farm – milking, making butter, feeding the pigs, haymaking etc.

In 1924, when Rachel was 15, she left the mayhem of family life and was sent to St Felix School in Suffolk where she met Brynnie, as well as Barbara Strachey, niece of Lytton Strachey, one of the founding members of the Bloomsbury Group.

Rachel's ambition was to go to Cambridge but she was not accepted, which was a huge disappointment to the Pinney family. Cambridge University was the family's preferred destination for further education, but Rachel twice failed the entrance exam, so in 1928, aged 19, she was offered a place to study philosophy at Bristol, an inferior establishment in the eyes of her family.

Rachel was thirsty for knowledge of the ordinary and was an anomaly for wanting to learn about the world outside her over-privileged life. Finding her own level became a lifelong struggle. She tried hard, but never quite managed to fit in. Wherever she went she stood out because of her unusual appearance which was rough and unkempt, contrasting with her upper-class demeanour. Arriving by motorbike at a spiritualist meeting in Cheltenham, Rachel was described by a fellow attendee Audrey Brodhurst as 'very fat, with bare legs and a red face bulging into a huge grin, a sort of square head, rather woolly, untidy, short hair, a tunic, somewhat muddy, and a blouse which had once been white with the sleeves rolled up ... her educated tones and polished manner were a great contrast to her rather coarse outward appearance.'

Rachel's background left her hopelessly under-prepared for university life.

All through my Bristol days I lived in a hostel (or hall of residence as it was snobbishly and euphemistically called).

I remember not knowing how to dispose of my disposable sanitary towels which we wore in those days; there was a wash stand in each bedroom which were used for small washes instead of the bathrooms. This stand had a jug of water... I tried wrapping up my sanitary towel and leaving it in the soap tray, but it didn't get taken away. I didn't dare ask anyone, I tried taking them in my pocket and finding a dustbin somewhere.

She lost her virginity, and had two platonic affairs with women while at Bristol, one with Margaret Eidsell whom she credits as the first of her crushes to return her affections. She says she had no knowledge of the word 'lesbian' or 'homosexual' nor any concept of who did what to whom. 'In spite of, or perhaps because of my sexual relationship with my father I would have been paralysed with fear had anyone spoken of anything sexual in my presence, let alone performed any act in any way related to any sexual part, primary or secondary.'

Her love for Eidsell, as she called her, was an innocent, unconsummated affair. They shared a bed together every night but there was no move towards a sexual relationship, which confused her. 'I reckoned that a close relationship between two people ought to do something else other than sleep in the same bed, but what was it? I knew the "facts of life" but that didn't seem to have anything to do with the expression of closeness between me and Eisdell. I never thought to discuss it with her, or I was afraid to.

'I do remember her telling me about another friend whom she no longer had a close relationship with, because she found her feelings were becoming more like a man's. I met this friend later and liked her.'

Intimacy, friendships and relationships were as confusing to Rachel as the Cambridge entrance exam, although she was beginning to discover life beyond the warped view of relationships her father had instilled in her. She was destined to experience many failures and disasters before she found any happiness.

CHAPTER TWELVE
The Bludy Beershop – Ruth Sherwood

A true Bohemian, Ruth Sherwood took the Gang to new levels of eccentricity and creative genius. She officiated over their ceremonies and rituals, held the Gang's official seals and had the final say over any disagreements.

Born on 18 August 1907, Ruth was from a wealthy but principled industrial family. Her grandfather founded the Workmen's Compensation, a non-profit-making insurance company for his employees. Ruth's mother, Wilhelmina 'Biddy' Parkes, was from a Staffordshire family whose company A. & F. Parkes & Co. Ltd made a fortune designing and making agricultural tools – the gardening fork and lightweight shovel, to be precise. Wilhelmina was a Girl Guide Commissioner. Ruth's father Wilfred Sherwood and his brother George ran the family's silverware and electroplated cutlery manufacturing company.

They married in 1903 setting up home in a sturdy detached house, called The Woodlands at Whitehouse Common in Sutton Coldfield.

Ruth had an older brother John and a younger sister Phyllis. John died in 1925, and Ruth's much younger and devoted brother Adrian was born the following year.

The Sherwoods moved to the Parkes's large family home, which had been built by Ruth's maternal grandfather in the 1880s. It was unusual in that it was the first house to be built with iron window frames.

Ruth was a day pupil at Edgbaston Church of England School for Girls in a suburb of Birmingham. She struggled with literacy, which her brother Adrian thought could have been because she suffered from undiagnosed dyslexia. She was creative and also a talented artist, a skill inherited from her paternal Welsh grandmother, Christine Griffiths from Lake Bala in Gwynedd. Painter Edward Burne-Jones was first cousins with Ruth's paternal grandmother, making her a distant relation.

A neighbour of the Sherwood family was Henry Tonks, principal of the Slade School of Fine Art, in London. He lived in Mulroy House, a large Georgian property. An influential art teacher, Tonks noticed

Ruth's artistic talent. Whether or not he helped her is not recorded, but in 1928, she was awarded a place at the Slade, moving into lodgings at 8 Airlee Gardens near Holland Park where Brynnie also lived.

The Slade was far from a conventional art school with a reputation for hedonism. Evelyn Waugh described the lifestyle in his novel *Vile Bodies*: 'Masked parties, Savage parties, Victorian parties, Greek parties, Wild West parties, Russian parties, Circus parties, parties where one had to dress as somebody else, almost naked parties...'

Graduates were influential and left their mark. Stanley Spencer, Dora Carrington (who associated with members of the Bloomsbury Group), her unrequited lover, the portrait painter Mark Gertler, and Augustus John all studied at the Slade. Rebellious and flamboyant, they lived life on the edge, but for some this world was too much and two of them, Gertler and Carrington angst-ridden because of failed loves, and Gertler also because of extreme poverty, killed themselves.

Little had changed by the time Ruth arrived. The artists were still poor and the parties plentiful. Ruth attended masquerade balls, and frequented clubs and cabarets where cross-dressing, comedy, dance, slapstick, acrobatics and body art were laid on as entertainment.

Henry Tonks was a strong influence on his students and Ruth's style was very much inspired by his rigorous and traditional approach to life drawing. Tonks was not an easy master. When irritated he would tell his female students to get on with their sewing or knitting.

His opinion of women was low. He said: 'Speaking generally, they do what they are told, if they don't you will generally find they are a bit cracked. If they become offensive it may be a sign of love. They improve rapidly from sixteen to twenty-one then the genius you have discovered goes off, they begin to take marriage seriously.'

Tonks had his favourites though and according to the Slade archive liked wistful, feminine students whom he described as: 'those girls with the greenery-yallery looks, nostalgic willows ... with long drooping hair through which their eyes peeped shyly.'

There was nothing shy, wistful or greenery-yallery about Ruth, whose hair was light brown with an untamable wave. Her features were heavy, not delicate, and at times she suffered with a lame leg and occasionally used a stick. Thoroughly Bohemian in appearance, she even smoked a pipe, albeit for purely practical reasons, as it left her able to use both hands to draw with. She was talented and won the second prize of £2 in a competition entitled 'Painting from the Cast'. She was certainly not like the debs described by fellow student Olga Lehmann, girls who flopped around on the lawn outside the art school.

The women had separate life-drawing classes to the men, but other classes were mixed, such as the antique class where students drew subjects from plaster casts. Students also took classes in anatomy (a standard practice for artists at the time) and perspective, and Margaret Alexander, calligrapher to the House of Lords, taught ornamental design with lettering and illumination.

Ruth developed an illustrative style. She was a good draughtswoman and her skill is evident in her pen and watercolour illustrations for the Gang. Using fluid lines she sketched portraits with pen, ink and watercolours.

By 1929, she had been appointed the Gang's official artist, their spiritual leader, and had adopted the grandest pseudonym: Is Bludiness the Lord Beershop of the Gladstone Islands and Mercator's Projection (a Mercator projection is a cylindrical map projection presented by the Flemish geographer and cartographer Gerardus Mercator in 1569). Inevitably her name was shortened, with several abbreviations including: Is B, Is Bludiness, The Beershop and The Bludy Beershop.

Although Peggy was the Gang member who was scholarly and highly knowledgeable about Britain's historical past, it was the Ruth Sherwood who performed the Gang's rites and rituals. It gave her another artistic outlet, something far more experimental than anything her contemporaries in the art world were doing. By incorporating pagan rituals into their meetings together with her own invented ones, Ruth created a kind of performance art.

CHAPTER THIRTEEN
The Artichoke and the Artichrix

The Gang's architect, John Macgregor, was an innovative, specialist architect who worked with the SPAB. He had already worked on Tattershall Castle and his integrity was beyond reproach.

The National Trust favoured John because there was nothing stuffy or conformist about him despite the fact that he was well respected by the establishment. He was 40 years old, and the Gang were in their 20s when they first met in 1931. He and his wife Janet were senior to the youngest of the Gang by 15 years but were struck by the vitality of Peggy and her compadres. They formed a strong bond based on a shared intelligence, the same appreciation of endangered buildings and a surreal sense of humour. The Macgregors, who belonged to an influential arty, socialist set in Chiswick, unhesitatingly welcomed this group of zany young women into their social circle.

Although he was older and much lauded, the Gang afforded John no reverence and teased him often, admitting him to the Gang with the title the Artichoke instead of the Architect. Janet became known as the Artichrix and, from then on, architects were known as artichokes. On one of their formal dinner menus the Gang served up a fine dish of Jerusalem Architects.

John was born on 4 October 1890 in the Chiswick area and grew up in Stamford Brook House with his two brothers, Alex and Norman. The community had strong socialist roots and was a magnet for artists and writers. Lucien Pissarro and his wife Esther were good friends and lived next door. Lucien, himself an artist, was the son of the influential post-Impressionist painter Camille Pissarro.

John's father, Archibald Macgregor, was an artist too and his sombre paintings depicted allegorical myths and legends. John's mother Ellen Miers, an active suffragist and political candidate, was concerned with child and family welfare and set up one of Britain's first mother--and-baby welfare centres in Hammersmith. The couple were caring lynchpins in the community. They hosted debates and produced elaborate pantomimes at the Mercury Theatre in Notting Hill to raise money for birth-control clinics.

John was educated at Westminster School, which he attended from the ages of 14 to 17. He hated it, and like Ruth he suffered from undiagnosed dyslexia, which held him back academically with the result that he had to repeat a year. Demotivated, John spent much of his time tossing postage stamps up onto the school ceilings and generally getting into a bit of trouble.

But there were some things he looked forward to, and one was school worship, which took place at Westminster Abbey. The Abbey is a work of architectural genius built in the 13th century. Listening to religious fables, such as the feeding of the five thousand, John struggled to relate to the miracle, but the Abbey always filled him with awe. He wrote about it in one of his sketchbooks:

> I leant back, cast my eyes up to the vault above me and observed the obvious miracle of the builders who ... had reversed the elemental power of gravity and virtually suspended those carefully shaped stones, that had held up there for some five hundred years... This was a human miracle I could understand and have no doubts about. Thus started my interest and enjoyment in the historic craft of building... Thus during the two years I spent at Westminster, I learnt and enjoyed the Cathedral while my scholastic advancement stagnated.

John's lack of education had hidden benefits and he became a master of lateral thinking, often coming up with unconventional and innovative ways to solve a problem. One thing he knew was that he wanted to become an architect.

He trained with Fred Rowntree & Sons in Hammersmith Terrace, where he developed an interest in modern functional architecture, before studying for two years with the Architectural Association.

John's talent was spotted early on and he was only 22 when he was employed by William Weir to help rebuild and repair Tattershall Castle. He recalled the scene on his first day:

The castle was a veritable ruin, the double surrounding moats were filled, being dug out by some fifty or sixty labourers, the building was roofless and floorless. For a couple of months I shared digs with Weir, simply observing and trying my hand in the various crafts on the castle. Twice I spent a fortnight working a shapeless lump of stone ... into a piece of medieval window tracery or chimney cap...

The kudos of the job could not be overestimated and laid the foundations, as it were, for John's conservation career. After that, the SPAB regularly employed him to survey properties and oversee their repair. By 1936, he was involved in their Scholarship Scheme, training architects and surveyors in conservation, and he eventually became chairman of the technical panel.

The Great War broke out while John was still working on Tattershall Castle and he enlisted immediately, which was something he had promised his father on his deathbed he would do. He decided that if he was going to fight, he would be in the thick of it, and he chose to serve in the Artists' Rifles, a formidable regiment.

While they were stationed in northern France, as a distraction from the horrors of war, he and fellow soldiers started 'The Cook's Club'. The club produced a satirical leaflet, 'The Cook's Club Artists' Rifles', which reads: 'The finest social club in Northern France, founded in November 1914, is situated on thick clay soil, 30 metres above sea level, within five minutes of the station and within range of the enemy's heavy artillery.'

Like so many others, he was gassed in the trenches, which left him with a sensitive constitution and although he rarely talked about his experiences, fighting in the war confirmed something he had always known, that he was a born pacifist. In the following years, the only time he ever lost his temper with his children was if one of them pretended to fire a gun.

Demobbed in 1917, John married Janet Udale in 1918. They set up home in a derelict Georgian house at 7 St Peter's Square in Chiswick, West London, about five minutes' walk from the Thames and close to where he grew up. John was still renovating all four storeys when their first daughter Janella was born in 1919. Three more daughters followed: Penelope in 1921, and twins Joanna and Sally in 1926.

Chiswick had a vibrant community, and the communal gardens in the middle of their grand Georgian square became a venue for Sunday coffee mornings where the neighbours would gather to debate the issues of the day while the children played happily in the background.

John and Janet lived in Chiswick at a time when everyone was talking about the Bloomsbury and Chelsea groups of writers and artists. Yet Chiswick had its own flourishing artistic community. As well as artists, the wit and writer G. K. Chesterton and the humorist A. P. Herbert were part of their social circle. Also an independent reformist MP, A. P. Herbert would accompany John on some extraordinary Gang adventures.

In 1925, the *Daily Chronicle* brought them all to the public's attention:

> In talking about the Bloomsbury or Chelsea groups of painters it must not be forgotten that Chiswick possesses a most flourishing artistic colony of its own … among the painters who now have their studios there are Polunin, who has done several designs for the Russian Ballet, and the McCances, that clever couple from Scotland who believe in cubist methods. Eric Kennington, the sculptor… As well as painters it also includes a number of writers such as A. P. Herbert.

Although John and Janet were highly professional, they also had a great sense of fun. They threw legendary parties; at one, John converted the final staircase of the four-storey house into a slide, which transported spirited revellers outside the front door.

He was an artist too, sketching and painting on holiday. In 1925, he and Janet went on a cycling holiday round the South of France with his close friend the writer Valentine Spalding and his girlfriend Bee.

Valentine wrote an account of the trip in his handmade book, *Allwither*, describing his friend:

> John's French is wonderful, he speaks like a native, but not a native of France, and certainly not of England. Grammatical inaccuracies differentiate him from the Frenchman and complete lack of self-consciousness from the English. But he

always succeeds in his main purpose of being understood – so he probably speaks like a Scotsman.

When Janet's two-speed gear developed a complicated disorder... All the ingenuity of John spent itself in devising substitutes for the missing instrument. The most radical defect of any kind of machinery can usually be made good by John with a hairpin. But in this case, even hairpins, prodigally offered by Bee regardless of results, were of no avail. How a man who relies so exclusively on hairpins ever came to miss-ally himself with a wife with bobbed hair is an insoluble mystery.

Inventiveness and ingenuity were part of the fabric of his life, and at home, he was the original recycler, once making a standard lamp out of a beer barrel and gas piping. John required nothing more complicated for his inventions than plywood, a bandsaw, simple wooden coat hangers and cotton reels, the latter two being used to produce all manner of toys and objects.

Meanwhile, his career continued. The SPAB was the first and the most respected authority on the conservation of ancient buildings, and John relished working for them. He illustrated *Repair of Ancient Buildings*, the SPAB book written by his business partner A. R. Powys (Powys was also Secretary of the SPAB) and first published in 1929. The Society had its headquarters in Great Ormond Street in Bloomsbury, which John remodelled for them.

The SPAB's ethos reflected John's personal approach and very quickly he was in demand for complex conservation projects. One was Montacute House in Somerset, a masterpiece of Elizabethan Renaissance architecture and design, completed in 1601. It was built by Master of the Rolls, Sir Edward Phelips, who was prosecutor during the trial of the Gunpowder Plotters. The honey-coloured stone mansion, decorated with ornate chimneys, figures and leaded windows, is said to be a textbook example of English architecture and it is certainly a statement of wealth, ambition and showmanship.

John also worked on buildings that were lesser known but equally as important to him, such as St Paul's, a tiny Saxon church in Elsted, Sussex. The nave had collapsed, leaving only the north wall and west wall standing. John had the task of integrating what was left of its thousand-year-old herringbone masonry with local, 20th-century materials.

Although John was a committed atheist, conserving churches was a passion. Despite never worshipping in one because he believed that religion was responsible for most wars and other troubles in the world, he looked on churches as interesting examples of architecture in their own right. Unsentimental about their main function, he always supported maintaining and finding new uses for redundant churches.

Functional considerations always underpinned any aesthetic decisions he made and, where possible, he used simple traditional techniques. This was never more obvious than when he worked on the painter, engraver and satirist William Hogarth's house in Chiswick. Built around 1700, the house suffered severe damage from a nearby explosion during a Second World War air raid. Instead of replacing the shattered roof like for like, John designed an overarching barrel roof, which opened up the interior.

In all, John worked on three projects with the Gang but the Artichoke was more to them than simply an architect. He was a friend, ally and Gang member himself. One July night in 1935, John borrowed A. P. Herbert's barge, *Water Gypsy*, called after his novel of the same name, and took members of the Gang to Tower Bridge where they docked under a dazzling full moon. From there, John rowed the Beershop and Kate O'Brien to the mouth of the Fleet in a sampan. The Gang called the outing an 'Oly X. Cursion' and recorded:

> ...the Artichoke rowed valiantly against the strong current, towards a sinister double tunnel intersected by a black Coffin... Up the right hand tunnel the sampan disappeared, according 2 Is B impelled or sucked by unseen 4cc. Their return was anxiously awaited, in view of the raucous yells of ghouls in the adjoining seminary. They emerged at last triumphantly bearing a bottle of Oly Fleet Water.

The water samples they collected from the underground tributaries of the Thames were prized possessions kept in five cut-glass water bottles.

CHAPTER FOURTEEN
Second campaign: the Old Town Hall

P eggy was staying at her mother's house on the Isle of Wight when a possible venture was suggested to her. At a dinner party hosted by her mother, Shalford Mill and conservation were being discussed, when Anne said, 'When is someone going to save the Old Town Hall at Newtown?' Instantly alert, Peggy went on a recce the next day, cycling the 8 miles from The Briary.

Newtown itself could be missed if you sneezed and boasted less than a dozen houses, an unsuccessful harbour and the dilapidated Town Hall. The tiny hamlet was formerly known as Franchville or Freetown and had once been the capital of the island. Its fortunes had faded, and the Old Town Hall, once its most important building, was crumbling almost beyond repair. If no action was taken, the building was sure to collapse. Its bricks were already being picked up by local farmers to mend their pigpens.

Peggy recorded in 'The Boo' that it was covered with 'a pretty (but destructive) shrub that had partly worked its way inside the building', causing the red brickwork and stonework to disintegrate.

She began to research its origins and discovered that the Town Hall had an appealing history. Built in 1256 on land owned by Aymcr de Valence, the Bishop of Winchester, Newtown began to thrive in 1284 after being awarded a Royal Charter by Edward I. The Charter, used by monarchs to help establish towns or cities, made available 78 plots of land. Any man who was interested and could afford the annual rent of 1s could lease a plot, and so be released from serfdom and declared a freeman.

Newtown began to prosper. Its population peaked in medieval times at 300, then lost around half its residents to the plague in 1348. In 1377, a second disaster struck when the town was razed to the ground by French invaders. Consequently, Newtown faded, but in 1584, Elizabeth I provided a brief reprieve. Under pressure from two wealthy, power-hungry, local landowning families, the Barringtons and the

Worsleys, she granted Newtown the right of Parliamentary representation. The Barringtons and Worsleys, keen to increase their power base, manipulated the system so that the tiny population of Newtown was turned into a rotten borough. (A rotten borough was the name given to a tiny electorate that was over-represented in Parliament.) Newtown held two parliamentary seats, being represented by two MPs.

Some of those MPs were very effective and two enjoyed a high profile. John Churchill, the 1st Duke of Marlborough, was MP for Newtown in 1679, and the Tory George Canning in 1793, later to become Prime Minister in 1827.

As intriguing as its political connections was the legend of the Pied Piper. Just as in the Hamelin story, the Pied Piper of Newtown was asked to clear a plague of rats that infested the town. The Mayor agreed to pay him £50 and the piper played bewitching music on his pipe, luring the rats away from the town to the Solent where they were all drowned. But when it came to paying the bill, the Mayor and Corporation tried to shortchange the piper, handing him just £20. The piper took his revenge, played his pipe and lured all the town's children to the wood; they were never seen again. Pied Piper legends became popular in towns and villages where numbers of residents had dwindled, as a way to explain the lack of townsfolk.

The shabby building that Peggy was looking at had been there since 1699 and had replaced the earlier structure. It was now owned by Sir John Simeon, a direct descendent of the Barringtons, who was also the MP for Southampton. The SPAB were already aware of it, as a local architect, Mr Troke, had sent a report to them in 1928, but there had been no available funds to repair it. The Gang made enquiries and discovered that Simeon was prepared to sell the Old Town Hall to the Trust for £5 and the land it stood in for £100. The Artichoke carried out a survey and advised the Trust to accept it. It might have cost virtually nothing to buy but it would be pricey to repair he said and quoted £1,000. Undeterred, Black Mary (Peggy's mother) immediately guaranteed the money, enabling the Trust's Mr Hamer to release the funds.

Bill Sticker's report in 'The Boo', dated July 1933 reads:

> The building is very derelict and almost past repair but the Artichoke says he can do it. He will assist and advise Mr Troke a little Artichoke of small experience but great enthusiasm.

The Gang were excited about their new project. The Old Town Hall had all the elements they loved: a murky history and intrigue, and it was a vulnerable, forgotten treasure in need of rescue. They all agreed that it was a perfect second venture and began to raise money in earnest.

Negotiations were concluded on 7 September 1933 and Mr Troke was notified that he could start work.

By December 1933, renovations were well under way on the Old Town Hall in Newtown on the Isle of Wight. On 2 December a local newspaper, the *Portsmouth Evening News*, announced:

BUILDERS ARRIVE IN NEWTOWN
RESTORING THE TOWN HALL
PIED PIPER LEGEND
AND THE POSTMAN-HISTORIAN

The builders have come to Newtown!

Not a very sensational announcement to you town dwellers, but it is a momentous occasion to ancient Newtown, where trowels and mortar have not been seen for generations.

Newtown Town Hall, probably the oldest public building in the Island, is being restored. The Society for the Protection of Ancient Buildings, with the assistance of certain private individuals, has stepped in in time to save this historic fabric from sharing the fate of so many of the buildings of the former capital of the Island, which have crumbled from ruins into mere bumps beneath the turf...

For years past the Town Hall has been derelict. An immense canopy of ivy grew over the building, even forcing its way into the banqueting hall, which had been the scene of many a great election feast. Vandal trippers, too, lent a hand in the destruction, tearing away the beautiful fan-tracery of the window-frames... Every window was smashed, the ivy had gouged huge holes in the brickwork, and scrawled 'Vote for' but the name of the long-forgotten candidate had failed to survive the elements.

The restoration has lent fresh life to Newtown, where keen interest is being taken in the progress of the work. An old inhabitant told me that the Town Hall had been last used for a wedding many years ago. 'Maybe we'll see another wedding there yet,' said he gleefully. Then he shook his head and looked thoughtful when he wondered how the National Trust might look at such 'goings-on'.

The following March, they planned a trip to check on the Old Town Hall's progress. Parties were a priority for the Gang who needed little excuse to plan a celebration. The night before the site visit was no exception. They loved a ritual too and on that occasion, Ruth as Lord Beershop was formally inducted as the Gang's spiritual head and chaplain giving her the authority to perform an important ceremony at Newtown.

Peggy wrote:

> The Induction of Is Bludiness 4mally took place with oly oil, oly Ring and oly Crooque. The Lord Beershop wore the Diadem, tunicle, cape, liturgical boots and running shorts. Sister Agatha wore the robes of her order, with wimple, veil and long black gloves. Bill Stickers wore jersey, burnous, earrings and running shorts. Kate O'Brien, T. N. wore official crimson narking robes. White Biddy wore a blue satin saque, scarlet turban and earrings.

After this the Gang had several drinks of damson gin and 'Is Bludiness danced in Is Liturgicle Boots'. And as the damson gin kicked in, the ceremony got under way.

Peggy's report was illustrated by a rare print of the Beershop's boots, a rather scruffy inkblot.

The Gang left for the Isle of Wight the following morning. In the evening, Peggy typed her report and pasted it in 'The Boo':

March 17th 1934 trip

Gang (with unavoidable exception of White Biddy) left the Cell in a body and proceeded to Waterloo where they took the 9.50 to Ryde. Black Mary's shofar met them and drove to Newtown where the Gang inspected the Town Hall. Very dismantled and full of ladders. Kate and Bill took photographs, and the building was entered by a cellar window. Is Bludiness cast aspersions on the Gang and also on the Town Hall with oly oil.

When they had first seen Newtown Old Town Hall it had been covered with ivy, now the ivy had been stripped back to reveal pretty floor-to-ceiling arched windows and a sturdy oak door. Like Shalford Mill, its window panes had been smashed but boards were in place. Huge wooden trusses supported the walls, while ancient gnarled tree roots had forced their way through the foundations. It was not a pretty sight and a grainy photograph of the Gang sitting in its large chimney shows them looking uncharacteristically grim-faced and serious.

The budget for the renovation was rising too and their conversation as they travelled home focused on the 'artichoke' for the project, Mr Troke, and his builders.

On 5 May 1934, at their tenth meeting, the Gang noted that it had been informed that renovations were not going as smoothly as hoped and were likely to be substantially over budget.

After a dinner of roast duck and new potatoes cooked by Peggy and Joy, followed by junket and cream, and once Brynnie and Joy had washed up, they debated two issues. The first concerned the Artichoke not agreeing with the conservation methods being employed by the builders and the second was about what use the Town Hall should be put to once the repairs had been completed. The Gang were very keen for the Town Hall to have a useful purpose and they unanimously voted in favour of Trevelyan's Youth Hostel Association having the use of it. It was decided to ask the YHA to admit the Gang occasionally to lodge in the building without it being obligatory for them to become Youths. The meeting concluded with a whip-round for the National Trust as Mr Hamer was retiring.

Although the Trust advanced the money to begin the repair of the Old Town Hall, the Gang needed to honour their pledge and reimburse them. On 1 October 1934, Joy was entrusted with the mission of delivering £500 to the Trust towards the Old Town Hall's renovation. She went, masked, with her father Silent O'Moyle and, on arrival, handed her business card to the concierge. It read 'Kate O'Brien the Nark of Ferguson's Gang', which seemed to guarantee immediate and unquestioned entry. She delivered the 'goat' and, after a brief discussion with Donald Matheson, the new Secretary, about whether the Town Hall should be a museum or loaned to the YHA, she left swiftly.

Her report read:

REPORT OF KATE O'BRIEN THE NARK

I took the goat, doccuments and card in the car this afternoon, collected my father as escort, called at Harrods for a mask, then drove to the Trust.

...The new secretary is a nice bloke, he was v charming & said it was an agreeable surprise as he hadnt expected such a big cheque so soon. (Receipt enclosed). He asked about our feelings re youth hostel V. Museum. I raised the points we had discussed, i.e. Curator and heat, & he quite agreed & said he had asked them if they thought of that. The local committee apparently hadn't. .... Our cards work lovely, no waiting. I dont wonder he was impressed with the goat, I ad never seen such another.

Two days later the donation was reported by the *Daily Mirror* and *Daily Telegraph,* then the *Daily Mail.*

It was after this that Rachel left the Gang and Shot Biddy was introduced on 16 December 1934.

Shot Biddy was Eileen Bertram Moffat. She is depicted on the Gang's map wearing a flamenco dress and pointing a pistol. Her 'den' was near Cable Street, East London, the scene of the famous demonstrations against Fascism in Spain and Britain.

Although she lived in Kensington she worked near Cable Street as a dress designer for a Jewish firm called Lawrence Hill in Aldgate. She also spoke Spanish, having grown up in South America. Her family nickname was Biddy but why Peggy chose the pseudonym Shot Biddy is not explained.

In 'The Boo' there is no announcement or fanfare surrounding her arrival; Eileen just appears at their 13th meeting on 16 December 1934 and was officially sworn into the inner circle three months later on 14 March 1934.

By 17 December 1934, the Gang was ready to deliver the second £500 instalment for the Old Town Hall. This time Silent O'Moyle, escorted by the Beershop, took the responsibility for handing over the cash. The night before, the Gang met at the Mill and handed him the money 'all split up into £100 kids' and a 'bottle of poison' bearing the label: 'Sloe Gin of Ferguson's Gang, gathered, matured and bottled by Black Mary and Bill Stickers, for internal use only'. They wrote their Christmas cards, sending the most special with photographs of the Mill and Old Town Hall to the Trust, and they indulged themselves with a dinner of braised pheasant with chestnuts, carrots, turnip, onion, barley and chipolata sausages, followed by green figs and cream.

The following day, Silent arrived at the Trust's offices and wrote his request to see the Secretary on a piece of paper, which he handed to the doorman. He delivered the money without uttering a word and, when asked any questions, put a finger on his lips to show that he would not speak. The newspapers were delighted. *The Times, Daily Telegraph, Morning Post, People* and the *Children's Newspaper,* a dedicated news publication for pre-teens with a 500,000 circulation, all reported the drop and after the Trust described it in their February 1935 bulletin, the *Morning Post* took the opportunity to write about the Gang again.

Before they delivered the final £400 to the Trust a few months later, the Gang decided to take another trip to Newtown to ensure that the work was up to standard. Eileen joined Joy, Peggy and Ruth on her first official excursion. They all piled into Joy's car while Joy and Ruth took turns behind the wheel.

It was a beautiful spring day in May 1935 as the Gang drove through the English countryside looking for the perfect spot for a picnic. They found it and Peggy wrote this report:

> At 10.30 the Gang set off 4 the I. of Wight in Kate's motor. Kate and Is B drove in turns. We stopped for lunch in a beechwood full of bluebells and cuckoos and solomon's seal, where we had chicken mousse, Russian salad, lychees and cream and a bottle of Chalian Larose Blanche. We caught the 2.30 ferry and drove 2 the Town Hall, which Is B solemnly blessed. We got inside and inspected. Then we returned and after a big tea in cowes of 5 waffles and 8 cakes caught the 7.30 ferry. Is B with a joyous yell charged off the boat in the direction of the

end of the pier, and we ad a narrow escape. E and Kate drove home in turns, dropping Bill and Biddy at the Mill.

It was, they all decided, one of the Gang's very best outings, but they confessed to missing Brynnie, who was in Australia.

That night, Peggy and Eileen stayed at the Mill. On the following day, 13 May 1935, they met at Silent O'Moyle's room at the Cromwell Hotel in South Kensington, put on their disguises, hailed a taxi and headed for the Trust offices in Buckingham Palace Gardens. They delivered £400, the final payment on the Old Town Hall, and scarpered. *The Times*, *News Chronicle*, *Morning Post* and the *Sunday Pictorial* all reported the drop and an article even appeared in the June issue of the women's monthly magazine *Good Housekeeping*, which said: 'Gangsters in England are not common, but this is a type of gangster who ought to be encouraged.'

CHAPTER FIFTEEN
Shot Biddy – Eileen Bertram Moffat

Eileen had joined the Gang just before Christmas in 1934 in time to help save Newtown Old Town Hall. She had no trouble acclimatizing, superbly completing her initiation with an act of petty larceny committed at a Trust dinner. At her second meeting at the Mill Eileen brandished a magnificent silver cup she had 'lifted' from the Dorchester Hotel. Her pilfering was rewarded by the Gang with loud applause.

Born 20 May 1910, Eileen Bertram Moffat was nothing like her alter-ego and friends knew her as a caring devoted Christian who supported all waifs and strays whether they were people or animals.

Descended from two aristocratic families, the Scottish Moffats and the Irish Bertrams, she was conceived in South America, where her father James Smith Moffat worked on the South American railways as a civil engineer. Determined his first child should be born in Scotland, he arranged for his pregnant wife Lucy to sail back to Edinburgh so that Eileen would have a Scottish birth certificate.

A fact that does not appear on the birth certificate is that Eileen was illegitimate. Her parents were very much together but not married and Lucy was still married to her first husband.

Lucy had grown up in India and age 18, married William Gardiner, a superintendent of post offices near Calcutta. They separated, and she began a family with James and moved to South America with him.

After registering Eileen's birth in Edinburgh, they sailed back to Buenos Aires and lived a peripatetic lifestyle. Like many Scots, Eileen's father was part of a pioneering movement to build a comprehensive railway network across the southern continent that would open up South America for international trade. As a railway director, his work took him to various countries and his young family moved with him. Lucy had two more children. Eileen's younger sister Kathleen was born in Venezuela in 1912 and Norah in Argentina in 1914. Most of Eileen's childhood memories are from Columbia.

They returned to England in 1915 after the outbreak of World War One and her father was seconded into the London Division Engineers as second lieutenant. By 1927 he was back in Venezuela, while Eileen boarded at Kepplestone school in Eastbourne, a school that catered for children whose parents lived abroad or travelled. She applied to Oxford, and seemed to be successful, but did not take up a place there. Her father wrote using his petname for her and expressed his pride.

'Dear Bo, I believe a father has more delight in the success of his daughters (or sons) than his own. The latter may become conceit – the former is pure joy and I want to thank you for the pleasure I have in your Senior Oxford success...

Mam, as you know, is speaking of France for a "finish"... I know you will take every advantage of what is offered to you in the matter of education. You will learn in time too Bo, that an educated mind is the best companion you can have thro life – no matter in what sphere of life your lot will be cast.

Eileen did not take a place at Oxford. Instead, in 1933 she began working in the textile and fashion industry while her glamorous younger sister got a job as a translator with the International Labour Organisation, a section of the United Nations in Geneva dealing with international labour standards. By 1936, Eileen was helping Jews fleeing Nazi Germany and 'The Boo' says she arrived late for Gang meetings as she was 'with the Jews in Margate' or the 'Germans in Golder's Green' an area popular with Jewish exiles.

Her flat was in fashionable Kensington in Mount Carmel Chambers which she shared with her friend Evelyn Booth. The Victorian mansion block, opposite a Carmelite priory, was almost exclusively occupied by single women, with at least one known suffragette.

Eileen designed ready-to-wear clothes that were sold in C&A and Marks and Spencer. M&S had introduced womenswear in the 1930s, its range including smart separates, overalls for busy housewives, along with glamorous dressing gowns, party frocks and knitted swimsuits.

Lawrence Hill were based in a large factory near the department store Gardiner's in Aldgate. The area became known as Gardiner's Corner and Lawrence Hill's vast four-storey warehouse was close by in Manningtree Street, tucked away in a narrow cobbled lane. It was one of the many Jewish tailoring workshops in the area and run by a Mr Goldblatt.

The area was long established in the rag trade but in 1936, became known for the Cable Street riots.

On an unusually hot day on 4 October 1936 Oswald Mosley led the British Union of Fascists in a provocative march through the East End, a march the predominantly Jewish community tried, but failed, to ban. It was the same day Republicans in Spain were preparing to defend Madrid against General Franco's fascists.

Mosley's thugs had been terrorizing Jewish stallholders in Petticoat Lane and graffitied 'Death to the Jews' on synagogue walls. Young and old protesters gathered together with communist sympathisers to block the demonstration. Bill Fishman, the Jewish professor of Modern History at Oxford University, was 15 and a member of the Labour Youth League at the time. He said.

'I remember standing on the steps of the Whitechapel Art Gallery, watching Mosley arrive in a black open-top sports car. He was a playboy aristocrat and as glamorous as ever.

I can still hear his plummy Oxford accent and, when he spoke of an "alien menace". I realised that he was talking about me and my family – my dad, who was an unemployed tailor, and my uncle Wolfie, who joined the army aged 14 and went on to win a Military Medal.

Back at Gardiner's Corner, I saw a tram pull up in the middle of the junction – barring the Blackshirts' way. Then the driver got out and walked off. I found out later he was a member of the Communist Party.'

The police diverted the march, instructing the Fascists to enter the London docks with its strong Irish population and there ensued the famous Battle of Cable Street. Rapidly, the protesters re-organised, making barricades of mattresses and hurling rotten vegetables and stones. Hundreds were arrested or injured, but they defeated Mosley and his Blackshirts and it was the anti-fascists who ended the day dancing in the street.

The office was full of talk of the riots on Monday, but it was business as usual.

CHAPTER SIXTEEN
Bobby Gladstone – Erb the Smasher

Bobby Gladstone had two roles in the Gang: Erb the Smasher, and as a stand-in for the elusive Ferguson when a physical presence was required. He preferred to keep a low profile though, because unlike his sister, he was quite shy. He was happy for her to take the limelight.

It was 1925 when Bobby arrived at Trinity College to read engineering, just as his sister was beginning her PhD. Dashing, handsome and quiet, with a penchant for sports cars, he gave away little about himself.

Peggy still adored him and loved having him around. He learned the Charleston, was sporty, playing tennis and golf, and he skied. He generally entered into the spirit of university life, but their friendship groups rarely mixed, as, in truth, Bobby was slightly embarrassed by his older sister and her louche friends. Peggy recalled:

> Once, and only once, Bobby condescended to come to a cocktail party given by my friend Geoffrey Gorer who said afterwards: 'My dear, your brother is so beautiful – I adore him – but I couldn't talk to him for half an hour!'
>
> Nor did I go down well with Bobby's friends, one at least of whom was notorious for buying old second-hand cars, souping them up, selling them for huge sums and buying more on tick. He owned a racing Mercedes and was known as The Motoring Body. Once I went to a party of his and suddenly there was a knock on the door and the landlady said it was a policeman. Instantly the room was empty and I was alone in it. All the others had dived under the sofa, into wardrobes or behind the curtains.

After his graduation in 1930, Bobby began a respectable career with paper manufacturer Wiggins Teape, inventing unique machinery for them. Then, at the age of 26 he married party-loving Naomi Trentham in 1933, an expert tennis player who had played at Wimbledon that year. Two years later Naomi gave birth to twins Anne and Jean, followed by Kitty in 1938. The family moved to Scotland as Bobby's job took him to Aberdeen, Glasgow and then Liverpool. Eventually, in 1945, they moved to London's stockbroker belt, settling in St George's Hill, Surrey, one of the most affluent areas of England. A faithful, if not ever-present husband, he preferred the sanctuary of his attic workshop where he built an enormous computerised railway system.

He valued his steady family life and presented a respectable face to the world, but Ferguson's Gang allowed him to secretly rebel and escape convention.

From the outside he seemed happy, although certainly less gregarious than his wife. He led what seemed an enviable life, with tennis and cocktail parties with a close-knit group of loyal friends and a steady job. The private lives of other Gang members were another matter altogether: Peggy was looking for passion outside of her marriage to Pollard; Joy, whose school had not predicted a bright future for her, was forging a solid career for herself, but she was still single; Ruth had graduated from the Slade, but was facing uncertainties about her artistic career; Brynnie's personal life was in turmoil, as she was embroiled in an affair with a much older married man; and Eileen was a welcome new member, as she could take Red Biddy's place while she attended to her busy and somewhat complicated personal life.

CHAPTER SEVENTEEN
Brynnie and Harold Jervis-Read

Brynnie Granger no doubt treasured the escape that the Mill and the Gang offered her from a private life that was growing ever more complicated.

Her course in domestic science and household economy at King's College had proved more of a challenge than she had hoped and her second-year exam results were unremarkable. She did well in physics, but only scraped through chemistry and failed dismally at biology. The failure gave her two choices, give up the course or retake the year.

On 4 July 1928, Miss Reynard, the College Warden, wrote to her mother. 'I cannot tell you how sorry I am that your daughter did not pass her examination. I know that it was not from lack of work and I am sure she did her best... I am glad to say that this reverse has not undermined her courage or her determination, and I hope that in the end it may not interfere with her career.'

Brynnie was reluctant to give up and wrote to Miss Reynard saying: 'My people are a little perplexed as to what to do for the best now. Is there any chance at all of the university accepting an Appeal if I were to do [the] second year of my Reformed Subject again?'

The College advised against it and after several lengthy conversations, Brynnie agreed to leave. She spent the summer recovering from her disappointment, spending weekends by the sea at home in Maldon.

An alternative direction was needed and one was found at St Thomas's Hospital in London. St Thomas's offered taster courses in almoner work. An almoner was a forerunner to today's hospital social worker, whose principal duties were to help poorer patients access free healthcare. There was no National Health Service then and healthcare could be expensive.

The almoner's role was originally a charitable one introduced by the Charity Organisation Society (later the Family Welfare Association), which was established by Octavia Hill and professionalised in the 1920s.

An almoner needed to have a caring nature so the role would suit Brynnie. Miss Reynard recognised that and wrote to St Thomas's: 'She is a very hard worker, has courage, grit and perseverance. She has an attractive manner and personality, a high standard of conduct and is unfailingly pleasant, courteous and considerate.' Brynnie was offered an internship.

Her senior was the pioneering almoner Anne Cummins, who during a lecture to hospital doctors, gave a picture of typical patients:

> At 9 o'clock there is a stream of women with their children outside the Almoner's Office for the Children's Department. They have been perhaps up and about since 6 o'clock and done their housework, washed and sent several children off to school, taken the baby to a neighbour to look after while they are at Hospital and put on the dinner to cook so there is something ready for the family at mid-day, and one child has had perhaps to be left in bed as she had a cold and was feverish.

Cummins was a caring rebel who taught her assistants to operate under the radar, placating male doctors who had little respect for women's opinions. She explained that the men would find any excuse to discredit them and, to avoid criticism of her staff, she implemented a strict dress code saying that the women would be taken seriously if they looked professional.

Brynnie trained for two years at the Institute of Hospital Almoners before accepting a job at Leeds General Infirmary, but she felt too 'southern' there and out of touch with the patients. In reality, she longed to be back in London where an affair of the heart prevented her from settling elsewhere. It was taboo but Brynnie was in love with a much older and very married man. Something was missing without him so when an opportunity arose at the Royal Free Hospital in Hampstead, she applied.

Her lover, Harold Jervis-Read, was a professional musician, composer and teacher with an impressive musical reputation. During his lifetime he composed at least 73 pieces – for piano, chorus and orchestra, violin and piano, and string sextets.

A romantic, he wrote a series of compositions putting poems by Percy Shelley, Francis Thompson and Oscar Wilde to music. In 1912, two of his works were performed as part of the Royal Academy of Music's Prom. He named one of the pieces 'Margery' after his wife.

That was before the First World War, when Harold's career was blossoming. Post-war, his own creative output declined, so he taught composition at the Royal Academy of Music. Nevertheless he did well and, in 1926, became Professor of Harmony there.

A passionate and intense musician, his relationship with music was intuitive and he held a deep and emotional connection to it. He was also in love with Brynnie, whom he had first met as a private pupil. Harold taught her piano at the family home, and grew to love her over the years.

On her 18th birthday, when he was 47, he sent his first letter to her. It was short and simple saying: 'I have been ill. But I wanted you to know that I had not forgotten your birthday, although I have not sent a present.' It cannot have escaped him that a married man in his late 40s writing to an 18-year-old girl was unconventional, but it seems he found Brynnie's innate caring and compassionate nature irresistible. Struggling to cope with family life, he was looking for a safe haven, an escape, and thought he had found it in Brynnie.

Harold had been an army Major in the First World War and suffered from what would now be called post-traumatic stress disorder. As a consequence, his mental health was unstable and he could be violent and prone to rages. He found family life noisy and troubling, and struggled with his duties as head of his household.

Harold was father to five children. His wife, Margery Vaughan, a solicitor's daughter, was aware of her husband's infidelity with Brynnie, and hints in a letter to her that she was not his first affair. She wrote: 'I expect you think me silly to mind my husband's infidelities – many people don't mind now-a-days. For 10 years we were divinely happy.'

That first decade was before Harold went to war. Like many soldiers who fought, he came back a changed man, unable to pick up his old life where he had left it. His rages were unpredictable and Margery described how he once kicked a bowl out of her hands. There was no romance left for her, she said; she was left short of money and burdened down with domestic drudgery. She wanted a divorce, but, scared of the shame, Harold threatened to kill himself. Margery wrote to Brynnie:

I didn't mind it as long as I had his love – no love remains but this endless performance of dull duties. I wanted to divorce him because I thought we should both be happier but I cannot if he says he would lose his job and commit suicide.

To make ends meet, she took a post as a live-in housemother at a girls' boarding school in Eastbourne. It was during one of Harold's week-end visits that she became pregnant with their fifth child, Christine, who was born in 1927. The headmistress was unsympathetic. She was clear that Margery would not keep her job if she tried to raise Christine on the premises and suggested they have her adopted. Harold and Margery felt they had little choice so when their daughter was about six weeks old, they gave her up for adoption. The eminent scientist, Quaker and pacifist, Dr Lewis Fry Richardson, and his wife Dorothy, welcomed her into their home and changed her name to Elaine.

Against this background Brynnie seemed refreshingly innocent and she soothed Harold's senses with her unjaded view of life.

For Brynnie, the attention from her piano tutor was flattering, confusing and overwhelming, but she responded. By the time she was 22, Harold was writing that he loved 'chatting twaddle to her' and that his children noticed he was much happier because of her. Brynnie fell madly in love but she battled feelings of guilt and remorse. She was very clear that she had no wish to break up his family.

In one letter she wrote of her 'dread of being an affair and you a married man whose family I know well'.

Harold's letters were focused mostly on his own feelings and needs. Brynnie's never seemed to be discussed or even recognised. She was someone lovely to cling to as his early promise slipped away and his latter compositions failed to attract the attention he hoped they would. In Brynnie he had a talisman, a peaceful existence and he reasoned she could help him restore his career. He told her: 'I should be very great with your help and encouragement. I know this and you know. I have always known it.'

By 1933, when Brynnie was 25, their relationship reached its zenith with a passionate exchange of dramatic, intense letters written every few days.

They would write, then meet, then write again, and their letters were filled with recriminations and declarations of love. Brynnie alternated between wanting Harold and wanting to be free of the affair while Harold would do and say anything to keep her. He wrote:

> I failed you yesterday Brynnie and again because I didn't trust
> you... Forgive me, make me strong... I am so happy with you...
> I'll try never to fail you again Brynnie.

She replied: 'Send for me if you want me, anywhere. If you are ill or tired or needing me.'

Their passionate relationship fulfilled both of them in many ways. Brynnie was a romantic and Harold responded lovingly to her romantic gestures, once waiting all day outside her flat opposite Regent's Park for her to come home. She spelled out messages for Harold in flowers on his doorstep. They shared a passion for music and wrote about recitals and concerts they had seen. When they were alone together he would lie at her feet for hours listening to: 'Wagner's marvellous music'.

Brynnie shared everything with Harold, even the Gang. He found them exciting and the Gang welcomed him. He would debate spirituality and Buddhism with Ruth and for a while lived with the Pissarro family next door to the Macgregors.

The affair was not kept secret from Brynnie's family, but her parents were on the brink of divorce and her sister was having lesbian affairs. Their own relationships were hardly traditional, but despite that, her parents were naturally concerned. They worried that the affair was not only emotionally damaging but could ruin her reputation. Her father wrote to Harold that it was his opinion that they had bonded over their love of music, but that the relationship should end.

Harold's response was to propose to Brynnie again and again, but she said no, suggesting a clean break would be the kindest thing for all concerned.

On 22 February 1933, aged 25, Brynnie wrote to him using his nickname Fitzjohn (he had lived in Fitzjohn Avenue, in North London) telling him: 'I am quite sure I have done the right thing... Today I have written to Mummy to say that so long as Margery and the children are faithful to you I shall not see you.'

Harold would not accept defeat and they began to bicker.

Brynnie wrote of their 'fruitless arguments'. He accused her of, 'jealousy whenever he achieved any happiness.'

Brynnie tried again and again to end the affair. In one letter she wrote:

> I ask you for my own sake to give up seeing me... You have had your love affairs, your marriage, your children and there is your work. You ask too much of a 'second Spring.' You must be blind if you don't see that I mean this.

He responded with a range of emotions: bitterness, cruelty and declarations of love. In a letter he began before bed and finished after waking up, he wrote:

> You'll tighten your life and feel virtuous, but you're wrong. All this is such fun to you – oh yes, you feel it a bit at times but your virtuous life strengthens you. You ruin me Brynnie: you have ruined me for should you beg me on your knees I would not come to help you now, for you withheld yourself and disgraced me.
> ...I hope I shall never see you again. I mean it: if I saw you now I should spit at you.
> You are wicked and selfish.
> Daylight – But I love you Brynnie I love you... I will start the divorce today if I have your promise. I cannot live without you.

It was emotional blackmail and placed responsibility for his happiness on Brynnie's inexperienced shoulders. Brynnie became desperate and grabbed any distraction.

Gang meetings were always welcome and once Brynnie hosted a meeting at her London flat after they met for supper at the Café Royal. She relished trips to the Mill and spent a late summer holiday with Peggy in Cornwall.

Even in Cornwall Brynnie did not feel free of Harold, so she took drastic and very brave action, securing a job in Australia. The post was as assistant almoner at the Royal Melbourne Hospital, where she worked alongside the British social work pioneer Agnes Macintyre. (Macintyre had set up the almoner service there five years before in 1929.)

Brynnie set sail for Australia in 1934, when she was just 26. The Gang met at the 'Beershop's palace' later that year, bereft that she had left: 'Sister Agatha was then ritually lamented for a minute... All keening expertly...'

CHAPTER EIGHTEEN
Joy and Ruth – finding their feet

J oy Maw also had her own troubles. After she became estranged from her mother she relied more and more on her father. She also needed to earn a living, so after graduation from King's in July 1929, she began looking for permanent employment. A job came up in administration at the Gordon Hotel Chain so Joy applied. (The Gordon Group owned high-profile London hotels such as the Victoria, the Metropole and the Dorchester, with clientele from the middle and upper classes.)

The faithful Miss Reynard, the King's College Warden, wrote her a lovely reference: 'I think that with experience she should make a good administrator. She is attracted to hotel work and if she could get the opportunity of beginning she would, I think, make a success of it.'

Joy was successful and was offered a post at the Victoria Hotel on a salary of £1 per week. Her role was to ensure that an efficient service was provided between front and back of house.

Joy had been in the Gang for two years by the time she began working, but her employers had no idea about her secret identity, and neither did the guests. Miss Reynard had written a reference saying that she was 'sober and respectable', so they would have been shocked to find that as Kate O'Brien the Nark, she was anything but.

In 1931, just after Joy had celebrated her 24th birthday, her mother died aged only 56. Although Joy had not seen her for many years, it was a difficult time. It made her appreciate how lucky she was that her father was so involved in her life. Arthur Maw's alter ego Silent O'Moyle meant he could be involved socially with his daughter as well as in his paternal role.

Joy stayed with the Gordon Group for five years before she felt it was time to move on. It was Brynnie's sister Isabelle who helped her find a new post. Isabelle had a teaching post at Channing High School, a boarding school in Highgate in North London and had been there for seven years. Through Isabelle Joy heard that a housekeeper's job was available. She applied, was offered the position and began working there in the spring of 1934.

Channing was a forward-thinking school that appealed to open-minded families. They offered a religious ethos, based on Unitarian grounds, and they believed in an all-loving God. Girls were encouraged to think for themselves too, also unusual for the time. Miss Alice Haigh, the headmistress, was very keen to nurture her students, and according to the school's history, aimed to 'stimulate her girls intellectually, rather than confine them to a rigid curriculum.' Throughout her time in charge she regarded every pupil as part of the Channing Family, kissing each boarder goodnight and following their later lives with interest and affection.

It was a place where Joy fitted in well, but after three years she left to join the Bergman Österberg Physical Training College in Dartford Heath, Kent, another forward-thinking establishment. Founded in 1895 by Swedish suffragette Martina Bergman Österberg, they trained teachers in physical education. Martina had radical ideas, and her first act was to abolish the generic corset and introduce a gym tunic, a much-copied design later adopted by most schools as standard uniform.

Students learned about anatomy, physiology, hygiene, massage and remedial exercises. The school had radical ideas about sport too and basketball was adapted for soft surfaces and given the name netball. Lacrosse was introduced and students played tennis, cricket, fives (a type of handball), swam and fenced.

Joy had a passion for sport and had found her vocation. She wrote to King's: 'I like the college very much so I hope it will be a long time before I worry you again.'

She was settled at work and loved her steady job, but also relished the unpredictability of life in the Gang.

Meanwhile, Bohemian life at the Slade tapped into Ruth Sherwood's unorthodox spirit. She no longer lived a sheltered life in a respectable, well-to-do industrial family, but was part of a vibrant if slightly mad artistic community.

To her fellow students she was a bit of a dark horse. Like her other compadres, she kept her involvement in Ferguson's Gang secret, even when Janet and John Macgregor attended the Slade's annual Christmas Ball, its summer Strawberry Tea or Vladimir Polunin's fantastic house parties. Polunin, who taught stage design at the Slade, lived near the Macgregors by the Thames.

In spite of this hedonism, life as an artist produced considerable heartache for Ruth. Her time at the Slade opened her eyes to a different world, one she found troubling. Ruth felt over-privileged and unentitled to succeed professionally. She clearly had talent and her lyrical, illustrative style, influenced by William Morris's Arts and Crafts Movement and the Bloomsbury Group, was in demand. On graduating, although Ruth was offered and took some jobs as a freelance commercial artist, she was wracked with a sense of guilt and discomfort at being surrounded by penniless painters. The Slade had its fair share of struggling artists desperate to earn a few shillings here and there to keep them in paint and canvas. Her family money meant she had no need of outside income. Hearing of the Slade artist Dora Carrington's well-publicised suicide, she took the altruistic decision not to deprive those more in need than her and not to compete with her contemporaries in the commercial art world. She did continue to paint and sketch, but only for her own pleasure.

Ruth was also grappling with more pressing personal concerns. Her health was deteriorating and she began to experience a numbness in her legs, which caused her to limp. Sometimes her limp was so bad she needed to use a cane. Fortunately her family provided her with refuge and support. They paid for her to take several therapeutic trips abroad, including a family holiday to the South of France, and a couple of years later she travelled via Bristol to catch a banana boat to Barbados in the Caribbean, leaving behind Brynnie at their shared flat in London. Ruth stayed in comfortable First Class and sketched her fellow passengers during the long crossing. Away for several months, she travelled alone, except for a tin of watercolour paints.

CHAPTER NINETEEN
Rachel and Lu Cox

While Ruth was travelling, Rachel was trying and failing as a student. While at Bristol, she applied for the third time for a place at Cambridge and again failed. Then, on her 21st birthday during the summer break, a bombshell letter from Bristol arrived at home at Racedown. She had been sent down. Rachel had been under the impression that her physical presence at university was enough to earn a degree. She had no concept of lectures or tutorials, and did not attend any. The university was not prepared to tolerate it.

The day after the letter arrived a house guest offered her a job at Stafford School, a special-needs school for teenage girls, which she accepted. But it was not what she wanted to do so she also applied to St Bartholomew's Hospital to train as a nurse. They turned her down because, at 5 feet tall, she was considered too short, but she did manage to land a training place at Middlesex Hospital. Sporty, like most of the Pinneys, she joined the student cricket team and immersed herself in her work. Although she liked the structure and routine at the hospital, she struggled with authority. While dressing a wound one day the ward sister told her to take her break. 'I haven't finished,' she said. 'That's an order,' came the response. Defiantly, Rachel left the ward, walked down the stairs, walked to the other side of the building, back up another set of stairs and back to the ward where she finished attending to the patient. Her disobedience was noted and, eventually, she was sacked. 'I loved nursing but my manners were not right,' she said. Another of her favourite sayings was: 'Obedience is a sin.' Rachel was lacking in social skills, she was tactless and could be overly disclosing. Although her intentions were good, she did not abide by the social norms and offended people because of her ignorance and bluntness.

Perhaps it was no surprise that Rachel seemed so emotionally illiterate. Her father had continued to abuse her throughout her childhood and was still. Now he arranged for the two of them to go to Scotland on a fishing trip. During the boat crossing, the General turned to her and, alluding to sex, said, 'You understand all these things, Rachel, being a nurse'. That was his contribution to a discussion on birth control and a suggestion of what was to come.

Her overriding memories of the Scottish trip are of her father climbing into her bed in their hotel and attempting penetration before saying, 'Here at last we have privacy and can do it properly, but we can't because I am old and you, old Bachel, are a virgin.' She was not, in fact, having had unsatisfactory sex with a student called Bill at Bristol. She had sex with Bill specifically so that she could lose her virginity, but the experience had not changed her opinion of intimacy with men, which she found uncomfortable and unarousing. Considering what she had suffered at the hands of her father, perhaps that was no surprise.

In 1930, Rachel went back to her studies and joined King's College, reading for an Applied Physics degree. Physics remained an enigma, although she was seduced by 'below stairs' experiments being conducted into atomic energy:

> I understood nothing of the Physics lectures. I did understand a little of the Mathematics and actually passed the BSc Hons Physics, Part I (Maths). That is the nearest to the degree I ever got.
>
> Instead of eating, studying and experimenting with my fellow students, I got myself to the tiny little space at the bottom of the narrow spiral staircase in the basement in which all the pre-atom-splitting research and experiments went on under the nominal leadership of Edward Appleton.* I was a close friend of Eva Widdowson,** one of the real geniuses. I didn't even begin to understand what was going on, but I had an ongoing account from her. It was like a parent keeping a ten year old informed of top scientific research. We made the first radioactive isotope in that lab. I hadn't the slightest idea what a radioactive isotope was, but I felt one of the team. The actual job allocated to me was to count the clicks on the Geiger counter while the researchers had coffee.
>
> Everyone in the lab was keyed up to what would happen when we could 'harness the energy of the atom'. Those were the exact words we used. Never did I hear a word about the atom being usable in war.

In 1931, while still struggling at King's, she discovered the Women's University Settlement (WUS) in South London. WUS was founded by women from Girton and Newnham Colleges in Cambridge and aimed 'to promote the welfare of the poorer districts of London, more especially of the women and children'. Women students were invited to live in the settlement in exchange for working in the community. Rachel had heard of the scheme through a visiting lecturer, signed up and spent a number of summers at their Blackfriars branch. 'My real life had started!' she said and she was excited to have a job she could relate to. Even though she was general dogsbody and messenger girl, she regarded WUS as her 'other home'.

Despite the abuse from her father and her unsatisfactory liaison with Bill, Rachel had not given up on men, and while she was still at King's, she met a carpenter, Luigi Cocuzzi. Lu was from Bethnal Green in East London, the son of immigrant Italians. But most exciting to Rachel was that he was a member of the Communist Party. She could only imagine, perhaps gleefully, her military father's disgust and distress if she brought Luigi home.

To escape the immigrant label, Luigi abbreviated his name and became Lu Cox, which made it easier for him to integrate. They met when Rachel was leasing a house in Oakley Street in Chelsea, near Cheyne Walk, and rented out rooms to make extra money. Most weekends Lu turned up to see Rachel's lodger Stella, bringing with him a pork chop, which Stella would then cook. As Stella was out one weekend Rachel offered to prepare the chop, although her cooking skills were nonexistent so he would have had to talk her through the process.

After he had eaten, she asked him to help her write up a physics experiment. Lu tried to help but was ignorant of anything to do with academia and quickly became bored. Instead, he kissed her. Rachel froze at first but according to her memoir, reluctantly had sex with him. Because of the relationship with her father, she had no concept of how to say no to men. So began a routine of Sunday visits from Lu: they would go for a walk, have supper then sex, but Rachel openly admitted she took no pleasure in it.

'Sex was just something that had to be done, rather like reading the directions for cooking on a packet of food, only rather more complicated,' she wrote.

Although their relationship wasn't easy, somehow, they began to talk of marriage. 'I remember telling Lu we couldn't get married because of the class and education difference. I am bitterly ashamed of that, but I am even more ashamed of the way I got round it. I arranged to hire an advanced student to educate him.'

She and Lu twice booked wedding dates at the registry office and rode there on their bicycles, arguing all the way, with Rachel objecting to Lu's antisocial road manners. By the time they arrived, they were so furious with each other they were no longer speaking, and both times the wedding was cancelled.

The safest way to get the job done, they decided, was to sleep in different houses the night before and arrive separately at the registry office. Witnesses were alerted, but told not to be surprised if their services were dispensed with at the last minute, and on the day, Lu was seen walking up and down Danvers Street trying to borrow money to buy Rachel some flowers.

On their third planned wedding day, 10 November 1934, Rachel felt deeply guilty, not because her family and friends were absent, but because she was due to play in a college cricket match and hadn't cancelled it. 'I think I was captain and that made it worse,' she said.

The wedding did go ahead but without the Gang or any of Rachel's family. Her parents and siblings had not refused to come but Rachel had only sent a telegram to them on the day, purposely too late. They wired back their good wishes and like Peggy's family a few years earlier, were thoroughly disapproving that Rachel had married beneath her.

Although she had enjoyed rebelling against her parents to marry Lu, there was no guarantee the marriage would be happy or successful.

She carried on working – she had to now as her allowance was stopped – but her career path was far from straightforward, partly because she suffered from dyslexia. Her writing was scruffy and she used block capitals, and the stress of her home and family situation made it hard for her to focus on much else. She was bright and intelligent but frustrated at her inability to achieve what was expected of her and what she expected of herself.

She felt overwhelmed and desperate. It was her failure in her studies, specifically her failure to master physics, which led to thoughts of suicide:

My difficulties with Physics spelt a failure to master any sort of living, I was also planning to kill my father at the same time. On the day my suicide didn't happen, I wrote a note to my parents, I said simply that I could see no future and couldn't go on. I wrote another note to Lu saying it wasn't his fault and I was sorry to be hurting him.

Nursing a loaded but uncocked revolver, sitting somewhere in the grounds of Racedown, she cried and wallowed in her depression until she noticed the family dog had become sexually excited. It was that distraction that saved her.

My intellect took over and I was interested. As the interest took over the depression ceased. This must have been some sort of cathartic experience. I felt calm, relaxed and in control of myself. I felt I had committed suicide. I thought, now I am dead, I can start all over again with that bit of my life behind me.

I walked home, destroyed the notes, unloaded and put away the revolver. I sought an early opportunity to have a proper talk with my mother. I had made a decision. I could no longer go on along the path I was on. For a start, I couldn't study; secondly, I couldn't read; and lastly, I couldn't understand a word the lecturers said.

My mother heard my story with utter seriousness, saying: 'What do you want us to do?'

'Pay for me to be psychoanalysed please.'

Rachel then spent three years in analysis but said she remembered very little about it.

Her analyst Karin Stephen was one of the early Freudians and also a friend of Rachel's uncle, Henry Head, who 'fiercely disapproved of all these "new-fangled" notions, and of one of his nieces getting into the hands of one of that gang.'

Stephen was married to fellow psychoanalyst Adrian Stephen, a member of the Bloomsbury Group and the brother of Virginia Woolf. Woolf unflatteringly described Karin as 'one of our lost dogs. She eats a great deal of food too, like a dog.'

Hard of hearing, Karin had an ear trumpet on a lead, which Rachel hated speaking into. She had sessions every day except weekends, each one costing a guinea. During the sessions, Rachel failed to tell Karin of the sexual abuse she suffered. 'People can't face up to what they can't face up to,' she said later.

Lu knew of the analysis and, in fact, they both attended lectures about Freud together. 'Neither of us understood a word of what was being said, but I picked up the essence of some of it and we both picked up a few clichés.' The one that she remembered was: '"Persons undergoing psychoanalysis have an opportunity of reliving their childhood under more favourable conditions." We had it as a signature tune, either to try to make up a quarrel or to consolidate one of our rare good moments.'

No amount of therapy helped Rachel to adapt to life, particularly a life without servants. Growing up, she had had housekeepers and nannies responsible for her wellbeing and upbringing. After she married Lu, however, her parents cut off her allowance and their minuscule budget just about covered their food bill.

Rachel left the Gang around that time too and was replaced a month after her marriage by Shot Biddy. Perhaps Lu asked her to leave or she had fallen out with Ferguson's Gang, but after 1934, she never appeared in 'The Boo' again.

Rachel became pregnant within the year, and she and Lu impulsively rented a shop with one week's rent they had in their pockets. It became 'Cox & Pinney', selling second-hand furniture. Her father was horrified that she was in trade. The shop was a disaster, with Rachel trying to please the customer at any price and Lu trying to make a profit at any price. They supplemented their income by becoming landlords.

> Lu and I always had lodgers. We eventually owned or rented several houses, using the proceeds from letting rooms to buy another property which, of course, was our capital. That may sound as if we had money, but we didn't. We were never solvent and were always in debt. I remember the large clip of unpaid bills hanging on the office wall.

Rachel raided the gas and electricity meters for cash and made futile attempts to make ends meet.

Their daughter Karin, named after Rachel's analyst, was born on 23 March 1936. With no nanny to take on the childcare, Rachel floundered. Von, the woman who had been the family's driver and who had also given birth to General Pinney's daughter Elisabeth, came to stay for a week or so bringing baby clothes. But after that, Rachel was on her own.

> I thought that in some magical way I would be told by someone what to do as the circumstances changed. I could not cope. My feeling of ineptitude was not limited to things like putting on nappies.

To her credit, she breast-fed Karin, but introducing her to food was another matter. When Karin was six months old, bone broth was suggested.

> I had got some bones, but didn't know what to do with them. The doctor never discovered that I couldn't handle the objects involved, let alone the baby. She never discovered that I couldn't make bone broth because I didn't know where to put the saucepan while I got the spoon ready, or the baby when I got the saucepan ready.

Karin lost all her baby teeth because of calcium deficiency and was in danger of serious neglect, so when Von volunteered to take her back to Dorset to look after her, Rachel and Lu agreed.

> Lu and I were struggling to make ends meet, feed the baby and run the furniture shop when Von turned up to stay. I realise now that she probably came on a rescue job as she well knew I could not cope.
>
> I did not feel I was doing anything wrong in letting Karin go. Karin went with Von to her rented bungalow near Bridport in Dorset and never came back. We tried to get her back and failed. First Lu went down ... and came back without her. Then I went down ... and came back without her. Then we both went down ... and came back without her. Finally we gave up.

I think probably Von decided she was going to have Karin right from the beginning, when she came to her birth. Later, she was heard to say, 'Now at last I've got even with the Pinneys...' whatever that meant.

Rachel fretted and missed Karin, but did not allow herself to pine, refusing to relinquish her stiff upper lip, although by now, her chaotic emotions were bubbling to the surface.

A few months before Von removed Karin, she was visiting Racedown when a family row broke out about the class system. After dinner, Rachel was sitting with her father, mother and two sisters, Hester and Mary, round a big fire in the drawing-room. An uncomfortable discussion began that grew more and more heated and in the debate that followed, Rachel revealed the truth about her father.

> I was feeling at home around that fire and was sad that they [her family] were so politically estranged from me. Dismally ignorant of political facts and not being able to make a clear case for communism or socialism, I blurted out about my father and me. Mary sprang at me shouting, 'You dare say things like that about your father!' It wasn't long before we were both in a clinch. I had my whole strength behind a hair hold on Mary. By the time my mother and Hester joined in with an effort to separate us, we had moved to the front where the curtains fell on to the floor.

Hester had hysterics and hid under the desk, their father left the room saying 'never darken my doors again' and their mother lost her false teeth (which she always clicked in agitation) as the big velvet curtains fell down on top of her. Hester ran to get a bottle for Karin, fearing Rachel's milk would dry up, then everyone went to bed, having resolved that Rachel was lying.

From that day, Rachel, at the age of only 27, was excommunicated from her family.

> I had become the baddie of the family from then on. I was no longer invited to any family occasions, such as weddings, with one exception: Hester made a point of inviting me when the

occasion did not involve any other member of the family, as for example when her husband was made Mayor of Chelsea. My sister Mary forbade me access to her children. As I was very fond of her eldest daughter Mary Ann, aged about three at the time, I minded the ban very much.

*Sir Edward Appleton won the Nobel Prize for Physics in 1947 for his work to establish the existence of the ionosphere, which led to the development of radar.

** Dr Eva Crane, neé Widdowson, trained in quantum mathematics, and in 1941, earned a PhD in Nuclear Physics.

CHAPTER TWENTY
Peggy and Pauline Tweedy

L ike Rachel and Lu, Peggy and Pollard knew how tough marriage could be, but continued their life together in St Mawes. While the newly wed Coxes bickered all the time, Peggy and Pollard achieved a reasonable harmony, outwardly at least. Peggy was a respected member of the community, seen as happily married and content, and she was all of those things, but she was unhappily still a virgin:

> I was suffering from a thundering inferiority-complex owing to my virgin condition after five years of married life, which I humbly attributed to my failure to attract Pollard.

Pollard never explained his lack of sexual interest in her and if he was unfaithful elsewhere, she never discovered a mistress; if he was a homosexual, that was never discovered either. He felt no need to conform in any way, living life as though he was a bachelor, going off on extended sailing trips and spending his nights in St Mawes in the Rising Sun pub.

Pollard was a powerful and skilful seaman who could whirl his boat in and out of tiny harbours that did not look big enough to park a soap-dish in. He also had a fantastic repertoire of raunchy sea shanties. One of his favourites was:

> *Please don't burn our shit-house down;*
> *Mother says she'll pay.*
> *Father's away on the ocean blue,*
> *Kate's in the family way.*
> *The man 'ere's got gonorrhoea,*
> *Times is effing 'ard.*
> *Please don't burn our shit-house down,*
> *Or we'll 'ave to wash in the yard.*

They loved him in the local pub where he entertained and impressed the locals with his encyclopedic knowledge of the world. He was a big drinker too and could down a gallon of beer in an evening. But with all that local brew, he gained weight, and his athletic build began disappearing behind a substantial beer belly. Pollard's physique went from toned sailor to that of a traditional tenor opera singer.

Peggy stuck with him but never broached the subject of sex. Her celibate marriage clearly disappointed her and she fantasised about experiencing a sexual relationship. She took no action to find a lover, but in the end, one found her.

Peggy met Pauline Tweedy at a local party given by Pauline's mother to announce her daughter's arrival in St Mawes. She was an attractive woman with a slim, shapely figure, her dark hair framing an impish face. A musical genius, Pauline studied the violin under the virtuoso and soloist Carl Flesch in Vienna. Peggy said: 'She was the perfect prodigy in every way and quite indescribably brilliant.'

At the party, Peggy invited her to their home at the Rope Walk and suggested they play a duet. Pauline chose a Brahms violin and piano sonata in A. 'At the sight of it my heart sank and I fell into desperation but resolved to get through the bloody thing somehow – and did.' Then Pauline produced the music for Mendelssohn's violin concerto.

I was now in the death-or-glory frame of mind and got through it tolerably well till the gallop of the last movement in which I came unstuck and at that moment was conscious of a violent karate chop across the back of my neck, spun round on the piano stool in consternation, not to say acute pain, and met the blazing eyes of Pauline, who looked ready to commit murder on the spot. For a moment we stared at each other, speechless; then Pauline burst into a shriek of laughter, plumped down on the seat beside me, flung her arms round me and kissed me, dropping the bow with which she had hit me.

I may say I had never been kissed before, in that manner. Pollard did not go in much for osculation... It was a positive earthshaking revelation to me. It cooked my goose, did my business, fixed my deck-chair. I was doomed from that moment. Nothing in the world was of any importance but only Pauline Tweedy.

Technically, Pauline was already spoken for as she was engaged to a violinist ten years her junior, Maurice Clare.* Determined to marry him, her plan was to push him to the top and make him famous. She was not ambitious for herself, saying there were no first-rate women violinists and never had been, but she was undecided whether to become a pioneer and try to forge a career for herself or focus on Maurice.

Pauline called Maurice Jimmy for some reason and, for a while, she wondered if she should ditch him and aim at fame for herself and Peggy.

> In the end, but reluctantly, she decided that Jimmy was better value from the long-term point of view; but he wasn't in England, and I was, and readily available.
>
> Things began to warm up. Pauline proceeded to further exploration; I lived in a state of combined ecstasy and alarm.
>
> By now I began to regard Pauline as exotically beautiful. She certainly had lovely long legs and looked just fine in a kilt (her heredity was Scotch and she claimed descent from Robert Bruce as well as a river-god, of the Tweed naturally). She assumed the dominant masculine role and I, for the first time treated like a woman, proved very gauche and inexpert.

Pollard was away when the affair first began and never found out. He had inherited £1,000, which he spent on a Brixham trawler called *Seaplane*. He had had it fitted out for a cruise to America, so while he was enjoying an adventure, Peggy had the house to herself. She took full advantage:

> I had a wonderful Jacobean bed, elaborately carved... It was too short for the vast form of Pollard, who slept in the other room in a bed specially made for his length. This bed, if it had concealed a tape-recorder (not yet invented) might have produced a regular Arabian Nights Entertainment with knobs on. Modesty forbids me to do more than quote the opening lines of a poem I wrote her...

> 'To your long hands of supple steel
> The last defences fell...'

Occasionally they forgot to be decorous and whilst enjoying a passionate embrace in the garden at Peggy's cottage one afternoon, they were interrupted by a peeping Tom.

> We concentrated on finding opportunities to go to't, and once we were doing so on the bit of grass that belonged to me in the Ropewalk, with tall hedges protecting us from observation, as we supposed; when suddenly Pauline hastily detached herself and muttered a wrathful observation, whereat I looked where she was looking and there was a dirty old man in the terrace behind fascinatedly surveying us through a pair of binoculars...

When Pollard returned from America he was penniless but happy, and none the wiser. He went back to his routine spending every day messing around with his beloved boat and every night at the Rising Sun.

> He did not seem to notice Pauline. But all of a sudden Jimmy marched onto the stage and issued an ultimatum to Pauline. Apparently he demanded that she should swear an oath not to see me for six years.
>
> Why six years I don't know; probably he thought by then he could have established himself on an unshakeable basis. However, Pauline and I settled down to a heated correspondence...
>
> We had another wild night at the Queen's Hotel, Penzance and a good many more after that. So Jimmy had to think of something else. He had lost the first round.

Peggy tried to content herself with simple correspondence, and while Pauline was away, took a trip to London where she met a Russian guitarist. Alexis Chesnakof (whose tutor would go on to train the classical guitarist Julian Bream) was a Cossack who had fought in the First World War and, according to Peggy, was a 'magnificent' musician. He had also had lessons with the great Spanish virtuoso Andrés Segovia, but lived in squalor in a basement flat near the Natural History Museum in London, supporting himself by joining the circus as a bareback rider.

Peggy had been taking guitar lessons but her progress was slow. She asked Chesnakoff if he would tutor her. He accepted her as a pupil but described her guitar playing as 'abominable'. Peggy was unfazed. She appreciated a direct approach, whether positive or negative:

> I liked him and he told me all his life story and in the well-known candid and naïve Russian manner said his trouble in England was he could not get a woman, and was in sore straights without one for such a long time. He wasn't going to pick one up on the streets who might give him a disease, they weren't clean – and he didn't know any respectable women who would answer his purpose. Whereat, infected by his naïve and simple attitude to life, I said, 'Would I do?' (I thought, this won't half nark Pauline when I tell her, and is a way to pay her out, if she thinks I am pining away for grief.)
>
> He enthusiastically accepted my offer and (Pollard being again away at sea) accepted an invitation to come and stay.
>
> The whole thing was a right cock-up (except that this is perhaps an unfortunate term to use...) and might allegorically be likened to a sheltered Victorian lady's saddlehorse being ridden by a bronco-buster from the Wild West. I was extremely shocked and revolted...
>
> I prefer not to dwell on the debacle. He left the next day, with mutual apologies, both of us admitting it hadn't been exactly a success, and I had sufficiently recovered my composure to wish him better luck with the next one. I never saw him again.

Peggy's first sexual experience with a man was humiliating and never-to-be repeated, but she turned it to her advantage. She immediately wrote to Pauline sending her a 'highly-coloured account which had the desired effect; she came rolling back. After that we had a lot of fun, and as Pauline had a large appetite, running chiefly to shoulders of mutton and rice pudding, I was periodically leaping out of bed to look in the oven and make sure it had not turned itself up.'

Their affair could never last unless Pauline was prepared to give up Jimmy, or if Jimmy was prepared to accept it. He was not and told Pauline that it had to finish. His ultimatum was beyond devastating for Peggy, who had had little in the way of emotional fulfilment. In Pauline, she had found a soulmate, a partner in crime, someone who found her attractive, and someone who was able to express physical as well as emotional love for her. Their break-up was deeply traumatic and proved to her that affairs of the heart, and loins, were a bad thing.

They decided to meet for a last time and, for their swansong, chose the small town of Lewes in East Sussex where they stayed in what Peggy described as a 'remarkable period hotel', which distinctly sounded as though it had seen better days.

There was a jerry under the (double) bed, which I regret to say had not been emptied. There was also a flea in the bed. Pauline had once told me that any flea which bit her would die. Next morning I was a mass of flea-bites from head to foot; on Pauline's lean form there was one small bite and on her side of the bed was a dead flea...

We went out for a walk on the South Downs and saw several of the strange Neolithic dew-ponds, full of dark clear slate-coloured water as cold as ice. There was also a quantity of a curious dark blue curly headed flower called rampion, which is local; likewise quantities of Chalkhill Blue butterflies, which are not common elsewhere.

We spent the last night under a haystack. I was more wakeful than Pauline and observed the rising of the Fomalhaut, a star rarely seen in these latitudes; and, just before dawn, Betelgeuse. And that dawn was the end. We said goodbye under a lamp-post.

But that was by no means the end. Pauline it always was who made the move back. And Jimmy had now to think up something in the way of a winner. I wonder if he read Colette's 'Le Mari Complaisant',** for he now proceeded to act out the plot of that novel, I later found out.

A close friend of Peggy's said that Jimmy joined in with the affair, which then became a ménage à trois. In the end, it finally did peter out, and Peggy knew that Jimmy had won.

Subsequently, Peggy professed to hate Pauline, but it is clear from the way she wrote about her that she did not.

> Nothing will ever kill me quite as dead again. If you do survive, you become invulnerable.

> For all that I don't claim I loved Pauline. I mostly hated her, I believe; I simply wanted her like nothing else on earth as I have never wanted anything or anybody before or since. And may I say I am devoutly thankful I never got her. Nor did she love me in any sense of the word. We simply wanted each other with a furious unreasoning passion, and she was the only person who found me attractive.

* Maurice (Jimmy) Clare did rise to the top and became a violinist of international repute. Eventually, he was offered the position as leader of the Australian Victorian Symphony Orchestra in 1962. His marriage to Pauline did not last, but he married for a second time.

** There is no novel called *Le Mari Complaisant* written by the French novelist and performer Sidonie-Gabrielle Colette (1873–1954), who is best known for her novel *Gigi. Mari complaisant* is French for a cuckolded husband.

CHAPTER TWENTY-ONE
Third campaign: open spaces

When the Gang met on 18 November 1934 to discuss new projects, they decided to change tack and decreed: 'THAT THE GANG DO NOT GO AFTER A BUILDING NEXT TIME, BUT AN OPEN SPACE'.

Small amounts of cash had already been sent by them to various countryside conservation schemes. There was £1 for the Appeal for Lake Buttermere in Cumbria and 7s 6d to the Sullington Warren Purchase Committee. Sullington Warren, a haven for birdlife in West Sussex, was saved from being flattened by housing developers. There was also a donation of £3 for the Appeal for Lansallos, a pretty cove in Cornwall, sheltering a beautiful white sandy beach, which was of particular interest to Peggy.

The Gang considered details for two woods for sale: one cost £3,000 and the other £2,000, but they decided they were too expensive. Bolberry Down, a dramatic clifftop near Salcombe in Devon with 'far reaching views' was more manageable at £900, and they would tell the Trust that they were happy to take on the appeal. Bill announced: 'This we can do in two years on our heads.' In the end, it was bought by public subscription not the Gang but still endowed to the Trust.

The driving force behind the Gang was always Peggy, and that continued although she lived furthest from the Shalford Mill headquarters

She threw herself into life in her adopted county of Cornwall, joining various groups including an operatic society and the Women's Institute. She wrote a folk opera based on German folk tunes called *The Ghost of the Inn*, in which the hero had deserted his lady-love and had fallen for a ghost. She also wrote a version of the pantomime *Jack and the Beanstalk* with Pollard as the villain. Always the linguist, she taught herself Cornish and helped to institute a revival in the language, eventually being appointed a Bard of Cornwall. For the role, she adopted a Cornish name, Arlohes Ywerdhon, which translated as Irish Lady.

Unselfconscious, direct and full of enthusiasm, she possessed end-less reserves of energy. She could be sharp, snobbish, and difficult at times, and some people found her intimidating, but she was fiercely loyal to her friends, doing anything she could to help them. She was described as formidable, which she was. She made things happen when she set her mind to them. Peggy was not one just to talk about a project; she also made sure she carried it through.

Moving to Cornwall only increased her passion for conservation and she turned her attention towards what she could do for the county.

Planning was only just beginning to be taken seriously in Cornwall and the local branch of the CPRE had been set up by Henry Trefusis in 1929. When Peggy's friend Bishop Hunkin, Bishop of Truro, took over as Chair in 1935, Peggy was the obvious choice for Honourary Secretary the following year. Together they campaigned tirelessly for local conservation initiatives.

Cornwall was becoming a tourist destination and as a consequence was suffering from the unsympathetic siting of hotels and holiday homes, built not in the Cornish vernacular of whitewashed houses, roofed with soft grey granite and slate, but in bright red brick that jarred with the gentle environment. Locals could see their beautiful coastline under threat. They worried that the rugged peninsula, secluded coves and the characteristic fishing villages clinging to the clifftops would be destroyed. The Cornish, with their own language and identity dating back to ancient Britain, did not want to see their culture diluted.

The book, *Cornwall, Coast, Moors and Valleys*, published by the CPRE in 1930 and written by W. Harding Thompson, a fellow of the Royal Institute of British Architects, described a common sight: 'At Polzeath there is an ill-assorted collection of shacks, bungalows, disused railway carriages, and old caravans, firmly established on the hillside of a beautiful little valley.'

Equally, some local authorities viewed the countryside as a conven-ient rubbish tip. Thompson lamented: 'It is still common practice for some of the inhabitants of these places to dispose of their rubbish over the edge of sloping cliffs, where it slowly decays and attracts vermin and flies... Porthleven, Mousehole, Malpas... These places possessed of harbours and rivers use them as receptacles for refuse, broken crock-ery, tin cans and utensils of all kinds.'

At Land's End, the southernmost tip of England, a hotel had been built on the headland and Peggy could foresee Mayon and Treves-can Cliffs, the coastland in the mile between Land's End and Sennen village, spoiled by unsympathetic bungalows, holiday parks and hotels.

They were unspoilt and beautiful. Gorse and heather cover the Mayon Cliffs, and the stretch of sea in front of it is one of the most interesting pieces of water in the world. From giant liners to tiny coasters, vessels bound for an English port from the Atlantic Ocean, or leaving home to cross it, would pass by Mayon Cliffs. *The Titanic* would have sailed past on her ill-fated maiden voyage to America in 1912.

Acutely aware that her own back yard was in danger of being despoiled, she began looking for suitable spots to save, using her own money and finding other benefactors to fund acquisitions.

The Great Western Railway had ambitions to extend its line along the south Cornish coast. The Gang had already contributed to an appeal to save Lansallos Cliff, just east of Fowey, but it was with the help of businessman Treve Holman, boss of Cornwall's largest mining equipment manufacturing company, and other benefactors including herself and Black Mary that Peggy secured it for the Trust for £580, effectively scuppering Great Western's scheme.

Lansallos Cliff overlooks a small, sheltered sand and shingle bay, the type you might picture on a desert island. Thanks to Peggy, it is now in the hands of the Trust and beautifully preserved. Then, much further west, by The Lizard, land surrounding the rugged, weath-er-beaten Predannack Cliffs at Mullion came up for sale, cited as a prime site for another headland hotel. She wrote:

> Treve Holman, [High Sheriff of Cornwall 1942] another valuable ally, and I did a sort of commando raid to save Lansallos Bay near Fowey, and was just in time. Henry Trefusis [Lieutenant-Colonel Hon. Henry Walter Hepburn-Stuart-Forbes-Trefusis, 1864–1948] and I did another commando raid and rescued an extraordinary old cottage on the Helford River which was haunted by the ghost of a witch. With a welcome legacy I bought the Predannack Cliffs at Mullion. It was a very exciting life.

Peggy also acted for third parties, once as a go between for a powerful and influential squire who owned Rosemullion Head, a stretch of rugged coastland west of Falmouth, again on the south coast of Cornwall. He wished remain anonymous, so made a deal that 'he would give me the money and I would write the cheque. Five thousand I think it was.'

The Trust were delighted and wrote in their bulletin:

> The National Trust announces to-day the acquisition, mainly through the generosity of MRS. POLLARD, of yet another stretch of the Cornish coast. The new addition to its properties will be all the more welcome for lying in a region where the Trust has hitherto had no foothold. Between Treen Castle, some ten miles south-west of Penzance and the Lizard Downs near Kynance Cover the Trust owned nothing along the whole coast until it was presented and entrusted with the property described...

> Trust's holdings on the Cornish coast make a brave show of red on the map in the most recent report. Tintagel, Pendarves Point, Trewarnavas Cliff at Gillan Cove, Nare Head (not yet open to the public, but safe from "development"), the Dodman (no fewer than 145 acres of headland and farmland), St. Catherine's Point and St Saviour's Point with Snail Park near Fowey, and Lansallos, between Polperro and Polruan in Lantivet Bay, where the Trust owns some fifty acres and protects 200 more by covenants – these, with the most recent acquisitions, are, it is true, mere fragments of the great whole, but fragments of inestimable value. In this coming spring and summer thousands of holidaymakers will benefit by the generosity of the donors and the energy and prudence of the Trust.

Close to Land's End stands the Irish Lady Rock, a gigantic pinnacle around which seas break even in calm weather, that stands a few yards offshore. It is said to be a memorial to the sole survivor of an ancient shipwreck, who fell into the sea before she could be rescued and whose ghost can be seen clinging to the rock by some. Overlooking the Irish Lady is Maen Castle, an Iron Age ruin, said to have been a refuge to which ancient Britons fled when attacked by sea raiders. The area is littered with prehistoric stones called Quoits, each one named by fishermen, who claimed they had been thrown by giants.

Peggy alerted the Gang, proclaiming that the tentacle of the octopus had finally reached the very end of Cornwall. They didn't hesitate to act.

Peggy and her mother, who was now living close by, visited Mayon Cliffs a couple of times before they purchased them. On the first occasion a strong south-westerly beat them back, but on the second Peggy wrote this report and composed a poem to mark the occasion:

BILL'S SECOND REPORT, June 19, 1935

Bill and Black Mary tried the Mayon Cliffs again. The day was fine and breezy. First they inspected the pond. It proved to be an interesting swamp, containing bog cotton, bog asphodel, lesser water plantain, spotted orchids, and other objects... He photographed the Irish Lady, which is not the one he thought but a tall shapely pinnacle shaped like a lady with a full skirt and a crown, right under the cliffs … afterwards she and Black Mary had lunch and a lovely long lie in the sun among the rocks. A seagull came and had lunch too, off Bill's Digestive Biscuits, and Bill saw a pretty viper.

THE IRISH LADY

'Wot as you seen by Mayon Castle,
Wot as you seen to make a fuss?'
'Up on the cliffs by Mayon Castle,
There I seen the Octopus!'

'Wot was the Octopus a-doing,
North of the Longships as you go?'
'E's some bricks and a load o concrete,
For to start on a bungalow.

Scarlet bricks and rubbery tiling,
Bright red boxes all in a row;
Tin ki-osk for the teas and petrol,
Parkin place for the cars to go.

Save me Castle, me old Cliff Castle,
Take it safe to the National Trus'!
Save me Barrow, me old Ring Barrow;
Save us all from the Octopus!'

'Ferguson's Gang will save yer Castle,
Save yer Barrow and cliffs and you.'
'Thank you, Sir,' said the Irish Lady,
'That is just wot I oped you'd do.'

Tiddy fa lol, fa lol, falady,
Tiddy fa lol, fa lol, fa lee:
Ferguson's Gang, said the Irish Lady,
Ferguson's Gang is the Gang for me!

The mythology of the area appealed to the Gang, who felt compelled to save it from ad hoc unsightly development. Galvanised into action. they raised £600 for the purchase of the cliffs and £450 to buy Treves-can Cliffs, which run adjacent to Mayon Cliffs.

On 25 June 1935, after the purchase of Mayon Cliffs was announced by the Trust, *The Times* reported:

> Once again 'Ferguson's Gang' have come to the help of the Trust, this time in Cornwall. They have now undertaken to find the money for the purchase of cliff lands between Sennen and Land's End, stretching from the Signal Station to Maen Castle. The property includes Castle Zawn and the Irish Lady rocks.

The *News Chronicle*'s headline read: '"Ferguson's Gang" to the Rescue Again'. The *Daily Express* and the *Daily Telegraph* also covered the story, as did BBC radio. The local paper in Cornwall, the *Western Morning News*, described the Gang in glowing terms as 'England's most mysterious philanthropic organisation'.

A year later, to celebrate buying Mayon Cliffs, Peggy invited the Gang to take a holiday in Cornwall. Arthur joined his daughter Joy and the other young women and on a late summer's afternoon the group clambered over the rocky cliffs and found a place to sit opposite the Irish Lady. It was a fine day, warm and windy, and a ritual blessing was performed which included throwing a bouquet of herbs and myrtle to the rock and a bottle of Spanish ale from Eileen, both of which landed safely. Ruth made a sketch of the Irish Lady from which Silent O'Moyle was able to design a unique tile. He instructed his tile makers at Maw & Co. to make one up.

Peggy recorded in 'The Boo':

Is B then settled down to draw the Irish Lady for Silent O'Moyle to make a tile for the Gang. The weather was bright and warm, with a strong wind. Another magnificent Gang outing.

CHAPTER TWENTY-TWO
'No defence but the National Trust'

B y 1935 Ferguson's Gang had been active for seven years and in that time had saved Shalford Mill, Newtown Old Town Hall and a stretch of Cornish coastline.

Ferguson and his Gang were well known by now, and people wondered who Ferguson was. In the Gang's minute book he was often seen to sign his name and at one point was referred to as a man with a full beard. The Gang had a rubber stamp made up at W. H. Smith with his signature, which they used on official documents, but he rarely appeared at meetings.

Ferguson was largely a phantom, but a physical manifestation was needed at times. Bobby was always happy to discard his respectability and become not only Erb the Smasher, but also to double as Ferguson. He agreed to make a rare appearance as the elusive Ferguson to give an appeal for the National Trust live on BBC radio.

The press were intrigued that the Gang's mysterious and reclusive figurehead would finally materialise, excitedly reporting the upcoming occasion. On 21 August 1935, *The Times* headline read:

'MAN OF MYSTERY' TO BROADCAST APPEAL FOR NATIONAL TRUST

The final paragraph of their report read:

No one, not even the officials of the Trust know who the gang are. They have come in various disguises and with fantastic pseudonyms. Ferguson has consented to come in person to the microphone on Sunday, but the National Trust do not know whether he will reveal how his gang collect their funds.

On Sunday 25 August 1935, Bobby raced up to the BBC in his sports car, arriving masked, and was then shown to a studio. He lit a cigarette, spoke to producers about the new Ramblers Association launched that year and discussed Alfred Hitchcock's film about spies and counter-espionage, *The 39 Steps*. He had one last rehearsal, took a deep breath, then delivered his appeal without once removing his mask. The full transcript of his impassioned speech read as follows:

> I am Ferguson of Ferguson's Gang. I appeal to you tonight for the National Trust. That means for the beauty of England: for all that is left of the England that belongs to you and me and is vanishing under our eyes.
>
> The land held by the National Trust is your land and nobody else's. The cliffs that you buy for the Nation will always be open for you to walk on. Nobody can turn you out of the woods and fields that are held for you by the National Trust. But no Government grant supports the work of the Trust; it is kept going by your efforts and mine. And it urgently needs more subscribing members to help in its battle against the Octopus: the Octopus, whose tentacles, in the shape of jerry-built estates and ribbon development, are stretching like a pestilence over the face of England.
>
> *'Green grass turning to bricks and dust,*
> *Stately homes that will soon go bust:*
> *No defence but the National Trust.'*
>
> Do you remember what happened about Stonehenge? In 1927 it was known that building development threatened the land round Stonehenge. All over England people were horrified at the news. People who had never set eyes on that strange circle of stones felt that in some way it was the historic heart of England, and they must save it at whatsoever cost. They did. They raised £35,000 in less than two years: and today the plain encircles Stonehenge, with only clumps of ancient beeches to break the skyline.
>
> Since then the work of the Trust has increased enormously. You can hardly open a paper without reading that some

beautiful piece of land or some historic building has passed into the safe hands of the National Trust ... into YOUR hands. Thousands of acres of Exmoor; lakeland fells and woods and crags; the fifteen Farne Islands; cliffs in Cornwall, New Forest commons, historic mansions like Montacute and East Riddlesden Hall, bird sanctuaries, naturalists' Paradises like Wicken Fen, buildings used as Youth Hostels like the City Mill at Winchester and the Old Town Hall of Newtown I.W. By subscribing 10/- a year, that is, what you pay for your wireless licence, you can save England from the Octopus and keep its woods and fields and ancient buildings for yourselves and the generations to come. Do anything but watch the Octopus at work and say 'Why doesn't somebody do something about it?' You can do something yourselves, whether, like Ferguson's Gang, you call at the offices of the Trust in a mask and deposit a sack of bullion, or join the Trust as a subscribing member, or become an Associate member, which costs only 2/6 a year, or simply give a donation ... anything you like, what you can spare.

Please send what you can to FERGUSON, c/o the National Trust, 7 Buckingham Palace Gardens, London, S.W.1.

The country was delighted and rose to the occasion. Hundreds of people sent donations and joined the National Trust. This was a massive boost because, although the Trust had celebrated its 40th anniversary that year, they still had only 5,000 subscribing members.

On 29 August 1935, the Trust's President, Princess Louise – Queen Victoria's sixth child – sent a personal letter of thanks to the Gang which became one of their most valued possessions. Aged 87, the Princess was a staunch supporter of women and delighted that it was women who were doing so well at furthering one of her causes.

The letter read:

HRH Princess Louise, Duchess of Argyll,
Kensington Palace, W.8.
Personal.

It has given me the greatest pleasure to listen to Ferguson's address last Sunday, on behalf of 'The National Trust'.

I have often wondered from where the helping hand to the finances came (a subject that has ever been the anxiety from all times to those who had its welfare closely at heart), and rejoiced of late to see how the Trust had been able to procure some of the many important historical and beautiful places and lands.

Therefore I feel greatly moved to say how grateful I am to those named 'Ferguson', who are doing so much splendid work in aid of the advancement of The National Trust. As its President may I thank 'The Fergusons' for the benefacting, true spirit, and express my admiration for the energies the 'Ferguson Gang' have evinced.

After this, Erb wrote to Peggy in a slightly more irreverent tone:

H.R.H. The Princess Louise, Duchess of Argyll has been greatly moved as by a dose of salts.

Such is the power of advertising that the gang is credited with almost the sole support of the Trust, which idea it is unnecessary to dispel.

I think the dear lady ought to get a nice line with the seal etc. attached. She ought to jump nicely if she is allowed to see the Bloody Bishop's signature...

Yrs. erb.

On 7 September 1935, the Trust wrote to the Gang with the official results of the appeal:

...we have really been inundated with subscriptions and donations for the last fortnight, and even now our post still includes letters addressed to Ferguson. The largest donation was £100 and the smallest 5d in stamps. We reckon that we have enrolled just over 300 Associates and 600 Members.

The final total of donations came to £905, a huge sum as the average annual salary then was around £200. The Trust also increased its membership by just over 20 per cent, an incredible achievement. What was unquantifiable and priceless though, was the upswell of popular support that the Gang was creating for conservation.

The following year, in 1936, the Trust held its Christmas dinner at the Mayfair Hotel, in Berkley Square, on the day that Princess Louise's great-nephew Edward VIII abdicated. The atmosphere was subdued and, according to the Gang, the meal was disappointing and 'no better than railway food', with what they described as mutton gristle, peppery soup, followed by unripe pear. They did manage to provide a light moment however. Peggy, disguised as a Dominican nun, nearly lost a £100 note donation by stuffing it inside a cigar, which she presented to Lord Zetland, who was officiating that night. The Gang then spent an anxious evening worrying that it would be smoked. 'It came through safe,' Peggy wrote in 'The Boo'.

CHAPTER TWENTY-THREE
Oly X.perditions

Nineteen thirty-seven was a momentous year for the Gang. It was their tenth anniversary and Brynnie was back from Australia. Determined to celebrate in style they organised a spectacular banquet, a visit to Stonehenge, a Mill Haunting and a holiday.

First came the dinner. On 27 May, 11 Gang members and guests gathered at a popular French restaurant, The Florence, in Piccadilly, London. The choice of The Florence was a natural one as it had become a favourite haunt. Gang members attending were: Bill Stickers, Shot Biddy, Sister Agatha, the Bludy Beershop (wearing the Regalia), Kate O'Brien the Nark, the Artichoke and Artichrix, the Pious Yudhishthira and Poolcat; Ferguson was represented by 'Samson is Shofar', and the National Trust was represented by Mr Matheson, the Trust's Secretary, who was 'Ghost of Honour'. Uncle Gregory, Erb and Black Mary were absent.

The evening started with drinks then the group headed upstairs to the banqueting hall where Peggy had decorated the table in an unusual manner with what she described as 'insex'. This could have meant anything from a scarab to incense. Games were paramount and they decided on a pea-eating competition with Samson being the official winner, balancing a total of 25 on his knife. The Artichoke caused much mirth by contesting his victory, accusing the chauffeur of using his moustache to hold the peas in place. The Gang reminisced over the past ten years and Poolcat recalled how it was he who had prepared the Gang's very first picnic at Tothill Fields.

The French menu that night was mouth-watering and included hors-d'oeuvre of smoked salmon or grapefruit, followed by roast lamb with minted peas, chicken salad, asparagus and filet of sole – a vast improvement on the Trust's ropey Christmas fare.

The finale of the meal was a dessert, invented especially for them by the Swiss chef, a lychee ice called a 'Bombe Ferguson'. 'A delight to the palate', if anyone could manage a spoonful at the end of their seven-course meal. During the dinner, Peggy was kept informed of the Bombe's progress, which despite the chef's warning that it had blown up and become more of a soufflé, was according to 'The Boo':

> ...perfexion. A ring of live lychees in their carapaces surrounded a big glittering white bomb, crowned with lychees as we usually ave em, and a delight to the palate.

The dinner was reported in the papers (although the cuttings in 'The Boo' do not indicate which ones). One says that: 'Matheson is still unaware of the identity of the Gang for no names were disclosed. He believes, however, that Ferguson himself was not present. During the even [sic] he was given a further £150 towards the acquisition of the land at Trevescan which brings the monetary gifts of the "Gang" to the total of £2,250.' (£2,250 was approximately enough to buy five three-bedroom houses then.)

Celebrations for their decennial could not pass without a trip, or 'Oly X.perdition' to their spiritual home of Stonehenge, followed by a haunting at the Mill.

The 2nd Oly X.perdition to Stonehenge, 26 June 1937, included just the inner circle of Peggy, Brynnie, Joy, Ruth and Eileen. They travelled First Class from Waterloo to Salisbury, and as they had done during their last visit, they entered the stone circle in pairs. The Bludy Beershop conducted the ritual at the altar stone where they vowed to preserve England as represented by Stonehenge NOT Whitehall and to destroy the Octopus. They then sat in the evening sun:

> ... olding profound conversation on world topics, and Bill took several 4ographs. We then had supper or eggs and eld a airdressing marathon in the train.
>
> Moved by Bill, seconded by Kate and carried: THAT THE GANG HAS HAD A LOVELY DAY.
>
> Kate went home 2 her pitch, the rest went to the Mill to aunt, arriving at quarter 2 11.

Joy could not stay for the whole of the midsummer celebrations as she had to return for the end of term at Highgate. She had handed in her notice as housemistress at Channing but had to be there for the final weeks of term.

At Waterloo, the group parted ways, and Peggy, Bryn, Ruth and Eileen dashed across the station forecourt to catch the 10 o'clock train to Guildford.

The fourth Haunting of the Mill began at midnight and ended at breakfast. Brynnie, who had become unaccustomed to the Gang's hedonistic schedule, barely managed to keep awake throughout the summer night. So after their usual 'swearing in' and a baptism by the Bludy Beershop, they sang hymns and played intellectual guessing games to keep her alert. Peggy and Ruth danced up and down the top gallery of the Mill and then played a game of 'Penitent Fathers' involving a rope and noose. Eileen and Ruth went downstairs to make coffee and drinking continued throughout the night until 3.15am when a cockerel crowed, at which point, they repaired to the Dawn Window. 'The Boo' says:

> ...they lay in a neat pile on a narrow board, Is B being at the bottom and Biddy on top. There was a melancholy suggestion by Ag, who was very doubtfully alive at all, as to whether 3 separate colours existed in the Artichoke's garden: but at 4 a.m. a pink rose, a red rose, and a blue delphinium were confirmed. The Gang then withdrew to bed.

Before the summer ended, the Gang decided to meet again. Outings came as a welcome reprieve for Bryn and Eileen who were working long hours developing their professional careers. Joy, the third money earner, had a free summer before starting her new post in Dartford. For Bryn, who had just moved closer to her work in Westminster Palace Gardens, in Victoria, an escape from the City and her ongoing turbulent relationship with Harold Jervis-Read was always welcome.

They would meet one more time that year. For their final decennial celebration they decided on a World Conference, a euphemism for a holiday, to be held between 9 and 15 August, in Portmeirion in Wales where they stayed at the hotel Castell Deudraeth, owned by Clough Williams-Ellis.

Peggy's five-page report is in irreverent postcard form and describes how they visited religious sites, one of them being the Moorish Castle, 'where the Gang was attacked by a party of Christians with a white woolly Chinese dog', glimpsed St Clough, bathed nude in a river (frightening away clergymen), played croquet, fought off flying ants and watched a beautiful display of summer lightning.

On 14 August, just before travelling home, they held their 24th meeting. The coffers were healthy, they reported, with £114 8s 1d in the bank. They needed to raise a further £85 11s 11d for Trevescan Cliffs, to add to the £150 already paid towards the purchase. They set a deadline to raise the balance by the next National Trust dinner.

CHAPTER TWENTY-FOUR
The Black Atropine Sisterhood

Although they were ten years old, Ferguson's Gang still enjoyed an eccentric, innocent and fun existence, but all that was about to be disrupted by unrest in the wider world. The Spanish Civil War was raging, and although the Second World War would not start for another two years, Jewish refugees were already fleeing Nazi Germany and beginning to arrive in Britain. The Gang were disturbed by these events and impressed that Eileen was working with refugees.

A retreat back to Ferguson's Gang for the women was still as welcome as ever and they indulged themselves with comfort food and a Christmas feast of roast loin of lamb, new potatoes, baby carrots and their favourite exotic fruit, lychees. For pudding they ate a peach brandy cake bought from a cake maker called Thœa Benia. (They had eaten her devil's food cake at a previous meeting and vowed to try every cake in her repertoire.) They drank toasts with vin rosé, followed by cherry brandy, and let the drink go to their heads.

They were in a festive mood and in generous spirit but did not ignore business. A small amount was still owed on Trevescan Cliffs, which they decided to deliver to the Trust on Christmas Eve:

> it was decided 2 ask Ferguson 2 deliver either on a sprig of olly or a little baby Christmas tree, a little silver tree like they ave in Austria, with a little goat anging down.

Ferguson was unable to deliver so Peggy volunteered and, inebriated, she made the delivery. Her report in 'The Boo' said:

Bill's Emma Gency Report
Distemper 24 1937

I kisses the goats goodbye and shoves them in a corf lossenge box and libels it with holly and a card showing various ugly Fishes and a greeting 2 say:

'This way Ferguson, as e best can,
Pay the debt upon Trevescan.
This ere design of various Fishes
We do enclose with our best wishes.'

A hit and run was best she decided and posted the cash in the sweet tin through the Trust's letterbox. The Trust would have liked more fanfare and wrote to the Gang afterwards saying they were disappointed the drop was so low key: 'we didn't think it was up 2 standard'.

Nevertheless, their bulletin carried a grateful note and was distributed to the Press. On 31 December 1937, *The Times* faithfully reported the 'hit':

'FERGUSON'S GANG' AGAIN
£200 FOR NATIONAL TRUST
It was announced last night that a menthol and eucalyptus pastille box, marked 'Highly perishable, deliver at once' was received at the offices of The National Trust on Christmas Eve and was found to contain £200 in notes...

A large part of the coast round Land's End has already been given to the Trust by Ferguson's Gang, and this is the Gang's final payment for the completion of the purchase of land at Trevescan.

The Gang's reputation was still growing and even the children's Press began to publicise their exploits. The *Children's Newspaper* printed caricatures of the Gang, sensitively omitting the Bludy Beershop in case the children were offended, they said.

Bill was portrayed as a man in glasses and a character called Boker Jake made his first appearance. He was never mentioned in 'The Boo' and may have been invented by the paper. Uncle Gregory also had his own caricature despite his lack of real activity in the Gang.

In the same year, 1937, the *Daily Mail* published the shocking news that the Gang was to retire. Although the Gang had formed in 1927, everyone considered their start date to be 1932, the time of their first drop. The *Mail*'s piece read:

It wasn't true, and the Gang didn't know why Matheson had decided to propagate the rumour. They made no comment but continued quietly contributing to other appeals, and had saved £100 to donate to the National Trust's Avebury Appeal. Avebury is a Neolithic henge, built around 2,600BC, containing three stone circles, one of which is the largest in Europe, surrounding the village of Avebury in Wiltshire.

What they didn't know when they were planning their drop was that Matheson could have been preparing the press and public for the arrival of a new group. In fact, a copycat gang calling themselves the 'Black Atropine Sisterhood' was already on the scene.

The Trust became aware of the Sisterhood one afternoon, just after their 3pm tea break, when the concierge announced that a group of 'Sisters' had arrived. The sisters refused to reveal their identities, but someone had spotted a pair of trousers just visible below the hem of one of the nun's habits. They left a £100 donation for the Trust's Dovedale Appeal, and went on their way. The Trust assumed it was Ferguson's Gang in another guise.

Unaware, the Gang went ahead with plans for an associate member known as Anne of Lothbury, already a benefactor to the National Trust, to make the delivery, accompanied to the door of the Trust by Joy. Anne had been looking for an occasion to wear her antique Venetian mask and thought this might be it. The Gang wrote her a letter 'empowering her 2 deliver the Avebury Goat' and included a verse that she should hand over with the cash:

> *This 'ere goat of ancient breed*
> *Did on the Bank of England feed*
> *When mature the same is found*
> *To be worth a hundred pound*

Which we sacrifice with zeal
To the Avebury Appeal.

During the delivery, made on 13 July 1938, Anne became the first member to hear about the new gang from Matheson. During their meeting, Mr Matheson swore to Anne he did not know who the rivals were and had been convinced they were part of Ferguson's Gang. Anne swore truthfully she had no idea about them and that Ferguson's Gang had no clue who the copycat gang were either. All anyone knew was that they were a clandestine holy order calling themselves the Black Atropine Sisterhood and were very similar to the Gang. They had the same ethos as the Gang, adopted pseudonyms and were anonymous.

The Gang received the news from Anne with a mixture of bafflement, amusement and shock.

The Times and the *News Chronicle*, sensing a feud, reported the rivalry with glee. The *Chronicle's* headline on 15 July 1938, read:

'Jealousy' Prompts £100 Gift

After a rather longer hibernation than usual, the 'Ferguson Gang' has made its beneficent appearance again, having left a £100 note with the National Trust for the Avebury Appeal.

It is suggested that the gang has been reawakened by jealousy of a rival gang, 'The Black Atropine Sisterhood', which recently presented a sum of money to the Trust for the preservation of Dovedale...

Dovedale, a network of pretty hills and deep-cut gorges in a stunning valley in the Peak District in the North of England, was under threat. Galvanised by the attention the Sisters received, the Gang also donated £20 to the same appeal and in August handed over £5 for the Punch Bowl Appeal in Hindhead, Surrey, a place now designated an Area of Outstanding Natural Beauty.

The Black Atropine Sisterhood was made up of eight members: Sister Niphetos Acherontia; Mother Maudez-Acherontia; the Virgin; Sister Budeaux; El Machetero; Forward Amanda; Sister Tertia; and

Sister Stychomythia. They said they were an order of the Symphorodox Church, a church proposed by an Anglican priest as a joke that would embrace heresies rather than denouncing them, therefore producing a church acceptable to all faiths.

The Atropines' pseudonyms sounded as though they could have been plundered from various holy orders, but most of them had their origins in nature. Their names demonstrated quite clearly that they shared the same intellect as Ferguson's Gang, and that they loved the natural world, were cosmopolitan and had a sense of humour.

Atropine is an alkaloid extracted from deadly nightshade, Jimson weed or mandrake and used to calm digestive complaints. Acherontia is the death's head hawkmoth found throughout tropical Africa, while the Niphetos is a simple antique white rose. The Machetero was an impromptu band of Puerto Ricans who fought the Americans during the Spanish–American War; Stychomythia is an ancient Greek arrangement of dialogue; and Forward is a common title used for socialist publications. The only religious associations were those of the Virgin, Maudez and Budeaux. Saint Budeaux derived from Saint Budoc, who was Bishop of Dol in Brittany around AD480, and Saint Maudez (also known as Mawes) was a Breton saint who lived around AD600.

It is not known where or when but the Trust introduced the two rival gangs. Rather than work in opposition to each other they decided it was a good idea to co-operate. Joy was even taken on as an honorary member of the Black Atropines, having been stopped for speeding and let off after producing a nun's habit. The Black Atropines thought this admirable and Joy was given the name Sister Spinosissima, from a wonderful cactus with a crown of red spines nicknamed the 'Red-headed Irishman'.

They began collaborating and both groups were keen to buy Beeleigh Abbey, a medieval abbey near Maldon, Essex, close to Bryn's birthplace, but at £5,000 it was a costly purchase and the Gang had been unable to find the funds on their own.

The Sisters attended an emergency meeting held by the Gang on 17 October 1938 and the Gang were willing to consider their opinions.

Peggy said that Sister Niphetos Acherontia (the Atropines' Honorary Secretary) should be invited to attend their next World Conference, wearing full robes, and wrote in 'The Boo': 'We shall then see how the cat jumps, the wind lies and the land blows.'

In a magnanimous gesture, Sister Niphetos offered to host the conference and to cater for it, which as food was involved, endeared her to the Gang. They accepted her offer and the Gang's second World Conference was held on 17 October 1938, at Sister Niphetos's Cell. Four Ferguson's Gang members were there: Peggy, Joy, Brynnie and Eileen, and Mr Matheson came as a representative of the Trust. Sister Niphetos, Mother Maudez and Forward Amanda represented the Sisterhood. It is possible that Amanda was one of the women working at the Trust, but according to the report she seemed uncomfortable and keen to leave. Peggy wrote:

> By 7.30 all had had enough sherry and withdrew to the Refectory where Mother Maudez and Sister Niphetos had prepared a simple and austere collation consisting of:-
> Petits Poussins Sacerdatales
> Roast Potatoes: Brussels Sprouts
>
> ~
>
> Glace de Framboises Maison Fortunée
> Les Mignardises Religieuses
>
> ~
>
> Wines:- Perrick's Blood. Château Carbonnieux
>
> ~
>
> Coffee

(Which, loosely translated, means priestly chicken, raspberry ice-cream from Fortnum & Mason, religious petit fours and red wine.)

> After this all repaired to Sister Niphetos' Cell and began a Conference. Matheson was more at home by a long shot than Amanda, who sat silently by the fire.

As the meet dragged on, Peggy noted that 'Forward Amanda was doing the wrist watch act something pitiful and so we let both of them go home.'

Conservation and the Sisterhood momentarily forgotten, the Gang focused instead on the next National Trust Dinner, to be held a couple of weeks later on 3 November, and their next drop, which they planned to make that same night. An uneasy alliance with the Sisterhood had been forged, though, and would continue for the time being.

The 43rd National Trust dinner, held at the Criterion Restaurant in Piccadilly, was presided over by Trust Chairman Lord Zetland.

Lord Macmillan proposed the toast and proceeded with a sarcastic criticism of the War Office. He said: 'There was an English process of saving beautiful places. First the War Office would select the most beautiful site for a gun emplacement. Protests would be raised and public-minded men like Professor Trevelyan would write to *The Times*, which would follow with a leader. After declaring that it was the only possible site the War Office would move elsewhere.'

In reply Mr Ronald Collet Norman, the Chairman of the BBC and in charge of the Trust's finance committee attacked the establishment and said that 'the tragic thing was that the dangers came from the hand of man. It was a most lamentable thing that half of mankind were trying to neutralise what the other half were doing. Threats came from the great public services, the War Department, the services of water, roads, electricity, and forestry. The National Trust might have to submit to arbitration under the Green Belt Act when there was a clash between the public services and amenities.'

However, he added, 'the Trust was making satisfactory progress, and in the last year had acquired a record number of properties.' They now controlled 80,000 acres, and their subscribers increased regularly.

CHAPTER TWENTY-FIVE
Fourth campaign: Priory Cottages

The Gang were used to successfully acquiring whatever they put their mind to but in September 1938, encountered their first failure. What they really wanted was a third property, a hideout that could serve as a home for Peggy, Eileen, Joy and Brynnie, either permanent or temporary. They envisaged each would have her own quarters all coming together in a communal area, where they could sit and plot their next hit. Peggy would embroider the Gang's robe, while Joy would read, Brynnie could play the piano and Eileen would cook.

A suitable six-bedroom house came up in Hertfordshire in Hunsdon, a pretty village that had been registered in the Domesday Book. An important yeoman house, the Old Pump House dated back to 1497 in parts and stood in 7½ acres of land. Now, it was largely 18th century in appearance, featuring a circular elm staircase. Seven cottages were attached to it and the grounds had an impressive walled garden. Rent for the Pump House was £52pa plus £24 rates. The rental on the cottages was £88pa, which could possibly provide them with an income. Peggy told the Gang about it and 'Interest was unanimous'.

A speculative builder had also been sniffing around the property but intended to sell the cottages for scrap, something the Gang considered sacrilege. The cost to buy the whole package was £2,200, a significant amount but income from the cottage rentals would be a big help.

Peggy contacted the Trust and spoke to Matheson who then wrote to the Chairman, Lord Zetland, who approved the purchase, subject to the Trust's survey. As with all the Gang's other purchases, he was prepared to advance the money, which the Gang would then pay back.

The Trust's Executive Committee had to meet to approve the project, but several members already knew the Old Pump House and felt it was too much of a mishmash of styles to be considered important enough to save. Reluctantly, the Gang's proposal was vetoed, which was a devastating blow. A highly apologetic Matheson broke the news in a letter:

They asked me to say that they very naturally looked with considerable sympathy on any proposal brought forward by Ferguson's Gang, particularly in view of the interesting properties which they have already presented to the Trust.

They felt, however, that the Old Pump House and Cottages were really not of such importance as to make it proper for the Trust to hold them for the nation for permanent preservation.

If the Gang are very keen on them and if it would be any help to them, I was asked to say that the Trust would, of course, be willing to hold the property but not inalienably...

I very much hope that the Gang will not be very disappointed by this news which represents a decision reached by the Committee only with very great regret.

The Gang were obviously sad but took it well and after a meeting to discuss Matheson's letter, Peggy responded:

There was a division of opinion. Some said they would not on any account permit points to be stretched by the Trust for the Gang and would rather look for something else. Others thought that if we let you take the property on such terms it would prejudice our relations with the Trust, which would thereafter regard itself as having been rather stung... and consider that it had gone out of its way to show the Gang a favour.

Others again said that we needed a bolthole and we should consider our own interests first and agree to your holding the property on any terms whatever. These were the ones who having seen the O.P.H. had immediately fallen in love with it.

But to another member of the Gang it occurred that by the time we were all dead we might have conferred upon the house sufficient historic interest to make it a desirable property for you to hold inalienably.

The suggestion was made that they might try the CPRE, which often gathered up the Trust's unwanted crumbs. They decided a World Conference was needed to debate what was best, but they were open to viewing other properties in the meantime.

The National Trust responded eagerly and wrote with several suggestions. Secretary of the Country Houses Committee James Lees-Milne was instrumental in trying to help the Gang find a property to buy that they could live in. He suggested several places that were both architecturally important for the Trust to take on and small enough for the Gang to run. He even wrote to them suggesting his father's property, The Manor House, in South Littleton near Evesham in Worcestershire, now a Grade II* listed building.

In the end, Lees-Milne's nominations and the Pump House became irrelevant because only a couple of months later, the Gang discovered Priory Cottages, in Steventon in Oxfordshire. Just before Christmas 1938, Peggy and Eileen travelled to the village for a site visit. Peggy wrote in 'The Boo':

> X.Perdition of Bill and Biddy to the Priory Cottages,
> Steventon, Sunday Dec 11th
> Once a Benedictine Monks' country lodge, built round an open
> court, with mighty timber frames, and stone fireplaces, and in
> one cottage a roof gathered up on a wonderful hammer-beam
> truss, having also a priest's bolthole in the chimney against the
> Re4m8ion. A nice big garden and orchard, and a little stream.
> The road bounds it all and beyond is the ole Church, Rectory
> and Tithebalm...

The asking price was a much more manageable £500 and it was decided that Peggy should go to the Trust immediately to ask them to take the cottages on.

Steventon had a medieval history and religious associations that intrigued the Gang, and like Hunsdon, Steventon was mentioned in the Domesday Book. In 1086, in a survey commissioned by King William I, Steventon was listed as being a settlement of up to 300 inhabitants.

Priory Cottages consisted of four 14th-century timber-framed buildings, which formed three sides of a courtyard. They sat at the end of an ancient cobbled causeway that formed the spine of the village. Opposite the cottages is St Michael and All Angels Church, a pretty stone church built by the Fleming family in the 14th century. The causeway would have provided a dry pathway for monks and residents to walk to and from church.

Henry I, King of England and Normandy, gifted the cottages, along with Steventon Manor, to the Abbey of Bec in Normandy. This meant that the cottages became what was known as an 'alien priory'. Alien priories were the English cells of Norman houses, and several Norman nunneries and monasteries had possessions in England.

Although Priory Cottages was built on British soil, it was considered one of the French religious houses belonging to the Catholic Church; its mother house was the Priory of St Mary de Pré, also known as Notre-Dame du Pré, in Rouen, itself a subsidiary of the Abbey of Bec in Normandy. Records showed that two monks had lived there along with a prior, a sub-prior and a lay steward.

On 14 December 1938, Mr Matheson wrote to Peggy at her club, the University Women's Club, South Audley Square, London. He said: 'The Committee agreed unanimously to accept the very kind offer of these to the Trust, to be held inalienably!'

Ferguson's Gang had found their bolthole and excitedly began allocating 'cells' for each other, and there was still room for a common area. There was a garden and courtyard too, which made it the perfect property.

Six months later, on 6 May 1939, thanks to the benevolent Black Mary, they delivered the first £100 down payment. Bard Gwas Arthur, a subscribing member, made the drop in his theatre mask with Shot Biddy, who kept watch while he delivered the cash. For the first time, the newspapers did not report it, and this bothered the Gang who resolved to deliver the next 'goat' in a 'snuphbox at the Annual Meeting'.

Once the first down payment was delivered the Artichoke was instructed to visit the cottages. He had big plans, but the Gang considered his estimate 'dotty and includes a pond in the courtyard'. The quote was in excess of £1,300, which they thought was too much and too ambitious. They needed to address his frame of mind, they thought.

Summer was approaching and it was time for a ritual haunting at Shalford Mill, but only three of the Gang could make it: Brynnie, Peggy and Eileen. Arriving there they found the Artichoke's family taking tea in the garden. Twins Sally and Joanna were naked except for ferns tied round their waists and hats made of upturned Indian rhubarb leaves.

The gang joined them, eating watercress sandwiches around the wheelie table, which had been cobbled together by the Artichoke out of an old church door and set upon four pram wheels. When Janet went into the kitchen to top up the silver teapot they nobbled John about costs for Priory Cottages. He explained that the main expense was for major repairs. The wonderful hammer beam needed a structural tie to keep the roof together. By the end of the conversation they saw that his estimation was as ever reasonable, even with his whimsical fishpond.

For the sixth year the Gang faithfully haunted the Mill, and it was an excuse for them to get together and regroup. For the first time, outsiders were invited. Sisters Tertia and Niphetos Acherontia were there representing the Black Atropine Sisterhood. Superhuman efforts were again made to keep Bryn awake:

> 4-part rounds were sung with the Sisters, and Ag compelled to learn some Greek songs. The Artichoke's child's proposal to distemper the Chamber of Horrors was discussed with disgust. Bill then played a Bolero to which Ag and Biddy danced with a certain degree of artistry.

They served a marshmallow fudge cake and Bill read the lives of the Saints until it was apparent that all the cocks had been silenced as it was now 4 o'clock. The Gang, scarcely showing the strain at all, repaired to the Dawn Window where three colours almost immediately presented themselves, including a beautiful red poppy.

The following day they began planning their next drop of £100 for Priory Cottages, and began to think about ways they could guarantee press coverage, not wanting their track record to slip. They discarded the snuff-box idea and the resulting stunt in July 1939 was Ferguson's Gang's unforgettable invasion of the National Trust's AGM with the pineapple that looked like a bomb. It elicited splendid headlines. The *Western Morning News* wrote: 'Received A "Bomb"'; the *Daily Telegraph* called it 'A Beneficent Bomb'; while the *News Chronicle* went with 'Ferguson Gang's £100 Bomb'.

These were fitting tributes to what would be the Gang's last purchase for the Trust, although they did not know it at the time...

War was brewing, and everything was about to change. This would eventually scupper their intention to live at the Priory, but not their wish to buy it. They planned to deliver £50 to the Trust at Christmas for Priory Cottages, which would take them to the halfway mark of the purchase price. They thought it would be nice to deliver it with a bottle of Nuns' liqueur.

For now, before war intervened, the Gang's most pressing issue was where to have their Christmas dinner. Joy proposed and Eileen seconded the motion that they have a Christmas celebration in London. The Gang hoped and the Sisters prayed that they could enjoy 'an Xmas Ganquet' the following year at Priory Cottages.

CHAPTER TWENTY-SIX
Sombre times

Ruth had been absent from meetings, rituals, dinners and Oly X.Cursions for about a year, and when the Gang met in Wales on 19 August 1939, only two weeks before war was declared, she was still not present. They were again staying courtesy of Clough Williams-Ellis at Portmeirion, not at Castell Deudraeth as they had two years before, but at what they described as 'the Priory of the Blue Campanulines', which was probably the Campanile, the blue-topped bell tower in the village. Present were Peggy, Joy, Eileen, a new member called the Public Recorder and Sister Stichomythia. To the shock and surprise of the other members, Bill announced the demise of the Rt. Bludy the Lord Beershop 'who had left a dignified and touching will'.

Handwritten in Ruth's sloping, untidy hand on transparent white paper, dated 22 July, and headed 'The Bleeding Will', it read:

This ere being my last will and testament I do desire to express one or two things:-

One is that Ferguson's Gang & other adhesive bodies thereunto, shall prosper & continue in the write way as is set down according.

Another is that some part of the Bludy Estaite, namely – Mercators Projection & the Gladstone Isles, shall be put to the use of the above Gang etc: & that the trustees shall be the advisors (M.F.&N.*) who shall breed coins & send P.O.'s to the above Gang.

One more thing, I would love it if Ferguson's Gang would scatter my ashes (enclosed herewith) threw the window into the Mill tail & throw a wreathe after them & perhaps make the occasion one for the drinking of something nice with some lychees & cream.

Lastly I would take it kindly if I were permitted to haunt the Mill occasionally.

The advisors are instructed to return the Great Seal & the Regalia.

signed

The Bloody Beershop

*male, female & neuter.

Ruth had not died, but she was suffering from a rare form of anaemia that had killed two of her brothers. She had every reason to think she might not survive and because of this, she felt she could no longer contribute to the Gang in the way she used to. She had moved back to Sutton Coldfield with the full expectation that she could soon be dead.

It wasn't only the loss of their spiritual head that was signalling great changes for the Gang and beyond. On 3 September 1939, Britain and France declared war on Germany and the Gang members were as disturbed as the rest of the country. On Boxing Day 1939, they held their 37th meeting and their '1st War Council' at Sister Niphetos's Cell.

Peggy, Brynnie, Eileen, two Public Recorders and Sister Niphetos were present. Peggy reread the Beershop's will and pledged that her ashes would be scattered as requested. Brynnie said she would compose an elegy and would send it. But they decided that, because of the war, personal delivery of money to the Trust was not possible. The Trust had now left London and were holed up with Baronet Sir John Dashwood in his Palladian mansion in West Wycombe, Buckinghamshire, which he would donate to the Trust in 1943, much to the chagrin of his heir. The Gang had no desire to make the trip out there.

Even if we run is butler's gauntlet we should ave 2 stay 2 lunch which would mean unmasking or starvation.

Peggy delivered £50 towards Priory Cottages with the enclosed note:

While fire is hot and water wet
Ferguson's Gang doth not 4get.
This Goat, though smaller than some goats,
The arf way mark at last denotes.

Signed Ferguson, Bill, Ag, Biddy. The rest of us are
serving in the Esprit de Corps, the Moustache Guards, and
the Crown Derby Tea Service.

During the meeting they declared that: 'there is a war on' and stated
that the future was uncertain. Peggy then announced the real deaths
of Anne of Lothbury, their associate member, and their most eminent
supporter, Princess Louise, who had died on 3 December at Kensington Palace at the age of 91. A Gang Howl was given in remembrance.

Even though Peggy had joined the Women's Land Army, which she
called the 'Old Mudguards', she continued showing her commitment
to the National Trust and by 17 June 1940, had sent another £50
towards Priory Cottages.

Mr Matheson sent her a personal note with the receipt, thanking
the Gang for the cheque saying: 'It is like Manna from Heaven to get
anything these days.'

In August, Peggy sent Matheson a poem with the final £250 for
Priory Cottages:

> *Hitler or no matter wot*
> *May afflict this nation.*
> *Ferguson defaulteth not*
> *on his obligation.*
> *More nor ruby, pearls and gold,*
> *sapphire and emERald*
> *He the National Trust duth hold.*
> *Yours sincerely Gerald.*
> *Ps. it isnt really Gerald but it rimes.*

The Trust replied, writing in rhyme:

> *The Secretary is away*
> *But in his absence may we say*
> *How glad we are to find the Gang*
> *Doesn't let its vows go hang*
> *But still gives money to the Trust*
> *Though most of us are nearly bust.*

We think it is a proper treat
So please accept our nice receipt.

The final payment had been made; the full cost of £550 paid. The Gang's next fund-raising effort would be money for the repairs.

As the war progressed, the tone of 'The Boo' changed, and a sombre mood crept into the Gang's minutes. It was obviously hard to carry on, but the Gang had no intention of surrendering. Nevertheless, a lot of their conservation missions were thwarted and meeting each other was becoming more and more difficult. At one point, they could do nothing but correspond.

At their 2nd War Council on 13 March 1940, again at Sister Niphetos's Cell:

> It was resolved that in view of the war only kids of £50 should be delivered and these inconspicuously by post as goats might give in4mation 2 Hitler.
>
> The Gang felt distraught and subdued, Bill being all muddled with is white slave traffic [Peggy's reference to running the land army] which was not going as well as it ought, and Kate having 2 cook in the trenches during air raid alarms.

They were also shaken by an assassination attempt on Trust Chairman Lord Zetland. A Sikh revolutionary called Udham Singh, avenging the Jallianwalla Bagh Massacre in Amritsar where hundreds of non-violent Indian protestors were killed by the British, tried to shoot Lord Zetland (who was also Secretary of State for India) during a meeting at Caxton Hall in London. Zetland had a lucky escape, being hit by a bullet just above the heart that ricocheted off his very thick pocket handkerchief. The bullet made a hole in his shirt and undershirt, and he was injured, but not seriously. Michael O'Dwyer, the Lieutenant Governor of the Punjab, who was at the same meeting, was killed.

At the meeting the Gang wondered what was going on and whether it was an omen. Looking for a silver lining, and trying to make light of the situation, Eileen suggested that the assassin might be sent to try his luck with Hitler. The meeting concluded with the Sisters singing their song with a new verse to bring it up to date:

The Nuns of Acherontia
Give no more money 2 the poor:
They put it in the War Loan
That we may beat the Boer.

The general feeling was that this could be the last meeting while the war was on and, given that the Gang met several times a year, this was to be a great wrench for all.

The huge events beyond the existence of the Gang were now taking over their lives. The Blitz was raging in London and across the country. A bomb penetrated Balham Tube Station, bringing tons of rubble down on scores of people underground sheltering from the Blitz. Those not injured by the blast were in danger of being suffocated by escaping gas or drowned in water from a burst main. It was a tragedy that shocked the world and the iconic photo published in foreign newspapers was of a number 88 bus, plunged into the crater created by the bomb. Over 60 died and the episode was a sombre reminder to the Gang of the grim reality of war. War was turning everything upside down and an uncertain future meant confusion. Nevertheless, the people of Great Britain rallied and got behind the war effort. The Gang were no different, each choosing their own unique way to contribute.

CHAPTER TWENTY-SEVEN
Peggy's war

In 1938, Frank Pollard joined the Royal Naval Volunteer Reserves and within two years had risen to the rank of lieutenant. By the end of the war, he was captain of a minesweeper and from then on, all the locals called him Captain.

Alone in Cornwall, Peggy embraced war like it was simply another project needing her attention. She was appointed Organising Secretary to the Cornish Women's Land Army and with Florence Peachey started a goat farm in Quenchwell. In true Peggy fashion, she gave her goats Hindu names, while the farm became Satya Goat Farm, a Sanskrit name which means truth or reality.

Goats, unlike cows, were not subject to rationing, which meant an endless supply of goat meat and butter made from their milk, whereas butter made from cow's milk was eventually rationed to just 2oz a week, and meagre meat rationing allowed for around 8oz of minced beef.

Children were evacuated from blitzed areas to the countryside in droves, and with Pollard away, Peggy offered her farm as a safe haven. She invited two children whom she already knew, eight-year-old Doris and ten-year-old Arnold Dick, from Sunderland in the north of England.

Sunderland was a shipbuilding centre that had become a target for German air raids, and the children's father William worked in a foundry making shells. Doris has no idea how Peggy knew her parents, William and Ellen, but remembers first meeting her when she was three years old. Peggy would invite Doris, her parents and her brother to London and treat them to expensive teas at prestigious hotels such as The Ritz and Claridges. Doris said:

> She was always sending us crates of oranges and presents. My father always talked about her and clearly had a lot of respect for her. We loved her and called her Auntie Peggy and she was always incredibly kind to us.

When the war started Arnold and I were told that Auntie Peggy would like to give us a long, long holiday and we were very happy at the thought. We arrived at Truro station and caught a taxi to the goat farm from there, then we were given a hot drink and a tablet and sent to bed. We were so excited and thought it was ever so grown up.

We truly had happy memories. The farm was lovely and included a stonewashed cottage, a dairy and an outside loo at the bottom of the garden. Two land girls stayed on the farm, Flo Peachey and another girl who didn't really speak to us, but Peggy and Flo could not have been kinder.

Auntie Peggy had about a dozen Anglo Nubian goats and I remember when they had kids, we had to drown them in a bucket when they were a couple of days old. It was horrible at first but we got used to it. They would be made into stews as Peggy couldn't afford to keep more than a dozen goats at a time.

Each morning, when we weren't at school, we were sent out with a bottle of goat's milk and a sandwich and the goats on a lead. We'd take them out for the whole day and not come back until dinner time.

In the evening Peggy would play the guitar and sing, or she would write down the beginning of a story for us to finish off. She was very keen that we learned to use our imagination. She was a fantastic needlewoman and taught me how to do invisible darning and embroidery and taught me how to knit. We had a much older brother, Alex, who was stationed nearby. I never saw him, but I knitted him a navy blue scarf on four needles, which Peggy sent to him.

I don't ever remember feeling homesick until after my brother went home. He left about a year before me and afterwards, my father came to visit me. He turned up at my school and I looked up, saw him and burst out crying. I was allowed the day off to spend with him.

William had arrived to sort out a rift that had developed between him and Peggy, who had offered to adopt Doris and Arnold. Although she was extremely fond of the children, she very likely had an ulterior motive. Her maternal instincts had never really surfaced. There was, however, a financial advantage to becoming a mother. Her inheritance was tied up in trust; her allowance had increased from £400 when she was a single woman to £800 when she was married, and would increase further if she had children. A born philanthropist, she would have wanted the funds for purely altruistic reasons but, in the event, Doris and Arnold's parents vetoed any ideas of adoption. Doris said:

> It ended badly and after my brother went home. Peggy said she would get a solicitor to sort it out so that I did not have to leave. I loved my mother and although Peggy was like a second mother to me, I would have wanted to go home. My father said no to the adoption so I left Peggy's before the end of the war when I was thirteen.
>
> Peggy took me to Truro station, gave me a little hug and put me on the train. There was no fuss. I met my father at Paddington Station in London, then we went back to Sunderland. When I got home my brother had a big pile of comics. Peggy never approved of comics, she always gave us books to read, but we loved them, so I settled back home as though I had never been away.

The ensuing tension between the Dicks and Peggy spelt the end of their friendship.

> My parents had fallen out with her over the adoption and we were told never to speak of her and we never did. I never talked to Arnold before he died about our time there, but I think Peggy must have sent us letters. She sent me a copy of a book she wrote about Cornwall* when I got married, with an inscription and I went to visit her once after she moved to Truro. Pollard was there but she had taken some students on a trip to India so I didn't see her.

* Peggy's book *Cornwall*, edited by Clough and Amabel Williams-Ellis, was published in 1947 and illustrated by Sven Berlin. It was dedicated to Dr J. W. Hunkin, Bishop of Truro. Chapter Two gives detailed descriptions of her goats.

CHAPTER TWENTY-EIGHT
Ruth, Joy, Brynnie and Eileen's war

The Gang had said their farewells to Ruth Sherwood and though she had stood down from her role, she stayed in touch. When war broke out Ruth headed back to her birthplace, Sutton Coldfield, and according to her brother Adrian, took a job as a factory worker with the Brooke Tool Company. Ruth was still ill with anaemia but able to work. After her house in Sparkhill, Birmingham, was severely damaged during an air raid, she went to live with friends.

Adrian wrote a short biography of his sister, whom he described as a delightful person, including brief information about her war years. He wrote: 'Ruth was walking to work [at the Brooke Tool Company] during hot weather after a heavy raid and passing the time of day with a rescue worker, who told her ghoulishly, "We can't keep bodies in this weather. Yesterday we buried one with two left legs."'

The tale did not put her off seeking a job as an ambulance driver at Hill Village and Boldmere, Sutton Coldfield. The service by then was mostly run by women, who worked part-time and full-time; full-time staff bearing the burden of the nightshifts. A driver and a nurse formed a team but at night they had to be accompanied by a man or two, who would do the heavy lifting if stretcher cases were involved.

The work was relentless at certain times, and then quiet at others, giving the staff plenty of time for recreation and other war work. Adrian wrote:

> In idle moments the women made gloves for men on mine-sweepers, did crosswords or played bridge... The ladies at Hill formed an acting group called The Mere Players. They gave performances in aid of the Red Cross, Prisoners of War and the Merchant Navy, performing a series of plays on the lives of famous women.
>
> One play was Victoria Regina by Laurence Houseman. Ruth's friend and fashion artist, Margaret 'Leakie' Leake

[who had studied with Joy and Brynnie at King's College] played Queen Victoria while Ruth played Prince Albert.

Ruth produced over 30 small, informal sketches of her co-workers, mostly in pencil. Some are caricatures, and many of the women are wearing their ambulance-driver's or nurse's uniform, some smoking, and some wearing headscarves tied in the 1940s fashion. There is also a humourless self-portrait, totally opposite in style to her other sketches. Whereas the drawings of her colleagues are lighthearted, bright and slightly irreverent, the self-portrait shows her sitting in front of an easel, looking serious, almost glum, with little light save to illuminate her face, the background being almost totally black.

Adrian tried hard to find out more about her war work and about those she worked with but could find very little information. 'Just snippets,' he wrote. 'Towards the end of the war, the air raids had ceased and her work was largely taken up with driving patients to the lunatic asylum at Hatton or taxiing the elderly to medical facilities in the Birmingham area.'

Ruth's health began to worsen. Knowing the fate of her two brothers, she must have feared the worst. Adrian wrote:

> At this time, she began to find that, on long drives, she was becoming more and more numb in her lower limbs. She was given a new, almost untried, drug, which happily turned out to be a cure for the disease.

When the war ended and the demobilised men returned to their jobs, Ruth went to live back in her family home at Sutton Coldfield and, incredibly, regained her health.

Joy and Bryn remained in London during the war. Brynnie had returned from Australia because Harold had pursued her relentlessly by telegram. She had absorbed herself with work and waited for the telegrams to stop, but before they did, her father died and she decided to come home.

Brynnie's father had always believed that Harold would 'bring her down' and he had obvious objections to her involvement with a married man. But Harold had ended his marriage, was living apart from

Margery and agreed to give his wife the divorce she so desperately wanted. With her lover divorced and no father around to object, there was no longer a reason not to commit to Harold.

Bryn was 31 and Harold 60 when they married in Westminster in the summer of 1939. She wore a straw hat trimmed with net and silk flowers, a tailored suit appliquéd with flowers, white gloves and a fox fur stole. She held a bouquet of dark roses and looked radiantly happy. Harold looked dapper in a single-breasted suit, check shirt and tartan tie, with a rose in his buttonhole, while a spotted silk handkerchief spilled out of his pocket. He looked just as happy as Bryn.

Despite the apparent fairytale ending, their future was far from steady. Brynnie suffered at the hands of Harold's irascible temper and their relationship could be volatile.

Bryn and Harold lived in Priory Gardens, in Hampstead. After their marriage, Brynnie's focus shifted from working with children and families of ex-servicemen. Through the Red Cross, she used her experience as an almoner to help returning soldiers, organising aftercare for those maimed and disabled. Part of her role was to find practical and psychological support and care for their families, widows and children.

With no possibility of having children herself, Brynnie's career became all important. Supporting families and men who were war casualties was her way of trying to prevent them being damaged in the same way that Harold had been. She was highly successful and gained several awards for her pioneering work.

Joy was still working south of the River Thames at the Bergman Österberg College when war broke out. By then, she was in charge of the kitchens and needed help finding a cook. She wrote to Miss Reynard at King's College, which had by this time evacuated to Cardiff.

Dear Miss Reynard,
I hope you will excuse my writing to you when I know you must be very busy but I wondered if you could help me over the appointment of a trained cook for this college.

We have now a very good new modern kitchen and we are anxious to run it with trained cooks. We are therefore needing an experienced person to take the post as head Cook and someone younger as assistant cook for next term.

I should of course very much like an old King's student to get the appointment. I thought perhaps you might know of someone suitable. There are 170 all told to cook for and two kitchen maids are in the kitchen.

At the moment I do all the menus and catering myself but of course with a trained cook I should be only too willing to co-operate with her and we could do the menus together and that would make the post more interesting for both of us.

I was very interested in your letter about college life in Cardiff. It must have been very sad to have to leave Campden Hill. I do hope that you will be able to come back soon.

We have been very lucky so far and there has been no falling off in the number of students although this isn't too good a locality as we are rather near the Thames Estuary.

The College has built three large and palatial trenches running underneath our college cricket pitch,

Yours sincerely

Joy Maw

(1926–1929)

Just as King's had moved to Cardiff, Joy's college moved out of London, relocating to Newquay in Cornwall, and renaming itself the Dartford College of Physical Education. It was 1940 and Joy chose not to go with them, giving up her post to remain in London.

Aged 33, a new interest had entered her life in the form of Philip Gaze, a certified electrical engineer. Her father had died two years earlier at the age of 72. (The Gang mourned too and a Gang Howl was given in memory of Silent O'Moyle.) Joy was ready to settle down and married Philip that same year. They lived not far from Brynnie and Harold, in Townshend Road near Primrose Hill in North London.

It was the first time since leaving Shropshire that Joy had lived outside an institution. Domestic life took over and she set about running her home. In 1943, she gave birth to her first son John and, two years later, just before the close of the war, had her second son, Henry.

Eileen was still living in Mount Carmel Chambers and designing clothes for Lawrence Hill.

By 1941, she was very involved designing utility clothing after the Civilian Clothing Act was introduced the same year. Her job was to make sure no fabric was wasted. The rules were no unnecessary pleats or folds, no velvet or fur trims, but women still wanted their clothes to look pretty and Eileen had to find a way to give them what they wanted.

It was the same year she married. Age thirty she settled down with John Souter, a chartered accountant and aristocrat destined to inherit the title Lord Audley and become the 25th Baron. (Under the reign of Henry VIII, the first Baron Audley of Walden succeeded Thomas More as Lord Chancellor and held the post from 1533 to 1544.)

After the wedding, work took him to Scotland almost immediately. Eileen his sent him off with homemade Seville orange marmalade. He wrote often to 'My Darling One' or 'Darling Girl'. They shared a passion for birdwatching and he sent news of birds he had sighted, pleased to have spotted a kestrel, chaffinch and a curlew. He was worried that new clothing rules, with 'less trimmings for women', might affect her work: 'I wonder if this means ruin for you, and am very worried. Poor darling – I wish I was at home but I don't suppose we can do anything.'

In other letters he complained that the weather was freezing. Eileen visited when she could and before one visit he implored. 'I think I can stand it without going back to winter undies but bring a pullover of some sort please.' In another letter he says his host's three-year-old is recovering from whooping cough, 'and whoops dreadfully at times.' All this seems insignificant but by November 1942 John himself was admitted to the Brompton hospital in London.

Eileen should have become Lady Audley but it was not to be, as John died nine months after their tragically short marriage, in December 1942, of tuberculosis. He was only thirty-one, as was Eileen.

Ironically, Eileen's parents married the same year John died – Lucy's first husband had died in 1941, so they were finally free to make their relationship official and their children legitimate.

Devastated by John's death, Eileen threw herself into the war effort, joining the Auxiliary Fire Service (AFS), a group of volunteers who supported the London Fire Brigade's 2,500 officers and firefighters.

Women were accepted into the Brigade for the first time, as most men had joined the forces. Women became fire watchers and drivers or managed the communications network, but were not allowed to fight fires. They manned mobile canteen vans too and became an indispensable part of the service.

Once the bombs began falling, Eileen climbed onto the roof of Mount Carmel Chambers to watch for fires caused by stray bombs, reporting any she spotted to the Brigade.

CHAPTER TWENTY-NINE
The Gang's War Councils

The Gang led full and busy lives, so it was hard for them to get together during the war. Towards the end of 1940, however, two of the Black Atropines, Peggy and Eileen managed to meet at Peggy's goat farm for their 3rd War Council meeting. Despite vehement bombing, Eileen and the Virgin travelled overnight from London to join Peggy and Sister Niphetos. Joy and Brynnie were missing in action and were not there.

At the meeting, they added up their funds, which came to a little over £13, and decided to put £10 into Defence Bonds. Whatever the future held for them, they had no intention of deserting the National Trust and planned to make as many small or large contributions as they could.

A motion was passed that 'the war does stop social things'. Another motion, that 'the Gang will survive the war and be present at the rebuilding of London', was also carried. They toasted Ferguson's Gang and the downfall of Hitler 'in various well-chosen words' and, at the end of the minutes, pasted a receipt for £20 from the Trust that they had sent to its general funds. In 1940, ten Players cigarettes cost around 7d, which meant you could buy over 650 packets for £20, so it was no small sum.

In July 1941, Peggy wrote a round-robin letter giving an update on Gang business and adding an adamant plea that they should not give up on Priory Cottages. It was sent to Eileen first, then Joy and finally Bryn. All added their comments and agreed that Priory Cottages should be proceeded with. They proposed a motion that: 'The Gang is holding the line firmly, has found its trench feet, is stronger than ever and will never die.'

Peggy wrote:

> All of us now bein married it dont seem quite so likely that
> we shall die in the cottages but (a) you never know and (b)

we could always ave them for lovely wee end olidays... we might think of celebererating with a banquet I ave a tin of black cherries nd ca perjuice any amt of butter they would charge corkage at a restaurant but we could pay if there aint no inflations eccept what we suffer afterwards.

Eileen replied:

Steventon must go on. We may all be whore widows or even know widows and Steventon is an object to werk for. A Gang meeting would indeed be a pleasure. I would offer a place if it suited everyone or it could be in a motel 1/2 way to Truro for all I care. Carry on with it. I might even get the cherries.

Bryn added:

I suggests that we do not lose site of our original plam and commitment at Steventon. That we shall ope to complete our objeg after the Whore, and that we consider it in detale then. P.S. A Gang meeting wood be a plesent relaxation, and i 4 1, wood injoy Timmed cherries and butter, and wod pay my share.

Joy was the last to respond:

By all means lets ang on to them cottages at Steventon. They seemed to me a very good thing & eaven only knows they might come in andy & even if we couldnt use them they could produce a nice bit of income for the Trust...

I'm all out for a Gang meeting & would try to get myself anywhere convenient for one & buy anything I could.

The following August, in 1941, Peggy and Eileen managed to meet at the Red Lion for their 4th War Council. They don't say which Red Lion, but they carried the motion that 'war is war and two is enough for a meeting'.

There's nothing more written in 'The Boo' until the following year when on 1 February 1942 Peggy, obviously concerned about what might happen if she did not survive, wrote BILL'S MANIFESTO AND REMINDER, which gave instructions on what to do with the 'war loan', their savings for Priory Cottages, should anything happen to her. She finished it with: 'Ale Gang, Ale Trust, Ale England, Doloj Gitlera [Russian for Down with Hitler].'

After 1942, Peggy stopped recording the year they met but the 5th War Council, held on Saturday 11 September could have been in 1944. It was held at Brynnie's joint and was just Peggy and Bryn, but they could see the end of war in sight and were looking to the future. Peggy proposed the motion that: 'We Begin Looking Ahead Again.'

They hoped to visit Steventon in February and look at the proposed works. Somehow they had raised £1,000 towards the reconstruction, probably with the help of Black Mary. At the meeting they made toasts to the war effort, the Trust, St Clough and the Gang, and as usual enjoyed 'another lovely lunch'.

On Sunday 20 February they held their 6th War Council meeting at Peggy's Hideout and their positive outlook had gone. Present were Peggy and Bryn. Peggy proposed the motion that: 'We stop looking ahead for the time being, for various reasons which we would rather not say.'

They had not been to visit Steventon and it looked unlikely that they could set any kind of date. Brynnie proposed the motion that: 'We go on doing our duty and live on dried eggs for the present, hoping for, but not depending on, an allocation.'

It was the last meeting they had before the end of the war, and they had no idea if they would all survive.

The fate of one of the Gang's properties was equally uncertain. Newtown Old Town Hall on the Isle of Wight was in a prominent position, being an island between the south coast of England and German occupied France. The Isle of Wight's boats were commandeered as part of the Normandy landings and between 1940 and 1945 the Luftwaffe made 125 attacks on the island, dropping a total of 1,392 high-explosive bombs and thousands of incendiary devices. Ninety-two men, 90 women and 32 children were killed and 10,873 buildings damaged. Some higher being must have been looking out for the Gang as, incredibly, the Old Town Hall was not one of them.

CHAPTER THIRTY
John's war

John's attentions were distracted from Gang business as he evacuated his family to Shalford Mill and joined the Home Guard. John and Janet's eldest daughter Janella, now 21, signed up for the Land Army, Penelope, aged 18, was at Cambridge following in her father's footsteps and studying architecture, and 13-year-old twins Joanna and Sally went to school in a nearby village.

Tank traps were erected at the top of the lane to prevent a feared invasion of German tanks and the Mill became a sanctuary for those escaping the London Blitz. It had always been a place where friends felt comfortable dropping in and now became even more of an open house. Visitors, refugees and friends slept on the floor or wherever they could find a space, using whatever spare mattresses there were. If they ran out of bedding, they kept themselves warm under coats. The Macgregors' antique furniture from their London home was packed up and stored in the old part of the Mill and the family sat on benches and ate from a trestle table.

A Viennese refugee called Lore Groszmann (now Segal), the only child of middle-class Jewish parents, had escaped to England on the first wave of Kindertransport in 1938. Her father's final plea to his ten-year-old daughter as she left was serious and poignant: 'When you get to England and meet an English person, say, "Please get my parents and my grandparents and my Uncle Paul out".' Lore learned English fast and began writing letters. Miraculously, her pleas succeeded and her mother Franzi, and father Ignatz, were allowed to leave Austria and settled with the Macgregors. Lore lived close by and visited them on Sundays.

The Groszmanns worked as domestic staff for the Macgregors. Franzi helped with the household chores while Ignatz, whose health was poor, helped in the garden when he was well enough. Lore later described her experiences at the Mill in her book *Other People's Houses*. Her account reveals a happy time with the 'MacKenzie' family, who were, in fact, the Macgregor family. She wrote:

Mrs MacKenzie, the lady for whom my mother was working, invited my father to stay with them so that my mother could look after him. The MacKenzies lived in an Elizabethan water mill belonging to the National Trust. Mr MacKenzie was an architect.

On Sundays, when I went out to visit my parents we all had our dinner in the living room, whose walls, floor, and ceiling were warm coloured, unvarnished old wood, at a great, heavy oak trestle table. That was a magnificent table, at which there was room for the four MacKenzie daughters, their school friends, an ancient grandmother, a simple-minded cousin, and, as often as not, some friends of Mr and Mrs MacKenzie – architects, writers, and ballet dancers, come to rest up from the nightly shock of the London Blitz – and there was room, too, for the refugee cook and the cook's daughter, and cook's sick husband.

I was in love with the MacKenzie family, and could have been in a state of happiness those Sundays had it not been for the presence of my father, who was always turning to my mother to have her translate what people were saying to him, and never understood the jokes going around...

John was still keen to contribute more and spent the war at his drawing board designing cities for the future. In 1942, at the height of the Blitz, he wrote several articles for the *Builder* magazine, illustrating his ideas for an effective post-war transport infrastructure.

The British Government was thinking ahead about plans for new cities when the war ended. To help, they commissioned architects with backgrounds in both conservation and modern design, such as Clough Williams-Ellis, and John, to work on those plans. John found working with modern architecture as exciting as historic buildings and put a lot of creative energy into building good-quality public housing. (His radical five-storey ziggurat design for Lennox House★ in Bethnal Green, East London, is now Grade II listed.) His reports for major cities, including Guildford, Plymouth, Exeter, Portsmouth, York, King's Lynn and areas of London, identified bomb-damaged buildings worth saving and how to incorporate these into a 'modern' city centre, were well received.

John continued to advise the SPAB, as well as the War Damage Commission, and wrote an article about the need to set a method for recording and listing damaged historic buildings. He contacted William Ansell, then President of the Royal Institute of British Architects (RIBA), and they founded an ad hoc committee, which included art historian, broadcaster and author Sir Kenneth Clark; and Walter Godfrey, the historian, architect and first director of the National Buildings Record. Together, they established the basis of what is today's English Heritage Archive.

The Trust did what it could from its temporary base, and acquired six major properties during the war, including, in 1941, the 13,000-acre Wallington Estate. In 1942 Viscount Astor donated Cliveden, built in 1666 by George Villiers, 2nd Duke of Buckingham; in 1943 Dame Margaret Greville endowed Polesden Lacey; the Acland family handed over Killerton in Devon, built in 1778; and the Trust also acquired the henge at Avebury, to which the Gang contributed. When Beatrix Potter died in 1943, she bequeathed Heelis Estate, comprising several fell farms in the Lake District.

*Built in 1934, Lennox House was awarded a Grade II listing in 2012. The design inspired many projects, including the larger Brunswick Centre, a shopping centre in Bloomsbury, just west of central London.

CHAPTER THIRTY-ONE
Adapt or die

As John prepared blueprints on how to rebuild Britain's cities, the Trust concerned themselves with the effect war had had in rural areas. In 1944, they launched an appeal to save Clumber Park in Sherwood Forest in Nottinghamshire.

Clumber Park spanned 3,800 acres and was once the country estate of the Duke of Newcastle. Its vast house had been demolished in 1938 because it was considered beyond repair, but the Trust were determined to save the woods, open heath and farmland for the Nation.

On 28 November 1944, the Gang posted a poem to the National Trust letting them know they were alive and active, along with a generous donation to Clumber. An exotic new member appeared in the poem, the humorously named, but unidentified, Sheikh Yusself. The poem read:

FERGUSON 2 THE NATIONAL TRUST
If you come 2 look 4 me
I still am on the run
And no ime in my castle
Enquire for FERGUSON

When i ears you break your rule
2 launch one more appeal
4 saving Sherwood 4est
It minds me of a meel

when up speak our Lord Zetland
no pear nor im mor good
and up & likens FERGUSON
2 famious Robbing Hood

that was some good time ago
and yeers is getting on
the Trust dont get no younger
no more do FERGUSON

but e likes 2 think that when
the Trust ad far 2 go
e lade sum littul steepingstones
4 it 2 rest its toe

Now Louise our good Princess
lies underneeth the moald
Silent O'Moyle and Lothbury Anne
Is likewise dead and cold

But you still can count on me
while i am on the run
And now ime in my castle
Enquire 4 FERGUSON

Triped by fergusons Free Arab Sheikh Yusself and sent with paper
munny 4 sherwood forest selam alickum

The receipt from the Trust was sent to Bryn and the amount they donated is not recorded, but there is a grateful letter from Matheson to Peggy and an anonymous donation of £500 is recorded in the Trust's 1944–5 annual report. The Sheik made another donation to Clumber a month later and Matheson wrote to Peggy on 20 December 1944. His letter read:

I am sending a formal receipt for a further generous donation to Clumber, which has been sent to us by a very literate, ex-free Arab, who, though he says he is a Trade Unionist, seems to me to be paid far less than Trade Union Rates. However, he does not seem to complain. Will you please give him our warmest thanks, as our typewriter does not write Arabic? Yours faithfully…

Germany surrendered on 8 May 1945. The Gang was immediately resurrected and, by June 1945, had sent the Trust £1 as a deposit for repairs on Priory Cottages. They promised the Trust 'untold riches' within the next six months. They sent a telegram too, which was read out at the annual luncheon and reported in the press, most likely *The Times*. It read: 'Ferguson's Gang salutes the National Trust'.

In early August 1945, America dropped the devastating atom bomb on Hiroshima in Japan, effectively ending the war and, by 15 August, *The Times* was reporting that the Trust 'will be more dependent upon the support of Ferguson's Gang, upon well-disposed owners who will both give and endow, and upon public-spirited taxpayers who may still have their mite to give or to bequeath.'

The war ended officially on 2 September 1945, also the year of the Trust's 50th birthday. It acquired a property in Queen Anne's Gate as its new headquarters, and it owned 112,000 acres of land and 93 historic buildings. It had a membership of 7,850.

To celebrate surviving the war, the Trust launched their Jubilee Appeal, aimed at increasing their membership and financial resources. The Government considered the Trust's survival of national importance and pledged to match any amount they raised pound for pound.

On 17 September, The Gang held their 43rd meeting at Peggy's Barracks. The upbeat, positive tone of the minutes is very different to those of the sombre, pessimistic war years. The full date was written and present were Bryn, Peggy and Sheikh Yusself.

Peggy proposed a motion, seconded by Bryn, that 'Ferguson's Gang do uphold the National Trust, which depends on it'. The motion was carried unanimously and a second motion was moved: 'That we see an opening ahead of us, and that we do invest ourselves in this opening. It was carried unanimously.'

They discussed asking the bank for £200 in cash as a further deposit on the repair of Priory Cottages. If the bank said no, for the first time ever they would have to fall back on a cheque. If the answer was yes, Peggy wrote: 'Sheikh Yusself may be called on 2 deliver: 4 a lady is only fitted for charge of littler nanny goats, not big billies... Bill will consult Erb and pore Old Arris about it.'

They began raising money in earnest for repairs. By 4 January 1946, they had received a receipt from the Trust for their largest deposit yet: £1,002 10s.

The National Trust bulletin reported:

> Gangsters are not desirable members of any community, but when one hears that 'Ferguson's Gang' have pulled off another coup it means that the exception to the rule has been proved once more. 'Ferguson's Gang' are good fellows and they have the interest of their country very much at heart (like Robin Hood). This time they have pulled off a property deal for the purpose of presenting to the National Trust the picturesque Priory Cottages, Steventon. For many years now the pseudonym 'Ferguson's Gang' has preserved the anonymity of a group of benefactors whose generosity is becoming almost legendary. That respectable organization for the National Trust has other connections with lawlessness too, for it has recently acquired from Mr. P. Thurburn the area known as Frenchman's Creek. The name suggests smuggling activities, but it is also known to thousands of people as the title of a book written by Daphne du Maurier which was also made into a colour film.

Frenchman's Creek is a serene part of the Helford River in south Cornwall close to the estuary. Seven-and-a-half acres was handed to the Trust on 2 February 1946 by Mr Thurburn, but Peggy added Frenchman's Creek to the list of properties in 'The Boo' acquired by the Gang. Acquisitions are usually accompanied by a sum of money, but Frenchman's Creek is blank. The fact that it is in their minute book suggests that they had some part to play in its acquisition, however. Perhaps Peggy knew Mr Thurburn and persuaded him to give it to the Trust, or maybe she acted as go-between. The Gang also made a donation to the Jubilee Appeal and on 26 November 1946, sending £2 3s 3d. They received a letter that revealed Bill Sticker's identity for the first time. It read:

> Dear Mrs Pollard
> As I was interviewing a most important visitor, a messenger handed me a very heavy Milk of Magnesia box which I couldn't resist opening forthwith and found inside Two Pounds three shillings and a rather rubbly threepenny bit

towards our Jubilee Appeal Fund. I suppose we shall have to call it £2.3.3. and if the Bank won't take the threepenny bit the Secretary will have to pay...

Yours very gratefully...

The Gang's final ever delivery to the National Trust in July 1947 threw the organisation into turmoil. Just like the occasion of the suspicious package delivered at the 1939 AGM, the Trust thought it was another bomb. The package was labelled as coming from 'Jew Billy', a play on the word Jubilee. It would have caused suspicion and fear though, as in 1946, the paramilitary Zionist group Irgun had bombed the British Embassy in Rome, destroying half the building and killing three. In April 1947, three months before the Trust's AGM, another bomb had been placed by Irgun at the Colonial Office in London. Thankfully, it failed to detonate.

There were no recriminations and the new secretary, Vice-Admiral Oliver Bevir, who had taken over the previous year, took it in good humour, although it must have been a heart-stopping moment when it arrived.

Bevir wrote a polite letter to Peggy at her new address in Truro.

It is nice to know that Ferguson's Gang are still up to their old tricks, although I am afraid, in view of Letter Bombs and the like, the contents of your letter were treated with the utmost caution lest 'Jew Billy' turned out to be a new form of Terrorist Organization. However, when all the usual tests had been applied we murmured to ourselves 'It really is Ferguson' and I enclose a receipt for the £3. 3s. 3d with heart felt thanks. By the way is there anything symbolical in this sum? It looks as if there might be.

The 1947 deposit was the Gang's last recorded enterprise.

Ferguson's Gang achieved all their goals, with one exception: although they saved Priory Cottages for the Trust, they never realised their wish to live there. For them, as for the rest of the nation, war had changed everything. After 1947, the Gang dispersed and, while they met occasionally, it was never the same. Brynnie and Peggy maintained their friendship for life and continued to meet well into old age. Brynnie also remained close to Eileen, writing to her until she died. Eileen also stayed close to Joy, taking annual holidays in Cornwall with her and her family, although they did not stay with Peggy. Rachel never really stayed in touch with the Gang, but Ruth made the odd appearance.

The Gang recorded one final reunion on 6 November 1956. Peggy, Joy, Bryn and Eileen gathered at Shalford Mill at their old headquarters. Ruth and Rachel were not present. The record of the meeting is unlike any other in 'The Boo'. Until then, Peggy always wrote in black ink, in a neat, careful, right-slanting hand, but the 1956 record is scruffy, lackadaisical and written in blue biro. Peggy would have been 52 then and perhaps her meticulous writing suffered after imbibing a few sloe gins. Her notes are still entirely legible and record that: 'Present were Kate O'Brien T.N., Biddy, Sister Agatha, Bill Stickers: Not nearly as drunk as you think.'

> Dinner. Reminininiscense. Everyone just as always. Ag as a sore throat & lumps & 3 of us as false teeth. But we are not dead but live. Resolved on somebody's motion that next year we ave a lunch at the Mill and then go 2 London 4 dinner as we are not as young as we were. Armoured Tubular Floors*.

The entry is signed by all four women, but there is no record of any lunch at the Mill, nor any further lunches, dinners or raids on the Trust. Ferguson's Gang had done its work, and done it well, but while the Gang lay fallow the lives of its members took some dramatic twists.

* Armoured tubular floors are used in buildings, but in Gang speak they are the tunnels that run under the floorboards at Shalford Mill. The Macgregor children used them as secret runways and the Gang practised their hauntings above one of them.

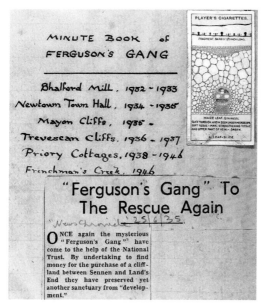

MINUTE BOOK of
FERGUSON'S GANG

Shalford Mill, 1932 – 1933
Newtown Town Hall, 1934 – 1935
Mayon Cliffs, 1935 –
Trevescan Cliffs, 1936 – 1937
Priory Cottages, 1938 – 1946
Frenchman's Creek, 1946

"Ferguson's Gang" To The Rescue Again

News Chronicle 25/6/35.

ONCE again the mysterious "Ferguson's Gang" have come to the help of the National Trust. By undertaking to find money for the purchase of a cliff-land between Sennen and Land's End they have preserved yet another sanctuary from "development."

An early page in minute book 'The Boo 2' lists National Trust acquisitions that the Gang had masterminded.

An illustration by Is B (Ruth) showing Bill (Peggy) and Kate (Joy) sewing curtains in their 'cell' at Shalford Mill, c1933.

The Crazy Gang: Peggy (front) and Bobby (back middle) larking about with friends at the Briary in the Isle of Wight.

Shot Biddy (Eileen), Kate O'Brien (Joy), Bill Stickers (Peggy) and Is B (Ruth) picnicked in a 'beechwood of bluebells and cuckoos', dining on 'chicken mousse, Russian salad, lychees, cream and a bottle of Chalian Larose Blanche' on a trip to Newtown in 1935.

Kate O'Brien (Joy) leapfrogging over Shot Biddy (Eileen) on the final day of their 1938 World Conference in Portmeirion.

Left An exuberant teenage Brynnie Granger (Sister Agatha) dressed as a native American.

Kate O'Brien, Shot Biddy and Bill in Cornwall on 10 April 1936, visiting the 'oly Quoit' of Zennor. They stayed at Boswednack Farm.

Is B, Bill and Shot Biddy (clockwise from top left) performing the 'Characteristic Dance of Ferguson's Gang'. Surrey, June 1935.

Is B, Ag, Kate and Shot Biddy at the Heel Stone at Stonehenge, celebrating their 10th Anniversary, 27 June 1937.

In 1938 the *Children's Newspaper* published their impressions of 'Ferguson and His Gang'. Bill Stickers is portrayed as a man.

(From top left) Irish Lady tile made by Silent O'Moyle. Water samples from underground rivers. A mask purchased at Harrods. Gang tapestry with figures representing the underground rivers Kilburn, Tyburn, Fleet and Walbrook. The shields show the Gang's personal heraldry. The Boa Constrictor represents Is B.

Embroidered panels from the Gang robe. (Left to right from top) An ode to the National Trust; Shalford Mill by Shot Biddy; 'England is Stonehenge not Whitehall', a Gang motto; The 'octopus' spreading its tentacles across England; 'No gains without pains', another motto; A tribute to Newtown.

Priory Cottages in Steventon, Oxfordshire, once a Benedictine Monks' country lodge. The Gang saved it and dreamed they would live there together.

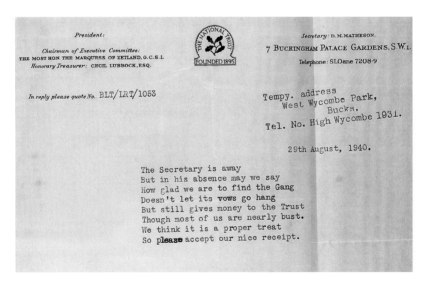

Tempy. address
West Wycombe Park,
Bucks.
Tel. No. High Wycombe 1931.

29th August, 1940.

The Secretary is away
But in his absence may we say
How glad we are to find the Gang
Doesn't let its **vows** go hang
But still gives money to the Trust
Though most of us are nearly bust.
We think it is a proper treat
So **please** accept our nice receipt.

A wartime poem from the Trust to the Gang, expressing their gratitude for a donation (1940).

Shalford Mill, c1960. The Artichoke's family and extended family at every window of the Mill.

Clough Williams-Ellis and Peggy c1972. Clough in his trademark canary yellow stockings, Peggy in her Cornish Bard dress.

Peggy in her room in Truro. In her seventies, she embroidered a 1,330 ft tapestry of the Narnia stories, entering the *Guinness Book of World Records*.

CHAPTER THIRTY-TWO
Afterwards

RUTH

Ruth Sherwood was the only Gang member never to marry and she kept her relationships extremely private. In 1949, she left Sutton Coldfield and moved to the south coast of Devon to take a post at the avant-garde Dartington College of Arts, part of the Dartington Hall Trust near Totnes.

Ruth was employed by the Adult Education Centre at Shinners Bridge on the edge of the estate, providing art classes to the local community. She also taught extramural art classes to the students at Dartington Hall.

It was a richly cultural environment. While Ruth was there, the music teacher was Imogen Holst, daughter of composer Gustav Holst, who ran a flourishing music department. The tenor Peter Pears and composer Benjamin Britten were frequent visitors. The same year Ruth started, Rudolf Laban and Marie Rambert arrived to teach experimental dance.

At first, Dartington did not run a full visual arts programme as most of the budget was spent on music and theatre. The arts were provided as an extramural course for the students as well as the local community. The Hall's newsletter, *News of the Day*, announced on 29 June 1949:

> An outdoor sketching and painting class has been formed and will meet next Sunday at 2.30pm. It also proposes a second class on Saturdays at Shinners Bridge, just outside the Dartington Hall estate. Beginners will be very welcome, and everyone may choose in what medium he wishes to work. It is suggested that people bring a picnic tea. The teacher is Miss Sherwood, a Slade student and a practising artist, who has a wide and varied experience under several distinguished artist-teachers.

Ruth lived in the Old Rectory on the outskirts of the estate and then in the nearby village of Weak. Bobbie Cox, the wife of the principal, taught her to weave using yarns coloured with natural dyes and she helped Ruth lay out a complicated, ambitious design for a tapestry, the motif of a white Hart, the emblem of Richard II. The finished tapestry was housed in the Old Tower Chapel where it lay hidden for many years until recently. Bobbie Cox, who still lives on the estate, cleaned it and it now hangs in the church of St Mary the Virgin on the Dartington Estate.

Bobbie said that Ruth was a very a normal person. She rode a bicycle and, in contrast to her Gang days, did not look particularly Bohemian. This description is backed up by Ivor Weeks who was employed to run the adult education courses at Shinners Bridge. He taught at Dartington from 1955 to 1993, and remembers Ruth well.

On learning of her colourful past this twinkly old man began to question what he had thought of Ruth all those years ago. 'I was 24 years old, terribly young, and Ruth – or "Toots" as she was known to us, would have been in her fifties. She taught a watercolour class. She did seem, I thought, spinsterish. She reminded me of my mother's Mother's Union friends. I'm beginning to wonder if I read her right.'

Ruth retired in the 1960s and moved to Minchinhampton in Gloucestershire to be close to her sister and widowed mother. Her brother Adrian says she attended a Gang reunion at the Mill. He said. 'My sister, I think, found it a little disappointing in that everybody seemed fearfully respectably dressed and conventional.'

A few months before Ruth's death in 1990, Adrian wrote to Sarah-Jane Forder, the editor of the *National Trust Magazine*, following an article about the Gang. He recalled Ruth's activities and his family having to hand over Victorian coins. In a letter he said: 'I do not think I suffered much, as my pocket money was a penny a week at the time.'

Adrian was keen for the National Trust to interview Ruth despite her memory being a 'rather dot-and-carry-one', as she could still recall much of the Gang's activities, but no interview is recorded. He asked for the surviving Gang members to be given lifetime memberships of the Trust as a gesture for their contributions to it. It saddened him greatly that his sister might slip silently from the world with little recognition of her contributions to the National Trust.

Her portraits of the women of the Civil Defence were donated to the library at Sutton Coldfield.

Ruth died at Northfield House in Uplands, Gloucestershire, in 1990 at the age of 83.

JOY

More than any other Gang member, Joy led what might be called a conventional life. Even during the heyday of the Gang, Joy was less Bohemian: completing her studies, taking respectable jobs and fulfilling her duties. Even after the Gang's activities ceased, she often spent weekends at the Mill with her husband Philip and their white Staffordshire bull terrier and went horse-riding at Lockner's Farm in nearby Chilworth.

Marriage dominated her latter years. After her mother-in-law died, and her father-in-law moved to Rhodesia, she and Philip took over their house in Radlett in Hertfordshire where they lived until they died. They had two sons, John and Henry, born in 1943 and 1945. Henry was severely disabled.

In the mid-1950s, Ben Simpson, a cousin of Joy's, would visit Shalford Mill when his father, the Chief Constable for Surrey, had meetings at the Surrey constabulary headquarters nearby. Sometimes Joy would be there with her son John. Grey-haired and in her 40s by then, she would give the boys jam jars and fishing nets so that they could go off and catch tadpoles and sticklebacks in the Tillingbourne stream. He recalls those visits with pleasure: 'She treated us like adults even though we were only ten or twelve.'

When Joy's son Henry died young at the age of 37, it affected her greatly. She died the following year, on 29 May 1983, aged 75.

BRYNNIE

Brynnie sacrificed much to be with Harold Jervis-Read, particularly her desire to have children, and sadly Harold died in 1945 after only six years of marriage. Not a rich man, he left her the value of his estate, which was just under £600. She never remarried but dedicated her time to working for the Red Cross. In 1964, she was elected Officer in the Order of St John and, in 1965, she was awarded an OBE for her exemplary service in the Ex-services War Disabled help department.

Brynnie never fulfilled her wish to live in a National Trust property, although she wrote to them in 1960 in the vain hope that she could take over the Mill tenancy. The Artichoke's relatives were still in residence, and still are, so it was not possible.

The Trust did try to accommodate her request but the properties they suggested were either in the wrong location or too expensive. Before his death, she and Harold moved to a Grade II-listed cottage in Essex. Cawdles, in Aythorpe Roding, was a beautiful 17th-century thatched cottage that Bryn infused with her own style. The property had a barn, which she converted after Harold died and where she lived when she could no longer afford the main house alone. Her close friend Joyce Conwy Evans, the textile and tapestry designer, often went to stay. On those visits, Bryn would hand her scraps of material, each with a personal tale to tell, which Joyce made into cushions. 'Everything in the house had a story attached,' said Joyce. 'She would hand me fragments of things that meant something to her. She liked things with a history.'

She built up good relationships with Harold's children, who although a similar age to her, gradually warmed to her infectious personality. Elaine, the youngest daughter who was adopted, described her as 'a lovely, warm, generous person'.

Diana Jervis-Read is Harold's son John's daughter. She remembers Brynnie as fun and scatty: 'Brynnie was spontaneous. I was there one afternoon and she put a leg of lamb in the oven, then we decided to go out. She left the lamb there, thankfully with the oven turned off, but it was still there two days later.'

Brynnie continued her friendships with the gang and combined this with her love of music. In her London flat she hosted intimate performances by leading figures in the music world, as well as up-and-coming musicians. She enabled Peggy's protégé Michael Maine to play in the organ loft in Westminster Cathedral. The Artichoke's family felt honoured to be part of a small invited audience of about 20 at Brynnie's London flat to listen to the tenor Sir Peter Pears, the young Australian pianist Geoffrey Parsons and the cellist Amaryllis Fleming, the illegitimate daughter of Augustus John.

In 1972, still with the Red Cross, she was promoted to the rank of Commander in the Order of St John, and in 1973 was appointed by Warrant from the Queen as Member of the Royal Patriotic Fund Corporation for a three-year period. The organisation provides assistance for the widows and orphans and other dependents of members of the armed services. She continued working with the Red Cross until 1985.

She and Peggy stayed close, bound by the insoluble ties of their youthful passion to preserve England's heritage and by all the fun they had shared. In the last letter Peggy wrote to Brynnie in 1990, six years before she died, she was still writing in mockney. She wrote:

> We ad guud times yew and me agg... I ave always lived in my own world, people ave come in and gone out, but I am glad yew are still there...

Brynnie died eight years after Peggy on 10 February 2004, at St Joseph's Nursing Home in Danbury, Essex, five days before her 96th birthday. She was the last surviving Gang member.

RACHEL

One of Rachel's favourite sayings was: 'If you're not a Communist in your twenties you haven't got a heart and if you're not a Conservative in your forties, you haven't got a head.' Her family would often say it to her to point out that her youthful idealism would wane and she would come to her senses. They were wrong; she never did change her opinions.

Rachel's life was a series of extremes and she had perhaps the most eventful professional and private life post-Gang, with a spell in prison, lesbian affairs and a controversial friendship with Moors Murderer Myra Hyndley.

Her son Peter describes his mother as 'an upper-class rebel'. A complex character, she fought constantly to come to terms with the sexual abuse she had suffered at the hands of her father. There is little doubt that her difficulty forming healthy intimate relationships with men and women was a result of the incest she had suffered. General Pinney died in 1943, when Rachel was 34, having never apologised to his daughter.

Because of the abuse, Rachel found it impossible to have a normal relationship. In her letters and autobiography she describes a catalogue of sexual infatuations with women and her repeated despair at not being able to unite sex and love in the same relationship. The difficult relationship she had with her mother did nothing to make her feel positive about her own femininity or that she was loveable. Many of her friendships seemed sexualised and she recounts how this sexual urge came to a crescendo one day when she left her job early to have anonymous and physically satisfying sex with a stranger on Wimbledon Common.

She did find happiness but not until she was in her 70s. Typically, there was nothing straightforward about it. She fell in love with Sally Maxwell, a younger woman and a Quaker, who was married when they met. Sally left her husband to live and work with Rachel (at the Children's Hours Trust). The first time Rachel publicly came out was with Sally, in the television documentary *Women Like Us*. She said: 'I had a series of girlfriends ... but no word would be spoken, and I denied it fiercely if anyone mentioned it. You've no idea how strong this thing was. Like if I'd committed murder, I wouldn't admit it, ever, to anybody.'

An enigma in some respects, Rachel was kind, chaotic, loyal and a fierce campaigner but her ferocious temper could be terrifying.

Her three children, Karin, born in 1936, Peter, born in 1940, and Christopher, born in 1948, were all Lu's, despite the fact that their marriage lasted such a brief period of time. Christopher was sent to boarding school age six, but unlike his siblings, lived permanently with his mother. All three were victims of her eccentricities and had unconventional childhoods because of her inability to parent. Peter, now in his 70s, who lived with both his mother and his father, cannot imagine growing up in a stable home. He said:

My parents never settled custody when they formally divorced so I felt free to spend time with whoever I liked. When I wanted a bit of anarchy and chaos I went to live with Rachel and when I wanted stability and regular meals I lived with Luigi.

There were never regular meals when I stayed with Rachel, you found what you could when you were hungry, and it was fine to have steak for breakfast. Manners were important to her though and she could take on a moralistic tone. We were on holiday in Scotland once in a boarding house and I hadn't cleaned the communal bathroom. She really tore me off a strip for that.

Karin's childhood memories of her mother are few but one is vivid. She said: 'One time she sent a large round parcel wrapped in many many layers of paper. Over breakfast Von and I took turns to unwrap the parcel to finally discover a handful of raisins, wrapped in a very valuable £5 note which had to be washed clean of raisin stain. Rachel was like that parcel of raisins. She had protected herself with multiple levels of fear, and her fear was of being accepted and loved.'

Her children survived somehow, gained an education (although Rachel took Peter out of school for a year when he was 12, which he spent reading comics) and all forged successful careers and are politically aware. Peter worked for the most part as a film editor on programmes as diverse as *The South Bank Show* and the children's programme *In the Night Garden*. Karin moved to the US, became a journalist and worked at one time for *Fortune* magazine. Christopher trained as a photographer and filmmaker and spent a portion of his career working on programmes about the establishment, covering the Ministry of Defence, the Royal Opera House, vicars and the aristocracy. He has also published a book of photographs: *Looking Back: Photography from the 1970s – United Kingdom and Ireland*.

Rachel's unconventional attitudes led to a varied and successful career. After 11 years training she finally qualified as a doctor. From 1945 to 1960, she practised as a GP at her surgery in Chelsea and as a doctor for the department store Peter Jones, in Sloane Square. Her approach to medicine was caring and patients at her surgery were very loyal, even though they might have a long wait because she would spend an hour with someone who needed to talk. Peter said: 'She told me once that 19 out of 20 patients were going to get better anyway. It's how you approach the 20th that's important.'

She also worked under the distinguished paediatrician Dr Margaret Lowenfeld, who at that time was developing Lowenfeld's World Technique, a form of sand play therapy for children.

In 1960, she wound up her GP practice and founded 'Creative Listening', a practice distilled from her Quaker roots. It was a technique of conflict resolution, which involved listening fully to what others of differing opinions had to say.

To spread the word, she and a friend set out across West London randomly knocking on people's doors, asking to listen to their views on homosexuality and hoping for hostile opinions. One associate remembered Rachel 'marching up to front door bells or accosting ladies tending their front gardens... She would explain that she had been touring Britain and Listening for Peace: 'Tonight [emphasised in a delightfully "you are especially privileged" tone of voice] I am listening on homosexual law reform!

We encountered only one forthright opponent, and he predictably said he was not prepared to discuss homosexuality in the street (or, I suspected, anywhere else). When pressed by Dr Pinney to give a reason, he replied: "I was forty years in the Navy, madam, and that's quite good enough reason. Good day to you!'"

Rachel joined the Campaign for Nuclear Disarmament (CND), protesting against the Polaris missile and the US Submarine base at Holy Loch in Scotland. After the march against Polaris, a group of protestors got together to discuss what else they could do to draw attention to the bomb. Rachel's contribution was to remain silent every Wednesday, a gesture she kept up for 30 years.

In 1981, she joined the Women's Peace Camp at RAF Greenham Common, where she supported anti-cruise missile demonstrations.

Rachel's life was a series of paradoxes. She said many times that her parenting skills were hopeless but helping children became a passion. She spent her life trying to become a better person, and succeeded and failed in equal measure. She followed her principles, even if they were not strictly legal, and made some hopeless decisions, which landed her in court on two occasions. The first time was for libelling a woman whose daughter she had helped to leave home. The case literally bankrupted her.

The second time was in 1970, when she was 60. Rachel was living in Oakley Street in Chelsea, in the house she and Lu had let out as bedsits. It was still rented out, filled with hippies and musicians, including the band Family, their guitarist Charlie Whitney, and the band Mighty Baby. Quentin Crisp, with his blue hair, often popped in to play chess with her and radio and television presenter Robert Robinson's wife and children would drop by.

One of Rachel's patients was Arthur Collings, the former partner of the sculptor Dame Elizabeth Frink. He married Rosalind Collings, an art teacher, who suffered from extreme bouts of manic depression. They had a young son, Matthew, whom Rachel looked out for after Arthur committed suicide.

Rosalind's mental health deteriorated. Aged six, Matthew was placed in care for his own protection, in what he later described as a loveless children's home with an abusive, bullying culture.

As he reached adolescence, Matthew began absconding and turning up at Oakley Street, and although Rachel disapproved of him hanging out with the drug-taking musicians, she would let him stay before sending him home to his ailing mother.

For some months the pattern continued, with 14-year-old Matthew seeking refuge on various people's floors and beginning to seek oblivion in heavy-duty sleeping tablets. Then Rachel suggested a way out and, in a flamboyant and extreme gesture, she gave him £200 to escape to Canada. An Interpol search was launched, and Matthew was eventually discovered by police in a down-market boarding house in Toronto and flown home.

Rachel was charged with kidnap. The charge read that '...she unlawfully kept and maintained Matthew Collings, a boy of the age of 14 years, out of his native England in some secret and private place beyond the seas and against the will of Rosalind Collings the mother.'

Labour MP for Glasgow Neil Carmichael wrote in support of Rachel.

> I am quite convinced of her very deep integrity and, in fact, I would suggest her integrity is perhaps the reason for her occasionally being at odds with authority. She does tend to carry things to the logical conclusion despite the disapproval of society. The one thing I am absolutely certain of is that Dr Pinney is incapable of consciously doing anyone any harm. She is rather the reverse and will go much further than most of us in order to help people.

The Crown was unsympathetic. She was sent to Holloway and received a two-year sentence. 'Oh, what fun!,' she said.

Rachel met Myra Hindley there. Like Lord Longford, who became a friend of Myra's and Rachel's, Rachel was convinced that although Myra and her boyfriend Ian Brady had been convicted of murdering five children, Myra had been unfairly vilified and should be given the opportunity of parole. She began a long correspondence with her, which continued until she died. She wrote about her fascination with the serial killer: 'Myra has been and still is and hopefully will continue to be a very big person in my life.'

Rachel was transferred from Holloway to Moor Court, an open prison in Stoke-on-Trent, where she was allocated number 968684. There she met Susan 'Shoe' Taylor, the hippy mistress of Jonathan Guinness, son of Lady Mosley, who was better known as the Hon

Diana Mitford. Shoe was serving a 12-month sentence for drug offences.

In Jonathan's 1989 biography *Shoe: The Odyssey of a Sixties Survivor*, Rachel is described as 'eccentric and a saint' and also as 'the eighth dwarf'. Shoe said: 'What a find she was for me... She became a friend for life. She was my confidante and my guardian angel. I could tell her everything... She later stopped me doing something very foolish that might have been the end of me.'

Despite a spell in prison, she was not struck off by the General Medical Council and held on to her doctor's licence.

After she was released, with her name blackened in the UK, Rachel moved to the States in the mid-1970s. She began treating a four-year-old autistic boy called Bobby with her own brand of child psychotherapy. Over many months of intense treatment, Rachel, and a few closely chosen helpers, followed Bobby as he explored the world. Her vibrant and moving account, written in her book *Bobby: Breakthrough of an Autistic Child*, describes his progress as he changed from being frustrated, angry, doubly incontinent and uncontrollable to a continent, emotionally responsive and happy child.

Rachel did not meet Matthew Collings again until he was in his 30s. Now a successful art critic, he credits Rachel with allowing him to flourish. 'She encouraged me and I'm proud of her,' he said.

There was a partial rapprochement with her family. Her mother always welcomed her at Racedown, and she visited her sister Hester often, but Mary never forgave her.

Towards the end of her life she lived in a council flat in North London, next to Pentonville Prison. Unconcerned with money, she lived on a state pension and a small amount from a charity. She was happy, worrying more about others than herself. So when her old governess Pilleo became incapacitated, Rachel took her in. Pilleo was 100, and Rachel was determined to nurse her so that she had a good death. Despite having little money, she cared for both of them and took her old nanny away on holiday whenever she could. Rachel died on 19 October 1995, aged 86.

EILEEN

Eileen continued to work for Lawrence Hill until she retired in 1963. Kind-hearted, she was once asked to sack an employee, but could not bring herself to do it.

She never remarried after John's death and, according to her nephew Christopher, never looked at another man again. Instead she threw herself into good works, becoming an ardent supporter of her local churches helping at St Mary Abbots Church in Kensington, St Paul's Church in Knightsbridge and St Andrew's Church in Fulham Fields. She also became patron of All Saints Convent children's orphanage in London Colney.

Eileen loved London. She stayed in Mount Carmel chambers and for 13 years after John died, shared her flat with his sister Pamela, until Pam married in 1955. They loved birdwatching, like she and John had, and wrote articles about birds for the RSPB. They are pictured in the *Star* in 1949 credited with a rare sighting of four pairs of woodlarks on Wimbledon Common. Afterwards, the RSPB asked them to keep an official watch on the Common for more rare birds.

They never lost touch, even after Eileen bought a small house in Baron's Court.

Pam had three children, Katherine (Katha), Richard (known as John) and Amelia (Mela) and they remember wonderful weekends with Eileen.

In 1951 her sister Kathleen developed breast cancer. To help, she invited Kathleen's son, her only nephew, five-year-old Christopher, to come and stay with her while his mother had treatment. Eventually, as Kathleen became more and more incapacitated after four operations, Christopher moved in with her permanently.

Once, as a treat for working hard in his exams, Eileen took him on the 715 bus to Shalford Mill to show him the Gang's room, but other than that, she never talked about her activities with Ferguson's Gang.

Christopher remembers Christmases spent with orphans from All Saints whom Eileen invited for Christmas lunch. There were up to 15 on Christmas Day, but they could be a handful. Nevertheless, Eileen would have as many as she could to stay overnight and would take them to the theatre on Boxing Day.

Christopher and Eileen were very close and would regularly holiday in Cornwall with Joy and her family, where Joy and Eileen would go surfing in Constantine Bay near Trevose Head. Eileen would also holiday in a house she owned with her friend Constance Rhodes on the Greek Island of Skiathos. Eileen had met Constance, whom she nicknamed 'Cecil', through her younger sister Norah. Cecil also worked for the UN as a conference organiser and was involved in talks about the discontinuance of nuclear weapons tests.

Aware she had no husband to support her in her old age, she looked for ways to provide herself with a pension and began buying and renting out property. She owned flats in the Cromwell Road and houses in Putney and Earls Court and inevitably looked after her tenants above and beyond the call of duty. She only sold her estate and left London after Pam and her husband Francis decided to retire to the small village of Ffair-Rhos in Wales. Eileen moved there too and they lived close but not long after moving, Pam became ill and died. Francis died not long afterwards in 1995.

She stayed in the village and she adopted cats. In the end she cared for 19. She owned a beautiful chair embroidered by Peggy and to save it from been destroyed by the cats, gave it to Pam's daughter Katha.

Eileen died on April Fool's Day 2002 in Bronglais Hospital in Aberystwyth after a series of strokes. She was 91.

PEGGY

Peggy did not receive her hard-won doctorate and degree until 1952, over two decades after she had earned them. Cambridge only awarded titular degrees until the fifties, when they finally decided to play fair with women who had overcome so much to gain them.

In the years after the war, she continued to make use of her extraordinary gift for languages. She taught herself Cornish, becoming an authority in it, and was appointed a Bard of the Cornish Gorsedd. In her later years a hint of a Cornish accent could be detected over her upper-class tones. She also taught herself Russian and German. She learnt Russian as she was bracing herself against a Russian invasion during the Cold War and was determined that when the time came she would be prepared. Realising there would be very few Russian-speaking English people, she was determined to have the upper hand.

She also taught herself the harp and played the guitar, piano and the church organ. It's not clear exactly when, but Peggy abandoned her kilt, Burberry and favoured baggy jumper and took to dressing like a Russian peasant, wearing heavily embroidered black dirndl skirts, headscarves tied under her chin and homemade, hand-embroidered hessian aprons. She would either be barefoot or wore men's boots.

Peggy and Pollard stayed together, living in a fine Georgian town house in Pydar Street, Truro, but the house was demolished after being the victim of a compulsory purchase. They moved to a rather less fine two-storey terraced house in Richmond Hill, Truro, where Peggy lived on the ground floor and Pollard on the first. Her friend Claire Riche, said that Pollard's room was covered with his papers.

Peggy's room had silhouettes drawn all over the left-hand wall where she would trace round a visitor's head instead of using a visitor's book. A bookcase full of leather-bound books stood next to a gas fire and there was one small gas ring on which Peggy cooked their meals, although she was happy with a diet of Kit-Kats. She had hung on to her beloved piano, a family heirloom that she had accompanied Pauline on when they played together.

Riche said: 'In the right-hand corner was a large grand piano, stacked high with music, a guitar lay on the floor. There were two life-sized paintings of monks and in the bay window, was a very old chaise longue, obviously antique but in dire need of repair. All the chairs, although broken and rickety, were upholstered in the most exquisite tapestry work.'

Peggy never owned a television and preferred to paint, embroider, write musical plays or perform music in her spare time and she loved 1920s musical-hall tunes.

Pollard died of a heart attack, aged 62, in 1968, having continued to gain weight throughout his life. Peggy missed their intellectual spats and shared pursuits and appeared to be lonely for several years after his death.

Religion was always important and she became involved with the Church, embroidering kneelers and tapestries, involving herself with the youth group and playing the organ at Truro Cathedral. She is fondly remembered for lustily playing out the congregation to the plinketty-plonk of the popular tune, 'Lily the Pink'.

Years earlier, having survived a fire, Peggy felt that God had saved her for a purpose, so she began to search for a faith that would fulfil that spiritual need. A trip to London with the church youth group ended her search after she attended a mass at Brompton Oratory in Kensington, the neo-classical Catholic church opposite their hotel. Peggy was mesmerised by its music, altars and priests in ornate vestments. She felt God strongly and began to think about converting to Catholicism.

Her decision was made in 1955 after Peggy had a vision of Our Lady, who appeared to her one night saying that she wanted to go home to Liskeard. Peggy told her that she needed proof she was real and said she would paint her portrait. 'If it is exhibited in the Paris Salon, I will do my best to help,' she said. The following day she painted *La Vierge à la Porcelaine* (The Porcelain Virgin), submitted it to the Paris Salon, and began to research Liskeard, an ancient market town in south east Cornwall.

She travelled to Liskeard. There she discovered a shrine called Ladye Park, a pre-Christian site of worship dedicated to the pagan Goddess Kerrid, the Goddess of Love.

On her return home, she opened an envelope containing an unexpected legacy and a cheque for £600. She handed the substantial sum to Father Hackett, the parish priest at Liskeard who promised to put it towards a fund to restore the shrine. Not long after that, she heard that her painting was to be hung in Paris. Peggy worked hard to preserve the shrine, which remains in private hands although pilgrims still visit every year.

She was received into the Catholic Church and took to wearing rosary beads. She formed relationships with African nuns and cultivated a network of 'brothers', lay people she would telephone before going to sleep to say prayers with on the phone.

In 1973, she built a modern Catholic Church in Truro called Our Lady of the Portal and St Piran. Its contemporary design is a surprise considering her passion for saving old buildings, but then, Peggy was never against progress, just the destruction of the past. For this she received the Benemerenti Medal, a special award from the Pope to honour her services to the Catholic Church. She said it was her greatest honour.

According to her niece Kitty Turnbull, money held little interest for her and she gave whatever she could away, prompting her brother Bobby to settle on her a monthly allowance of £50. Bobby died before Peggy, aged 74, after a routine operation in 1981.

Peggy had become close to C. S. Lewis after responding to a letter he wrote to *The Times*. They shared an intellectual and spiritual debate, slipping between heady philosophy and down-to-earth humour with Lewis recounting in one letter the story of a law-abiding dog, which had taken to stealing sausages from the butcher, however it eventually came to light that the dog had been keeping alive a fellow animal that had fallen down a disused tin mine. She also became friendly with a young organist, Michael Maine, who had a passion for C. S. Lewis's Narnia books. Peggy began embroidering scenes from the books for him. Once finished, it measured a record-breaking 1,338 feet and in 1983 Peggy entered the *Guinness Book of Records* with the longest embroidery ever stitched.

She became frail and in her last letter to Ag wrote:

> i makes a czreer out of being bedridden, i can manage jobs in the house given plenty of time, all that is wrong wiv me is arthuritis from ip to nee and deficient sight...
>
> And wot do yew think my latest apostolate is, Marka and Spenfer ave put my tallowphone number in their catalogue by mistake and people ring up every day and as soon as they say sorry i got the wrong number i ses, well ave you got a pencil, put a 1 where theh got a 2 and try again... Because if it was anyone else they wood be yelling Bloody hell yew are the tenth in half an hour... but when they get me i ca cheer them up instead without any trouble or expense which is nice...
>
> i got a lot of notices in my window saying that the rosary is said in this house every day, if you want to be prayed for shove your name in the letter box...

Peggy supported the National Trust all her life and sent her last £10 note donation in 1994. She received a card from Sarah-Jane Forder, editor of the Trust's magazine, who, in true Gang spirit, Bill called the Dutch Doll. Forder's note, handwritten in mockney, thanked her and asked for her help. She wrote: 'I as a "last request", Bill, as I know you is a good man and sommat of a poet. The NT is 100 years old next yere – 1995 – could you rite me a pome to celebrate?' Delighted, Peggy wrote the following:

> *For 100 years the Trust has fought*
> *And the battle is still to win –*
> *You sit there moaning and wringing your hands?*
> *You say it's a shame and a sin?*

> *Hedges and fields and forests*
> *Vanishing one by one –*
> *Get your pen and your chequebook out,*
> *Load and fire your gun!*
> *Save what is left of England*
> *Give what you can and more –*
> *Once in the hands of the National Trust,*
> *It is safe for ever more.*

> *(Bill Stickers 1994)*

She helped whatever cause she could, whether it was in England or not. She sunk three or four wells in South Africa and became known as Ma to 40 black nuns there, and she was called Nkhono or M'E by more nuns in Lesotho.

> All my life I have preserved my anonymity and am still doing it to purpose. I have about thirty names and am now operating as Sister X.

As she began to foresee the end of her life, Peggy had a last wish. Although Ferguson's Gang had lain dormant for nearly 40 years she had one final mission and drafted a letter to *The Times* to be opened after her death.

> Having depleted all worldly goods in pursuit of Ferguson's Gang, my final request is that the Gang be opened to all members… To this end I have appointed the first new member of the gang who goes by the pseudonym 'Pegasus'.
> My dying wish is (yes I confess to being Bill Stickers of Ferguson's Gang) that *Times* readers be invited to send donations to the National Trust to start a fund for the purchase of Ladye Park.

Pegasus accepted the honour in 1995. Like the original Gang members, he had an unconventional past: an orphan, ex-paratrooper and self-taught silversmith, capable of exquisite work.

By the time she died, Peggy was almost blind, but she did not allow her lack of sight to prevent her writing to friends and the National Trust. She wrote in bold capital letters, with a marker pen, or a 'tripe-writer' when she could find one. Peggy died in a nursing home on 13 November 1996, aged 92.

In 2006, according to her wishes, Pegasus and Peggy's friend Claire Riche took her ashes to the small town of Vierzehnheiligen in Germany, famous for its Baroque-Rococo Basilica of the Fourteen Holy Help-ers. Peggy had been there on many pilgrimages and now her ashes are scattered there.

CHAPTER THIRTY-THREE
The Artichoke and the Mill

John Macgregor enjoyed a richly satisfying career. He became a Fellow of the Royal Institute of British Architects (FRIBA) and continued to work with the SPAB, developing ideas on conservation and repair. His daughter Penelope worked with him and both received the Esher Award, John in 1974, and Penelope in 1996. The Esher is not presented every year but is given to those who, purely on altruistic grounds, further the cause of building conservation and the work of the SPAB.

The National Trust valued the contribution John made to their historic buildings and when he retired as their architect, presented him with an engraving of Tattershall Castle. In 1964 he was awarded an OBE for his work.

But John was always a family man at heart and it gave him great pleasure to see his daughters, grandchildren and great-grandchildren enjoying Shalford Mill.

After the war John and Janet returned to London. Then in 1952, their daughter Joanna and her husband Brian Bagnall took over the tenancy. Penelope moved into Watermill Cottage next door, single-handedly continuing her architectural conservation practice.

Brian, also an architect and later a cartoonist for *Private Eye*, often acted as a go-between for the Gang and the Trust and labelled the Gang's 'relics' to be housed in a cabinet made by his son Adam. He kept up a correspondence with Peggy after she became a Catholic, as he was a Catholic too, and he also helped negotiate the wishes of the Gang to remain anonymous when approached by journalists and scriptwriters.

Thirty-four years after the Gang first met at the Mill they decided to relinquish their use of it and, in 1966, the Gang's room was handed to the Bagnall family. Joyce Conwy Evans, Bryn and Geoffrey Parsons were there and Joyce remembers having a lovely tea. 'Bryn handed the key to the Bagnall family and Adam had built a cabinet to house the

Gang's relics. It was ceremoniously mounted on the wall in the Gang's room then Geoffrey took us rowing on the river. It was a glorious day and the banks were covered with buttercups.'

The transaction was celebrated officially with a black-tie supper, on 27 May 1967, lovingly prepared by Joanna. Brynnie and Joy attended, representing the Gang, bringing with them their first Minute Book, which they handed over to the Trust's Historic Buildings Secretary Romilly Fedden, Area Agent Ivor Blomfield, the Trust's Chief Agent Ivan Hills and Secretary J. W. Rathbone. John and Janet Macgregor were special guests.

Whilst half of the house was kept as a private residence, the original machinery housed in the other half was kept open to the public. The lucam contained a ladder, trapeze and wooden rocking horse, which young visitors could enjoy, and inside was the two-storey dolls' house John had built for his grandchildren, which had featured in *Vogue* magazine in the 1950s. Made out of packing cases it was a replica of his Georgian house in Chiswick. Visitors' children were welcome to play with it, putting the dolls to bed upstairs or making tea in enamel cups for when their parents returned from their tour of the Mill.

The family always treated the Mill as a home rather than a relic, but not everyone was so happy with their laissez-faire attitude to history. In recent years the dolls' house was moved to the Rural Life Centre in Farnham in Surrey.

An angry letter written by a visitor to the Mill in 1974 read:

> I lately paid a visit to the Mill and found my way obstructed by a table tennis table and a motor cycle.
>
> There is a rope ladder, a single rope swing, a double rope swing, the seat of which looks like part of the mill, a trapeze made of a pick-axe handle all fixed to the structure of the overhanging storey.
>
> I am glad to say that most of the items that were stored in the mill have been removed. However the following items were still being stored in the mill:
> outboard motor
> fire screen
> wicker basket
> a kind of metal cage

2 off [sic] rubber hot water bottles
? basket
Child's scooter
2 off bicycles
cycle storage racks (2 off)
Logs and wood stored in meal bins
2 off glass panels
sawing trestle
a kind of ? fixture

The Gang would have approved wholeheartedly.

The Gang's association with the Mill was never forgotten and, in 1982, to celebrate the 50th anniversary of the Gang rescuing the Mill, the Bagnalls organised the planting of a Weeping Pear in the mill garden. Brynnie and Philip Gaze, who came in place of his wife Joy who was ill, represented the Gang. Brynnie gave a speech relaying cryptic messages from Peggy and thanked the Macgregors who had been 'Honorary Godparents' of the Mill. She said:

> For twenty years they occupied the house with their four daughters, and brought it all to life. The Mill pond was often full of young naked Macgregor children dipping. For the last thirty years the Mill has been blessed by Joanna and Brian Bagnall – and their delightful brood. They too have added tremendously to the beauty and character of the Mill and garden.
>
> We all owe the Macgregors and Bagnalls a tremendous debt, and we all thank Joanna and Brian for to-day's memorable Jubilee Party.
>
> Lastly, I want to thank, on behalf of us all, the National Trust which has shown that it can administer huge estates of National importance, but that equally it can care about tiny properties like ours – and can hold them in trust for the future generations of this country. We all thank them sincerely.

The July Mill party became an annual affair and whilst John's numerous grandchildren and great-grandchildren played on the grass John could be found bathing in the Tillingbourne, lying on his back, his big toes sticking out of the water and the sun bouncing off his bald head.

He died on 31 January 1984, aged 93 and his ashes were scattered in the Mill stream, joining the ritual ashes of the Bludy Beershop. John and Janet are toasted every year at the party when all the family gather together.

Shalford Mill remains open to the public and in 2015 is still lived in by Joanna, the current custodian.

EPILOGUE

PRESERVING ANONYMITY

When Ferguson's Gang ceased to be active they could have waived their anonymity. There is no doubt that both broadsheet and tabloid newspapers would have relished revealing the women who had inspired such headlines as:

'RED BIDDY' AND HER GANG ARE AT IT AGAIN – SCOTLAND YARD KNOWS IT!

---

and

BENEFICENT GANGSTERS – £500 'RAID' AND NOT A WORD SPOKEN

Ferguson's Gang could have dispersed with a flourish, but they chose not to. Instead, they slipped out of view and directed their efforts elsewhere. By 'going quietly', they kept a promise they had made to each other when they formed and swore that they would take the Gang's identities to their graves. They pretty much kept that promise and so did all their associates, including the National Trust.

A handful of people knew that Peggy Pollard was Bill Stickers. For practical purposes, the Trust needed a bona fide contact and, as the Gang's leader, Peggy was the obvious choice. Clough Williams-Ellis knew, and outed her in his 1971 autobiography, *Architect Errant*, divulging that Ferguson's Gang was Peggy's creation. But it was a niche book and the information went largely unnoticed.

While Peggy and Joy recruited family members to the Gang, only select friends and relatives of the others knew. Rachel's son Peter was aware that she was involved with the National Trust and remembers hearing the names Red Biddy and Bill Stickers, but never more than that. When Rachel wrote her autobiography, she did not mention Ferguson's Gang or her work with the other members, although in the archive of her old papers, the Gang's names are all in her address book. Ruth's younger brother Adrian knew that his Bohemian sister was a member of the Gang, as Ruth constantly requested Victorian coins from him and the rest of her family. Eileen's nephew heard her talk about Ferguson's Gang but she gave no details and Pore Old Arris's identity is still a mystery.

The Press and the Trust did try to persuade the Gang to go on record and talk about their activities but they resisted all temptation. In 1978, Ivor Blomfield, Secretary of the National Trust, wrote to Brian Bagnall, the Artichoke's son-in-law, asking for more information on Ferguson's Gang for a short article in their spring newsletter. After a meeting with the Artichoke, Brian Bagnall spoke to Joy and Brynnie, who said firmly that they did not wish to make any statements about the Gang beyond what was already common knowledge. Two years later, in 1980, the Artichoke received a letter from Lawrence Rich, the Appeals Secretary at the Trust, who had been asked to write a short article for the Trust newsletter about the Gang. Brian Bagnall spoke to them again and reported to Rich that 'The Gang still do not wish to expose themselves any further.' In 1990, a filmmaker wrote to Sister Agatha via the Trust, wanting to dramatise the Gang's story, but Brynnie was adamant that the contents of 'The Boo' were kept a secret, never to be reproduced or published.

Brynnie turned up on the Isle of Wight in 1989 and presented a six-panel collage by her friend the tapestry and textile designer, Joyce Conwy Evans, depicting the history of the Gang. Having abandoned her mask, she was happy to explain that she was Sister Agatha, but declined to reveal her identity. When she was asked why the Gang had done what they had done she said: 'We cared about helping to save England and wanted to be involved in something of permanent value. Together we decided to pool our wits into battle ... and we were in our early twenties and it was fun.'

LEGISLATION AND LOBBYING

When Ferguson's Gang began in 1927 there were few conservation laws and no national planning acts. There were no national parks or areas protected from development by the green belt. Ferguson's Gang played a significant role in raising public interest to push for tighter conservation laws. When Ferguson's Gang were active, the following legislation was passed:

The Housing Act 1930, requiring all slum housing to be cleared in designated improvement areas.

The Ancient Monuments Consolidation Act 1931, post-Stonehenge, was amended to restrict development in an area surrounding an ancient monument. The Act excluded inhabited buildings. Had it included them, much that was destroyed before the Second World War could have been saved.

The Town and Country Planning Act 1932 was chiefly concerned with development and new planning. It was the first planning act to consider the countryside as well as the town in regulating new development. Although the Act had too many loopholes to be effective, it established the desirability of universal rural planning. It also permitted a town council to prevent the demolition of any property within its jurisdiction.

The Restriction of Ribbon Development Act 1935, designed to prevent the sprawl of towns and cities across the countryside. George Trevelyan submitted a Town and Country Planning Bill in 1929 but although it was supported by the first Labour Prime Minister Ramsey MacDonald, himself an open-air enthusiast, it wasn't passed. It would not be until 1935 that legislation in the form of the Restriction of Ribbon Development Act and the Preservation of Old Buildings Act was passed.

The Trunk Roads Act 1936 gave the Ministry direct control of the major routes and a new classification system was created to identify these routes, which gave rise to A and B roads. When motorways were introduced in the late 1950s, a new classification 'M' was introduced.

The Metropolitan Green Belt Act 1938, a policy for controlled urban growth around London. It was first proposed in the same year as Ferguson's radio appeal. It constrained the spread of the octopus and allowed local authorities to purchase land to be designated as open space.

The Town and Country Planning Act 1944 introduced listing to protect historic buildings. Grade I buildings like The Palace of Westminster and Blackpool Tower, were designated as being of exceptional interest, Grade II* buildings like Battersea Power Station and the Coliseum Theatre, were designated as special interest, and Grade II properties included railway stations, swimming pools and houses and more utilitarian buildings, and homes designated as being of special interest warranting preservation.

The New Towns Act 1946 was an ambitious programme for building new towns. It gave the government power to designate areas of land for new town development. A series of 'development corporations' set up under the Act were each responsible for one of the projected towns. Stevenage, in Hertfordshire, was designed to accommodate the overspill from London and was the first new town created under the Act. It was built in 1946. Ten others followed by 1955.

The Town and Country Planning Act 1947 allowed local authorities to include green-belt proposals in their development plans. By 1955, the Minister of Housing, Duncan Sandys, the son-in-law of Winston Churchill, was encouraging local authorities around the country to consider protecting land around their towns and cities by formally designating clearly defined green belts. The legislation stopped sprawl in its tracks. It established the principle that a contained settlement would be the norm, with definite boundaries, and that with any development, a conscious decision would be taken about where was the best place to put it.

The National Parks and Access to the Countryside Act 1949 finally created what Peggy had lobbied so long and hard for. There were two statutory proposals: to conserve and enhance the parks' natural beauty, wildlife and cultural heritage; and to promote opportunities for the public understanding and enjoyment of these special qualities. There are now nine National Parks in England, plus the Norfolk and Suffolk Broads, which have equivalent status, and these 11 areas account for 8 per cent of England's land mass. Unfortunately, there is still no National Park for Cornwall.

Successive governments have continued to legislate to protect the countryside and buildings of interest, and to curb urban sprawl.

Ferguson's Gang was part of a revolution that helped protect what we now take for granted: important historic buildings, small and large, and open spaces. Green-belt campaigners have often claimed that Greater London could have stretched from Reading in the west to Colchester in the east and from close to Cambridge in the north to Brighton in the south, covering almost 140 miles from one side to the other, an area of around 10,201 square miles.

The Gang's activities are perhaps best summed up by Philip Venning, who was Secretary to the SPAB from 1984 to 2012. He said, 'The help provided by the Gang to the National Trust was valuable both as a source of money and more importantly for its publicity value, something modern public relations and media specialists would have jumped at.'

Dame Fiona Reynolds, who was Director-General of the National Trust between 2001 and 2012, and is a former Director of the CPRE and an alumna of Newnham College, Cambridge, said:

I've always admired the women who made up Ferguson's Gang. They were visionary, brave and just a little eccentric, raising money and stealthily leaving it on the doorstep. At a time when women were not meant to take the initiative they refused to be told what to do.

Today, the Trust is a huge organisation, far richer than the members of Ferguson's Gang can ever have imagined. But it learned from them how important it is to act swiftly when it's necessary, and how to stand up for what really matters. Some of their exuberance and style has rubbed off in the passion everyone in the Trust feels for rescue and conservation. Without Ferguson's Gang, the Trust would be a duller place and our country not as beautiful.

The Trust's Chairman from 2008 to 2014, the journalist and writer Simon Jenkins, sums up their life and work:

> The Gang's wish to bring history to life by giving these smaller old buildings of local interest a new lease of life is very much the ethos of today's National Trust, creating a living history which captures the public imagination and is accessible to all. Ferguson's Gang act as a reminder to the National Trust today that conservation needs to be fun.
>
> The Gang rose to fame through their theatrical stunts. The need for such anarchic activism was less necessary after the Second World War when conservation legislation was rolled out nationally, but the Trust lost some of its most colourful characters. Revealing the background to Ferguson's Gang opens a door to a fascinating piece of our history.

FERGUSON'S GANG
Lady, a nameless life I lead,
A nameless death I'll die;
The friend whose lantern lights the mead
Were better mate than I.
Yet sung she: Shalford Mill is safe,
And Steventon also;
We dun it for the National Trust
So many years ago.

By Peggy Pollard, July 1990

APPENDIX

THE ROLE OF WOMEN AT THE TRUST

The activities of Ferguson's Gang coincided with a dynamic phase of the National Trust's development. When Sam Hield Hamer was Secretary of the National Trust between 1911 and 1934, it was a laid back institution. The Trust's efficient running was in part due to having a solid structure with two main committees focusing on Finances and Estate Management respectively, and on a clutch of hard-working and committed women.

Hamer could not have been described as go-ahead. He worked a very relaxed four-hour day, with an hour spent at his club for luncheon, whilst his very capable and knowledgeable Assistant Secretary, Victoria Spencer-Wilkinson, deputised for him, writing his letters and drafting important appeals.

Victoria and Florence Paterson, who was also known as 'Snooks' or 'Miss P', were Hamer's only staff. Both women visited Trust properties and advised local committees. Spencer-Wilkinson, a town girl, genned up on countryside management so that she could advise, for example, on the correct way to lay a wattle hedge, having only just discovered the technique for herself. After a day out in the country she would return back to the London office in time for tea and hot-buttered toast, which she shared with Snooks.

Victoria was appointed Assistant Secretary in the 1920s and worked under Matheson after he took over as Secretary until 1942, when a young Cambridge graduate and rival, Bruce Thompson was appointed in her place. Her career prospects thus thwarted, she left the Trust to travel around south-east Asia.

The Trust had been founded by a woman, Octavia Hill, and from the start, women had been instrumental in the organisation. Hill's co-founder, Sir Robert Hunter, had three daughters, the youngest of whom was Dorothy. Dorothy Hunter inherited her father's powers of persuasion, but whereas her father was a quiet, thoughtful man,

Dorothy was a powerful orator, speaking out compellingly on subjects such as women's suffrage and Free Trade.

Dorothy Hunter joined the Trust in 1913, the year her father died, and was an active and dynamic presence. Committed to conservation, she served on the Executive Committee until 1964, resigning aged 83.

The Trust's workforce was small, and included committed women such as Janet Upcott, who worked with the Trust from before the First World War until after the Second on the Finance and General Purposes Committee. She studied at the London School of Economics, training in housing management. She was also a founder member of the Association of Women Housing Managers.

Upcott was responsible for managing the finances of the National Trust's properties and instituted income-raising systems so that properties should 'pay for themselves'. She spent 15 years working in finance and a remarkable 56 on the Estates Committee, but in spite of her tremendous value to the Trust, she was a modest woman, playing down her contribution and speaking little in Trust meetings.

It was surely not surprising therefore that someone with the intellectual guns and dynamism of Peggy chose not to work within a hierarchical institution such as the National Trust in a professional capacity. She preferred to be her own boss, and even her period working for the CPRE in Cornwall was only possible because she had immense respect for Bishop Hunkin and the two of them worked as a double act, pushing out unsupportive people within the local organisation. Peggy of course did compromise at times and was Secretary whilst Hunkin was Chair, but she had free rein to run meetings and follow her own agenda. Had she joined the staff of the Trust she would doubtless have found it hard to hold back in meetings, like Janet Upcott, nor would she have been content to settle down in the background for tea and toast with Snooks.

MEN AT THE TRUST WHO SUPPORTED THE GANG

Donald Macleod Matheson took over as Secretary to the Trust from 1934 to 1945, the period when Ferguson's Gang was most active. He formed a close relationship with the Gang, and it was his name that appeared on most of the Trust's receipts.

Although he was born into an aristocratic Scottish family and 'educated at Oxford University he was not really interested in money and was happy to work for the National Trust at a lower salary than he might have expected. His friendship with the Gang was genuine and like Peggy he was interested in comparative religion and also worked as a translator. He was thought to be a good secretary, being described as sensitive and somewhat shy, and his interests lay in the open country. He had injured his back badly during the First World War and during his tenure he was often ill, taking almost a complete year off in 1944. While the Trust's minutes reveal nothing of Matheson's character, the Gang's minutes record him at many of their dinners entering into their games, performing sword swallowing acts and encouraging the introduction of the Black Atropines into their midst.

Matheson did not disguise his fondness for the Gang. In his book *The National Trust Guide to Places of Natural Beauty* he describes the acquisition by the Gang of Sennen Cove in Cornwall:

> This romantic tip of England was given in 1937 by Ferguson's Gang, who found the money to buy it against an imminent threat of development. Ferguson's Gang gave quite a number of properties to the Trust, but this is a suitable point for a word about them. Who were the members of the gang remains unknown; it can only be said that none of them were rich and all of them were young, at least in spirit. When they heard of a chance to buy for the Trust some threatened land or building for a sum within their scope one of them rang up or one of them called masked and unannounced, on the Secretary. Would the Trust buy and trust them to raise the money? They never failed to fulfill a promise to find money, and on more than one occasion they found much more than had been promised. Truly a new generation of such gangsters is needed.

Matheson's stand-in during his year of illness in 1944 was James Lees-Milne, who was appointed secretary of the Country Houses Committee, which had been set up in 1936 as a way to protect stately homes. He was similar in age to the members of the Gang and attended Eton while Bobby Gladstone was there. He is mentioned often in 'The Boo' and attended Gang dinners and celebrations. An architectural historian, novelist and biographer, he was shy, droll, diligent, well-connected, enigmatic and provocative.

Lees-Milne came from a prosperous manufacturing family and grew up in Wickhamford, Worcestershire, near Ruth and Joy. He married Alvilde Chaplin, a prominent gardening and landscape expert. Both were bisexual, and while Lees-Milne enjoyed an affair with author Harold Nicolson, some years later, Alvilde embarked on a passionate relationship with Nicolson's wife, Vita Sackville-West. It was Sackville-West who recommended Lees-Milne for the National Trust job. For his part Lees-Milne was passionate about art and was incensed about its wanton destruction. In 1930, whilst a student, he had been invited to a party at Rousham near Oxford and was horrified that for sport a crowd of drunken undergraduates started taking potshots at a statue of Apollo.

> The experience was a turning-point in my life. It brought home to me how passionately I cared for architecture and the continuity of history. That evening I made a vow ... that I would devote my energies and abilities, such as they were, to preserving the country houses of England.

The Country Houses Scheme was a way of allowing the landowner to stay resident in his home, whereby death duties would be waived on condition that the house was open to the public. When Lees-Milne took over, the Trust only owned two stately homes, Montacute and the Tudor manor house Barrington Court, both in Somerset.

He was ambivalent about power and class, at one moment sycophantic and in praise of the old social order and at the next outspoken and critical of the arrogance of the aristocracy. He was ruthless when it came to acquiring property for the Trust, often turfing out owners' 'vulgar' possessions and leaving them strangers in their own home.

He persuaded the Astors to endow Cliveden and Dame Margaret Greville to endow Polesden Lacey to the Trust and, by the time he retired, in all, he had acquired 17 properties and had restrictive covenants on 5 others. The Country Houses Scheme was responsible for protecting many of Britain's 'great' houses and developing the character of the National Trust as it is known today. Lees-Milne's relationship to the Gang was one of mutual need. Many people found him rather intimidating, but the Gang was intimidated by no one.

LIST OF FERGUSON'S GANG DONATIONS

Objects furthered:

£5 General Fund

£5 Watersmeet Preservation Scheme

14s Golden Valley Preservation Scheme

£1 Chester Roman Amphitheatre

£5 General Funds

7/6 Sullington Warren Purchase Scheme

£1 Whiteleaf Cross

£1 Buttermere Appeal

£3 Lansallos Appeal

£905 BBC Broadcast Appeal

£100 Avebury Appeal

£5 Hindhead Appeal

£20 Dovedale Appeal

£1 Pembroke Appeal

£20 General Fund

£ Clumber Park. An amount is not written in 'The Boo' for Clumber Park, but an anonymous donation of £500 is recorded in the Trust's 1944–45 annual report

£2 3s 3d Jubilee Appeal

£3 3s 3d General Fund

PROPERTIES PRESERVED

1932 The Old Mill, Shalford, £500

1934 The Old Town Hall Newtown, Isle of Wight, £1,400

1935 Mayon Cliffs, Sennen, £600

1936 Trevescan Cliffs, Sennen, £450

1938 Priory Cottages, Steventon, £1,553

1946 Frenchman's Creek (no amount recorded)

TOTAL £5,578 14s 0d

ACKNOWLEDGEMENTS

It was never going to be easy to research the lives of women who made it a life's ambition to remain anonymous. We could not have done it without the help of many people who generously opened their archives and gave their time to help us. Their interviews, letters papers and photographs made it possible to build a picture of the unique women and men who were Ferguson's Gang.

We would like to thank the following people for their enthusiastic and unstinting help. Our agent Diane Banks, and our publisher who believed that the Gang's story was an important one to tell. Our dear friend Kerry Bradley, who brought together the two authors during the making of a short film about the Gang. We thank the many friends and family who gave their time freely, in particular Clare Nicholson, Luke Batterham, Philip Dobree, Millie Dobree and Arthur Dobree. Also Bibi Khan and Rhiana Khan who did not complain about the many weekends we had to spend working on this book.

Veronica Gates, Mill Officer, and all the National Trust volunteers at Shalford Mill; Darren Beatson, who adopted a Gang name and became our good old 'Dad'. Dad happily burrowed through the National Trust Archives retrieving snippets of information and made us smile by corresponding in Gang mockney. He deserves this 'akolade'.

Megan Clark-Bagnall, Freelance Artist, without whom the exhibition 'Taming the Tentacles' in 2012, the stimulus for this book, would not have happened. Simon Webb, who worked tirelessly on the exhibition catalogue and all the artists who contributed, including Cathy Lane and Sebi Messerer.

Special thanks goes to Sue Watts, the Maw family archivist, who became so much more than that, diligently digging through family ancestry forums for information about the Gang members and their many friends and relatives.

Interviews with the following people have added the all-important colour to the factual information: Kitty Turnbull, Jean

Gladstone, Michael Maine, Claire Riche, Doris Bird on PEGGY POLLARD; Diana Jervis-Read, Diana Dollery, Elaine Richardson, Joyce Conwy Evans on BRYNNIE JERVIS-READ; Joanna Bagnall, Penelope Adamson, Sally Lewis; Lore Segal; Jane Nicholas; Tony Spalding; the Macgregor grandchildren including Anna Pohorely, Kirstie Clark, Alistair Adamson, Caroline Bagnall, Adam Bagnall, Kate Bagnall, Sarah Cage, Barbara Lewis, Gabriel Lewis, Hugh Lewis, Jane Lewis on JOHN MACGREGOR AND OTHER MEMBERS OF THE GANG; Ivor Weeks and Bobbie Cox on RUTH SHERWOOD; Peter Cox, Karin Cocuzzi Tetlow, Matthew Collings, Hannah Lowery on RACHEL PINNEY; Christopher Clayton, Trish Mackinnon, Amanda Souter, Jenny Carrington, Katherine Evans, Richard Harvey, David Kass and John Nairn on EILEEN SOUTER; Ben Simpson and Christopher Clayton on JOY GAZE; Robin Godwin-Austen on MAJOR ROBERT ARTHUR GODWIN-AUSTEN.

Conversations with the following people contextualise the events in this book:

FROM THE NATIONAL TRUST: Simon Jenkins, Chairman 2008–12; Dame Fiona Reynolds, Director General 2001–12; Dame Helen Ghosh, Director General since 2012; Sarah-Jane Forder, the National Trust magazine Editor 1989–96; Sue Herdman, the *National Trust Magazine* Editor 2005–12; Yvonne Rainey, resident at Priory Cottages; Becky Noyes, Custodian The Old Town Hall, Newtown, Isle of Wight; Sarah Crawcour, Visitor Services Manager, Wey Navigation.

OTHER ORGANISATIONS AND PEOPLE: Matthew Slocombe, Society for the Protection of Ancient Buildings (SPAB) Secretary since 2012; Philip Venning, SPAB Secretary 1984–2012; Oliver Hilliam, Senior Communications and Information Officer, Campaign to Protect Rural England (CPRE); Simon Banton, Historic Property Steward, Stonehenge; Merlin Waterson, Art Historian and writer on donors to the National Trust; Julia Elton, on her father Arthur Elton; Edward Hoare on Stourhead; Nick Swankie on Benthall Hall; Joanne Ruff and Diana Manipud, King's College London; Dr Andrea Tanner, Archivist at Fortnum & Mason; Anthony Richards, Head of Documents and Sound, Imperial War Museums.

Finally, we would like to thank the Macgregor sisters, Joanna, Penelope and Sally, whose recollections have been invaluable.

CREDITS

Photographs reproduced by kind permission of the following people.

FIRST PLATE SECTION IMAGES

Bill Stickers: Kitty Turnbull; Red Biddy: Peter Cox; Sister Agatha: Diane Jervis-Read; Shot Biddy: Christopher Clayton; Is B: Sutton Coldfield Library; Kate O'Brien: Kings' College Archive; Uncle Gregory: Kitty Turnbull; The Artichoke: Bagnall family archive; Erb the Smasher: Kitty Turnbull; Black Mary: Kitty Turnbull; Gang map: Bagnall family archive; *England and Octopus*: CPRE; Constable cartoon: Daily Express; Postcard of mill: Bagnall family archive; Rachel and Luigi: Peter Cox; *The People* article: © Mirrorpix.

SECOND PLATE SECTION IMAGES
Is B drawing: Bagnall family archive; Crazy Gang: Kitty Turnbull; Brynnie as Indian: Diana Jervis-Read; Gang treasures: Bagnall family archive; Photo of mill c.1960: Bagnall family archive; Clough and Peggy: Kitty Turnbull; Peggy in her room – photographer: Ander Gunn.

All other images are from 'the Boo', by permission of National Trust with thanks to Wiltshire and Swindon History Centre.

TEXT EXTRACTS
Extract from 'The General' copyright Siegfried Sassoon by kind permission of the Estate of George Sassoon.

Extracts from *The Times* articles dated 23 November 1932, 1 February 1933, 21 August 1935 and 31 December 1937, copyright *The Times*, courtesy News Syndication.

BIBLIOGRAPHY

BOOKS AND MAGAZINE ARTICLES

Patrick Abercrombie, *The Preservation of Rural England*, Liverpool University Press, 1926.

Polly Bagnall, *Ferguson*, Private publication, 2012.

N. J. Barton, *London Rivers*, Historical Publications Ltd, 1962.

Mavis Batey, David Lambert and Kim Wilke, *Indignation!: The Campaign for Conservation*, Kit-Cat Books, 2000.

Stanley Bernard, *Peacehaven and Telescombe Through Time*, Amberley Publishing, 2009.

Mary Bowers, *Glimpses of the College Edgbaston Church of England College for Girls*, Edgbaston Church of England College for Girls, 1985.

Kevin Cahill, *Who Owns Britain Based on a Census: Return of Owners of Land, 1873*, Canongate Books, 2011.

Stephen Chaplin, *The Slade School Archive Reader*, UCL Special Collections.

Reginald Coleman and Shirley Seaton, *Stamford Brook: An Affectionate Portrait*, Stamford Brook Publications, 1992.

Margaret Dierden, *Scenes of Shalford Past*, Private Publication, 2002.

Max Egremont, *Siegfried Sassoon: A Biography*, Picador, 2006.

Tony Farrell, *Shaping London*, John Wiley & Sons, 2010.

Ferguson's Gang, *Ferguson's Gang*, Unpublished, c.1950.

Judith Flanders, *A Circle of Sisters*, Penguin Books, 2002.

Sarah-Jane Forder, 'Death of a Bandit', *National Trust Magazine*, 1997.

Sarah-Jane Forder, 'Frustrating the Octopus', *National Trust Magazine*, 1990.

Juliet Gardiner, *An Intimate Portrait of the 30s*, HarperCollins, 2011.

John Gaze, *Figures in a Landscape: A History of the National Trust*, Barrie & Jenkins, 1988.

Miles Glendinning, *The Conservation Movement: A History of Architectural Preservation – Antiquity to Modernity*, Routledge, 2013.

William Gray Fearnside and Thomas Harral, *The History of London, Illustrated by Views in London and Westminster*, Orr and Co, 1838.

Jonathon Guinness, *Shoe – The Odyssey of a Sixties Survivor*, Hutchinson, 1989.

Alexandra Harris, *Romantic Moderns*, Thames and Hudson, 2010.

David Boyd Haycock, *Crisis of Brilliance: Five Young British Artists and the Great War*, Old St Publishing, 2009.

Sue Herdman & Merlin Waterson, *Interviews Relating to Ferguson's Gang – Transcript*, Unpublished, 2008.

Sue Herdman, 'The Cloaked Crusaders', *National Trust Magazine*, 2008.

Jane Hill, *The Sculpture of Gertrude Hermes 1901–1983*, Lund Humphries, 2011.

Simon Jenkins, *England's Thousand Best Houses*, Penguin Books, 2004.

Harold Jervis-Read & Brynnie Granger, *Personal Letters*, Richard Ford Manuscripts, 1927–1940.

Brynhild Jervis-Read, *Talk by Sister Agatha*, Unpublished, 1982.

Sue Kirkland and the National Trust, *Shalford Mill*, National Trust, 2010.

Janet Leeper, *English Ballet*, Penguin Books, 1944.

James Lees-Milne, *Some Country Houses and their Owners*, Penguin Books, 2009.

J E M Macgregor, 'Highway Grid', *The Builder Magazine*, September 1942.

J E M Macgregor, 'Remodelled Cities', *The Builder Magazine*, October 1942.

J E M Macgregor, 'Squash Court, Rivercourt, Hammersmith', *The Architect and Building News*, March 1942.

Peter Mandler, *The Rise and Fall of the Stately Home*, Yale University Press, 1999.

Neville Marsh, *History of Queen Elizabeth's College*, King's College London, 1986.

D M Matheson, *National Trust Guide: Places of Natural Beauty*, Batsford, 1950.

David Matless, *Landscape and Englishness*, Reaktion Books, 1998.

Catherine Moorehead and Rob Burns, *The K2 Man (and His Molluscs): The Extraordinary Live of Haversham Godwin-Austen*, Neil Wilson Publishing, 2013.

National Trust, *The Curious History of Newtown Old Town Hall*, National Trust, 2007.

Virginia Nicholson, *Among the Bohemians: Experiments in Living 1900–1939*, Penguin Books, 2002.

Biddy Passmore (Editor), Sue Limb (Author) and 5 others, *Breaking Bounds: Six Newnham Lives*, Newnham College, 2014

Rachel Pinney, Bobby, *Treatment of an Autistic Boy*, Harvill Press Ltd, 1983.

Rachel Pinney, *Creative Listening*, 'A to Z' Printers & Publishers Ltd, 1968.

Rachel Pinney, *Rachel, Finding What I Can Do and Somewhat Doing It*, Unpublished autobiography, 1995.

Lucien Pissarro, foreword by Miriam Macgregor, *Pastorale*, Whittington Press, 2011.

Peggy Pollard, *Cornwall*, Paul Elek Publishers, 1947.

Peggy Pollard, *Memoirs*, Unpublished, pre-1996.

Eileen Edna Power, *Medieval English Nunneries c.1275 to 1535*, Cambridge University Press, 1922.

A R Powys, illustrated by J E M Macgregor, *Repair of Ancient Buildings*, J M Dent & Sons, 1929.

Isabel Raphael, Carolyn Postgate and Catherine Budgett-Meakin, *Channing School: A Chronicle of 125 Years*, The Channing Association, 2009.

Lawrence Rich, 'Light Under a Bushel', *National Trust Magazine*, 1980.

Anthony Richards, 'Inside The First World War: The Sardonic Humour of 'The General' by Siegfried Sassoon (1886–1967)', *The Sunday Telegraph*, 2014.

Julian Richards, *Stonehenge: The Story So Far*, English Heritage, 2007.

Claire Riche, *The Lost Shrine of Liskeard*, The Saint Austen Press, 2002.

Vita Sackville-West, *English Country Houses*, William Collins of London, 1941.

Angela Simmons, *A Profession and its Roots: The Lady Almoners*, Michelangelo Press, 2005.

Valentine Spalding, illustrated by J E M Macgregor, *Allwither*,

Unpublished, 1926.

Lore Segal, *Other People's Houses*, The New Press, 1964.

Herbert Spencer, *Social Statics, Or The Conditions Essential to Human Happiness*, D. Appleton and Company, 1873.

Simon Thurley, *Men From The Ministry – How Britain Saved its Heritage*, Yale University Press, 2013.

W. Harding Thompson FRIBA, *CPRE CORNWALL, Coast, Moors and Valleys 1930*, Council to Protect Rural England (CPRE), 1930.

G M Trevelyan, *Must England's Beauty Perish?*, Faber & Gwyer, 1929.

G M Trevelyan, *The Call and Claims of Natural Beauty*, University College London, 1931.

Merlin Waterstone, *A Noble Thing: The National Trust and its Benefactors*, Scala Publishers Ltd, 2011.

Clough Williams-Ellis, *England and the Octopus*, Council to Protect Rural England (CPRE), 1928.

ARCHIVES

Wiltshire & Swindon Archives (Home of the Gang's two 'Boo' minute books)

National Trust Archives, Heelis

Slade Archive, Slade School of Fine Art, University College London

The Newnham College Archives, University of Cambridge

Cambridge University Library

Bristol University Archives

King's College London Archives

Dartington Hall Trust Archive, Devon Heritage Centre

Channing School Archives, Channing School

The British Library

Imperial War Museum, London

Ironbridge Gorge Museum Library and Archives

Shropshire Archives, Shropshire Council

Sutton Coldfield Library, Birmingham City Council

Fortnum & Mason Archives

Women's Library, London School of Economics

Guildford Museum, Guildford Borough Council

Bishopsgate Institute

Royal Academy of Music

Saint Felix School, Southwold

The National Archives

Oxford University

Bagnall family personal papers

Michael Maine personal papers

Kitty Turnbull personal papers

Diana Jervis-Read personal papers

CONTEMPORARY NEWSPAPER ARTICLES

The Birmingham Post
'Beneficent Gangsters', 15 May 1935.
'A Stronger National Trust', 1936.
'The Pembrokeshire Cost Appeal – Nearly Two-Thirds of Needed Sum
    Obtained', June 1939.

The Children's Newspaper
'Good Gangsters Ferguson and the Rest – Masked Band Going About The
    Countryside', December 1934.
'Ferguson and His Gang', 1938.

Country Life
'A Ballad of the By-Pass', 11 February 1939.

The Daily Express
'Erb The Smasher Pays A Call – £200 Gift from "Gang" to Save Beauty Spot',
    7 November 1933.
'Ferguson's Gang Act Again – Unknown Benefactors', 26 June 1935.

The Daily Mail
'Masked Woman's £100 Gift in Silver – "Red Biddy"', 1 February 1933.
'"Ferguson's Gang" to be Disbanded', 15 January 1937.

The Daily Mirror
'Woman in Mask Gives £500 – "Kate O'Brien the Nark"',
    2 October 1934.

The Daily Sketch
'Gang with Good Heart – Masked Woman's Gift of a Bag Full of Silver',
    1 February 1933.
'Ferguson's Gang Busy Again – Mystery Band with Terrible Names Complete
    Endowment of Beauty Spot', 7 November 1933.
'Ferguson, of Ferguson's Gang to Broadcast', 21 August 1935.

The Daily Telegraph
'The "Ferguson Gang"', 8 November 1933.
'Ferguson Gang Gift to National Trust – Masked Woman's £500',
    2 October 1934.
'"Masked Gang" Visit National Trust – Anonymous £500 Gift',
    19 December 1934.
Untitled news item, 26 June 1935.
'A Mystery Man to Broadcast – "Ferguson's Gang" Leader – Anonymous

Helpers of Nation Trust by Radio Correspondent', 21 August 1935.
'Beneficent Bomb', 18 July 1939.

Estate Magazine
'Ferguson's Gang Again', 1945.

The Evening News
'Masked Woman's £100 Gift In Silver – "Red Biddy"', 1 February 1933.

Good Housekeeping
Untitled news item, June 1935.

The Morning Post
'"Ferguson's Gang" Active Again – Masked Woman's Anonymous Gift of £100',
   1 February 1933.
'The "Ferguson Gang" – Further Gift of £200 for Beauty Spot', 8
   November 1933.
'Developing the Countryside', 19 December 1934.
'Men of Mystery', 7 February 1935.
'Beneficent Gangsters – £500 "Raid" and not a Word Spoken – Ferguson's
   Again', 8 February 1935.
'Benefactors in Disguise', 18 May 1935.
'Ferguson Speaks for "the Gang" – Unknown Voice Broadcasts', 26 August
   1935.
'Ferguson's Gang', 27 August 1935.
Untitled news item, 7 September 1935.
'Ferguson's Gang Again – Cornish Cliffs for Nation', 8 January 1937.

The Motor
'Saved', November 1932.

The National Trust Bulletin
'Shalford's Old Water Mill', November 1932.
'Kate O'Brien, Nark', November 1934.
'Silent O'Moyle', February 1935.
'Recent Happenings', February 1936.
'"Ferguson's Gang" Again', December 1938.
'Priory Cottages, Steventon, Berkshire', March 1939.
'Steventon: Priory Cottages', June 1939.

The News Chronicle
'"Ferguson's Gang" at Work Again – More Money Given to National Trust', 15
   May 1935.
'"Ferguson's Gang" to the Rescue Again', 25 June 1935.

'"Jealousy" Prompts £100 Gift', 15 July 1938.
'Ferguson Gang's £100 Bomb', 18 July 1939.

The Observer
'A Hidden Hand', 10 January 1937.

The People
'"Red Biddy" and her Gang are at it again – Scotland Yard Knows It! – Here's Another £500 Raid', 23 December 1934.

Portsmouth Evening News
'Builder's Arrive in Newtown – Restoring the Town Hall – Pied Piper Legend – and the Postman-Historian', 2 December 1933.

The Radio Times
'The Week's Good Cause', 26 August 1935.
'The Week's Good Cause', 13 December 1935.

Rand Daily Mail
'"Ferguson's Gang" – More Money to Buy Cliff Lands', 9 January 1937.

The Star, Johannesburg
'£100 Note Round a Cigar – Anonymous Gifts to Trust Fund – The Preservation of Beauty Spots', 9 January 1937.

Sunderland Daily Echo
'"Ferguson" to Broadcast – Mystery Leader of Masked Gang', 21 August 1935.

The Sunday Pictorial
Untitled news item, 19 May 1935.

The Sunday Times
Untitled news item, 5 November 1933.

The Surrey Advertiser
'Shalford's Old Water Mill Taken Over by National Trust', 26 November 1932.
The Times
'Old Surrey Mill Saved', 23 November 1932.
'Saving of an Old Mill – Some Benevolent "Gangsters" – Masked Lady Weighed Down with Silver', 1 February 1933.
'Quiet Corners', 8 March 1933.
'The National Trust – 13 Properties Acquired During the Year', November 1933.
'Ferguson's Gang – Another Gift of £200 to National Trust', 7 November 1933.
'Masked Woman Gives £500 – Aid for The National Trust', 3 October 1934.

'For the Nation', 5 October 1934.

'Ferguson's Gang – Christmas Gifts to National Trust', 19 December 1934.

'"Ferguson's Gang" and The National Trust', 15 May 1935.

Untitled news item, 25 June 1935.

'"Man of Mystery" to Broadcast – Appeal for National Trust', 21 August 1935.

'National Trust's Record Year – Acquisitions in 1935 – The West Country', 17 December 1935.

'"Ferguson's Gang" at Work Again – Cornish Cliffland for the Nation', 8 January 1937.

'Cornish Cliff Land Preserved – Gift to The National Trust', 30 March 1937.

'"Ferguson's Gang" Again – £200 for National Trust', 31 December 1937.

'Gang Warfare for National Trust – Ferguson's Catspaw', 15 July 1938.

Untitled news item, 18 July 1939.

'The Disfigurement of Salisbury', 26 July 1939.

Untitled news item, 15 August 1945.

The Times of Ceylon

'Land's End for the Nation – "Ferguson's Gang's" Gift', 16 January 1937.

West Briton

Untitled news item, 14 November 1935.

The Western Morning News

'"Ferguson's Gang" Again – "Red Biddy's" Gift to National Trust', 1 February 1933.

Untitled news item, 26 June 1935.

'Cornish Cliffland for the Nation', 7 January 1937.

'Preserved for the Nation', March 1937.

'Received a "Bomb"', 18 July 1939.

'Bill to Check I.R.A.', 18 July 1939.

YHA Rucksack

'Fragment of a Mediaeval Romance', January 1937.

'The Knight of the Ferguson Gang – and how he is Thwarting the Octopus', Springtime 1937.

INDEX

"RED BIDDY" AND HER GANG ARE AT IT AGAIN

SCOTLAND YARD KNOWS IT!

HERE'S ANOTHER £50 RAID

Special to "The People"

"THE YARD," they say, ha[s] "cleaned up" gangla[nd] in London; driven th[e] gang leaders out of the countr[y] made the West End safe f[or] every citizen. But HAS IT?

There is one powerful gang which flourishes under the very nose, so [to] speak, of Lord Trenchard!

The "Ferguson Gang" it calls itse[lf] and its exploits in recent times h[as] gained for its members more start[ling] publicity than any American gang co[uld] hope for!

But the peculiar thing about

'FERGUSON'S GANG' AT WORK AGAIN

CORNISH CLIFFLAND FOR THE NATION

The mysterious "Ferguson's Gang [ha]ve again been active on the Cornish [co]ast, close to the scene of their las[t] [re]corded exploit near Land's End.

Their usual method of doing good by [ste]alth is by now familiar. At interval[s] [in] the last few years masked men and [wo]men, emissaries of the gang, have [vis]ited the prosaic offices of the Nationa[l] [Tr]ust in Buckingham Palace Gardens t[o] [ha]nd over bags or wads of currency [re]quired no one outside the gang know[s h]ow or where. Their latest gift is th[e] [sec]ond and final instalment of the pur[cha]se price of 15¼ acres of cliffland, in [ord]er to keep it safe for the nation for al[l] [tim]e. Exactly how this money reached [the] Trust has not been disclosed. But i[t is] now known that the first instalmen[t] [cha]nged hands last month. During the [an]nual dinner of the Trust on Decem[ber] 10 a messenger arrived with an urgent [com]munication for the secretary. He [fou]nd that it was a cigar, round which [wa]s wrapped a £100 note.

Earlier in 1936 "Ferguson's Gang" [pre]sented to the Trust the Mayon Cliffs, [bet]ween the village of Sennen and Land's [En]d—24 acres stretching from the signal [stat]ion to Mayon Castle. Their new gift, [joi]ning that of last year, runs from the [May]on Cliffs to Carn Clog, which is a [qua]rter of a mile from the First and Last [Ho]use, the hotel at Land's End. Thus the [com]munity, through the benevolent work [of t]he gang, is now the permanent owner [of v]irtually 40 acres of Cornish coastline [that] ranks among the finest cliff scenery in [grea]t Britain.

'Erb The Smasher Pays A Call

Tuesday Express

£200 Gift From 'Gang' To Save Beauty Spot

Another gift has been made by the "Ferguson Gang"—a group of anonymous philanthropists—to the National Trust.

Last year the "gang" bought Shalford Mill, near Guildford, and presented it to the trust. They put it in a condition of thorough repair, and promised to endow it with a sum of £300.

Early this year a masked woman who announced herself as "Red Biddy" called at the offices of the National Trust and handed the secretary a bag containing £100, all in silver.

The remainder of the endowment has now been paid in an equally unusual manner. A masked man called at the offices of the trust and handed in his card which read :—

A MYSTERY MAN TO BROADCAST

"FERGUSON'S GANG" LEADER

ANONYMOUS HELPERS OF NATIONAL TRUST

BY OUR RADIO CORRESPONDENT

"Ferguson," a mystery man, is to broadcast on Sunday.

For some years masked men and women, members of "Ferguson's Gang," have called at the offices of the National Trust from time to time with bags of money or bank-notes for the purchase of properties in which the Trust was interested.

None of the officials of the Trust knows the identity of the members of the gang or its leader. Their "raids" have, however, resulted in the raising of over £2,000 and the acquisition and repair of Shalford Old Mill, near Guildford, and the Mayon Cliffs, between Sennen and Land's End.

Mr. D. M. Matheson, secretary of the National Trust, told me yesterday that the broadcast, which was to be a "Good Cause" appeal, had been arranged by a "go-between."

MASKED VISITORS

"Members of the gang leave cards with fantastic pseudonyms like 'Kate the Nark'

SAVING OF AN OLD MILL

SOME BENEVOLENT "GANGSTERS"

MASKED LADY WEIGHED DOWN WITH SILVER

Anonymity is a quality not unkno[wn] among donors of gifts to the Natio[nal] Trust, but rarely is generosity conceal[ed] by a disguise so mysterious as t[hat] assumed by the benefactors who recen[tly] gave Shalford Mill, near Guildford, [to] the Trust.

They are known to the Trust [as] "Ferguson's Gang." Experience sho[ws] that they are not "gangsters" of the ty[pe] that have haunted Chicago or engaged [in] smash-and-grab raids in the West End [and] other parts of London, although one [of] their number, a masked lady, recen[tly] astonished officials of the Trust when [she] made a flying visit to the office in Bu[ck]ingham Palace Gardens. But she speed[ily] proved that her mission was one [of] beneficence. Without lifting her mask [she] gave £100 in silver to the secretary as [an] instalment of the Shalford Mill endo[w]ment and then fled, leaving the offic[ials] more mystified than ever concerning [the] "gang."

Shalford Mill is an early eighteen[th] century watermill in the village of Sh[al]ford, on the Tillingbourne stream. T[he] National Trust, in announcing the g[ift] stated :—

"It has been given to the Trust by

GOOD GANGSTER[S]

FERGUSON AND THE REST

Masked Band Going Abou[t] the Countryside

TWO YEARS OF THEIR WO[RK]

For some time past a mysterious [band] has been going about the cou[ntry] making accurate observations of [the] land's most valuable treasures.

Sometimes they travel disguise[d as] ordinary motorists interested in bea[uty] spots, sometimes they go ma[sked.] Until now little has been known a[bout] them save that they go by the na[me of] Ferguson's Gang, and that, unlike [real] gangsters, they are bent on doing g[ood.]

It is impossible to discover wh[o the] members of Ferguson's Gang real[ly are,] but the C.N. has ascertained that, in [addi]tion to their leader, there are nine ot[hers—] Bill Stickers, Black Mary, The Bi[g...,] Sister Agatha, Arris, Erb, P.P. [...,] Gregory, Kate O'Brien, and White B[...]